RACE

TO

FREEDOM

RACE

TO

FREEDOM

A Tale of an Impossible Around the World Journey

By Vladislav Murnikov

7 Seas Publishing

Library of Congress Catalog Card Number: 99-97548

ISBN 0-9676657-0-1 $19.95 soft cover

7 Seas Publishing
P.O. Box 394
Sudbury, MA 01776
E-mail: publisher@fazisibook.com
Web site: www.fazisibook.com

For all my companions on FAZISI's journey

"... ³⁷A furious squall came up, and the waves broke over the boat, so that it was nearly swamped. ³⁸Jesus was in the stern, sleeping on a cushion. The disciples woke him and said to him, 'Teacher, don't you care if we drown?'

³⁹He got up, rebuked the wind and said to the waves, 'Quiet! Be still!'. Then the wind died down and it was completely calm.

⁴⁰He said to his disciples, 'Why are you so afraid? Do you still have no faith?'"

Mark 4-37:40

" It was answered, that all great and honorable actions were accomplished with great difficulties and must be enterprised and overcome with answerable courages."
"...Their condition was not ordinary. Their ends were good and honorable, their calling lawful and urgent, and therefore they might expect a blessing of God in their proceeding; yea although they should lose their lives in this action, yet they might have comfort in the same; and their endeavors would be honorable."

Governor William Bradford
"History of Plymouth Plantation"

CONTENTS

FOREWORD

The nation of immigrants has no end of immigrant stories, a heritage of moving, inspiring tales of landfalls made on America's promising shores. Vlad Murnikov's story now takes its place among them. Be prepared to be moved and inspired, not to mention entertained, for this is a compelling narrative of a courageous quest. It is a story so tightly packed with drama, adventure, humor and tragedy that one is tempted to describe it as incredible. Yet it is true.

Race to Freedom is more than Vlad's story. It is the story too of kindred spirits, freedom-craving Russians who signed on to sail around the world in an unlikely pursuit of one of yachting's holy grails; and of a motley collection of vivid characters, the likes of Juki, the well-muscled Georgian sailor with rugged good looks of an ex–boxer, known for his feats of strength at sea and feats of romance in port; the doctor of the galley, a Russian physician who longed so desperately to sail in the Whitbread Race that he agreed to serve as a cook though he was unable to read the English instructions for preparing the freeze-dried food on which the crew subsisted; the ambivalent American hired gun Skip Novak; and a Ukrainian navigator who had last seen the American coast through the periscope of a Soviet submarine. There is even a cameo appearance by Dennis Conner, whose ability to absorb prodigious quaffs of vodka won the hearts of Russian sailors.

This is also a story of a boat named FAZISI, a remarkable character in her own right. This low-slung, 80-foot sailboat, whose predatory lines suggest a great white shark, met the daunting ocean challenges of the 1989-90 Whitbread Round the World Race with elan and shocked doubting observers by reeling off an astonishing 386 nautical miles in 24 hours. But even that achievement paled beside the feat of just making it from Soviet Georgia to the starting line.

The Soviet Union of the late 1980s, where corporate sponsors, up-to-date yacht building technology and experienced offshore sailors were foreign concepts, was one of the most frustrating places on earth from which to mount a Whitbread challenge. Though the collapse of the Communist Empire was underway, the political atmosphere was far from favorable for such a decidedly capitalistic endeavor. Even as the Fazisi project began its shaky progress, Vlad felt the pressure of a system that once required him to design sailboats in secret for fear of being prosecuted for the economic crime of carrying on private business. The dearth of offshore experience among FAZISI's crew was a residue of government restrictions on ocean sailing designed to prevent Soviet citizens from sailing away to freer shores.

Vlad Murnikov was one Soviet citizen who decided not to return to his homeland after his incredible Whitbread adventure, not to stay, at least. He lives now in the United States with his wife Tatiana, designing and marketing fast, innovative sailboats in the cradle of free enterprise. He didn't set out to design FAZISI, chase sponsors, organize construction, recruit a crew and sail in a grueling race around the world in order to find a new life in America. It just worked out that way. And therein lies a great American immigrant story.

William F. Schanen
Editor and Publisher
SAILING Magazine

Vladislav Murnikov

FAZISI's route during the
Whitbread Round the World Race
1989-90

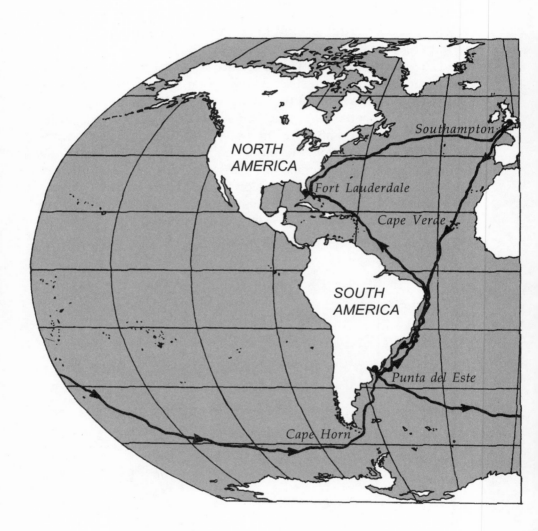

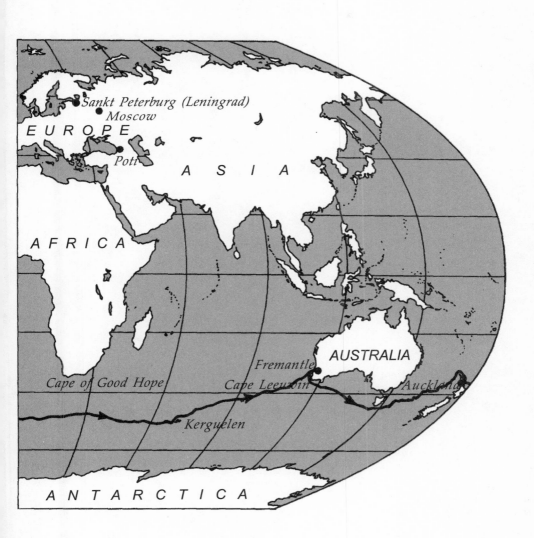

RACE

TO

FREEDOM

PART I

AGAINST ALL ODDS

1

THE DREAM

My first watch on FAZISI had come to an end but I didn't want to go below—not yet. I knew I wouldn't sleep anyway, I was too excited. Leaving my position at the backstay winch behind Dale Tremain, who took his turn at the steering wheel, I headed to the afterdeck, my steps careful and unsteady on the boat's bouncing deck. I hadn't developed a feel for her motion yet. All my previous sailing on FAZISI had been in the much more sedate conditions of The Solent and off Punta del Este. Surrounded by the stormy Indian Ocean, as we sailed farther and farther south around Australia, it was different now.

It was evening on December 23, 1989, and we had just started the third leg of the Whitbread Round the World Race aboard the Soviet Maxi racer FAZISI. We — the first-ever Soviet entry in the world's most grueling ocean race with the American Skip Novak as the skipper. Indeed an unusual mix but there was much more of the unusual in our entry. In the height of *perestroika*, which would change not only Russia but also the entire order of the world, our entry FAZISI with her international crew bravely challenging the most treacherous waters of the planet was, in a sense, like a dove sent out into an uncertain future. Like perestroika itself, FAZISI's entry was an experiment in survival.

Well, wet and cold, totally exhausted after my first watch, I was in no mood at this moment to reflect on the world's issues or, for that matter, our mission. All I cared about now was a cup of hot tea and a bite to eat, even if it was an awful freeze-dried, cosmonaut-type ration. Then I would crawl deep into the warmth of my sleeping bag for a short rest.

For the two weeks leading up to the start, the weather had been absolutely delightful, a mixture of bright sunshine with a nice fresh breeze—not too strong, just enough to make the hot Australian summer comfortable. But on the eve of the start, a gale off the Indian Ocean brought cold rain with a strong westerly. By the start it was blowing at Force 8. The first day at sea, typically a time of adjustment, was especially uncomfortable. The storm wasn't helping our acclimatization. Everyone felt at least a little seasick, but that was okay. It would go away in a day or two.

By dawn, having already rounded Cape Leeuwin, we turned southeast. The wind remained strong but on a spinnaker reach now, the boat felt much more comfortable. Her speed increased as she hit a plane more and more frequently. Flying through clouds of spray, her acceleration was quick and so abrupt the deck seemed to spring forward away from my feet as the Speedo bounced upward from 14 to 18 to 20 knots.

For the first time in my life I was sailing in conditions far beyond my wildest dreams. The rain had ended and rays of sunlight, breaking through the torn, fast flying clouds, painted bright turquoise patches on the dark surface of the ocean. The menacingly howling wind complemented the wild beauty of nature surrounding us. The following seas, coming at 120 degrees to the boat, increased to 15-18 feet. Occasionally an especially big wave would slam hard into the quarter, rise up into the air and break into a myriad of sparkling diamonds, then flush the deck with the power of a fire hose. Everyone was wearing full foul-weather gear and inflatable life vests with safety harnesses hooked on to the boat. Yuri Doroshenko, sitting next to me on the weather rail, wore two harnesses. He explained that when moving on deck he would never unhook one without first securing the other in front of him. Then he pulled out the emergency strobes that he kept in his pocket. "Just in case," he said. "You never know if you'll end up in the water. I'm well prepared for anything."

I listened with visible respect. After all, with two legs of the race under his belt, he was something of a veteran Whitbreader now. But I felt he was a little full of himself and had gotten carried away with safety precautions. So far the ocean had been neither scary nor hard on me, just beautiful and exciting. Well, we'll see.

About a mile to the south, a big cargo ship was struggling to make its way westbound against the seas. At times half of it was covered by waves, then it would slowly emerge, shaking off the water. The sight provided a good perspective on what the sea conditions really were and sobered me somewhat. I wondered how we looked to the crew of that ship -- just a tiny speck of a boat flying among the waves in a cloud of spray...

The ship disappeared in minutes as we flew past. All in all that first day we covered more than 320 miles, maintaining a position right in the middle of the fleet. Ahead were the usual leaders, the two New Zealand ketches, STEINLAGER and FISHER & PAYKEL, with MERIT and ROTHMANS right on their heels.

By sunset the wind had abated somewhat and the seas, though still high, became less steep. Now the conditions were even better for surfing. Coming on watch, I took FAZISI's helm. Steering her for the first time in planing conditions, I was a little nervous to start with. But it was so easy; the helm was so sweet. It seemed as if she knew where to go and required only the slightest input from me. In no time we had established a harmony. To a large extent this boat was my brainchild and at that moment I was extremely proud, as any parent would be. The long days at the drafting board and the many struggles that led up to this moment in the Southern Ocean had finally paid off.

Because it was my first experience, and at night to boot, the speed sensation was intense. In the darkness FAZISI seemed much larger, her bow so far away. With each swell she would dip forward, the bow sinking till the water came nearly up to the deck. Then she would lift her transom and start sliding down the wave faster and faster. Fluorescent spray would grow higher and higher until it formed two wide, roaring walls almost 10 feet high on each side of the boat, which flew by, disappearing into the darkness. Reflecting her running lights, the foam and spray sparkled emerald green to starboard and ruby red to port. At this point, the boat rode as smooth as an express train on polished rails, with only slight vibrations revealing the strain she was under. Absolutely awesome.

The lighted digits on the jumbo Speedo would jump to 20, sometimes to 22 knots, and stay there for half a minute, or even longer if I could hold the wave just right. I didn't break any records but I felt like a helm wizard, guiding this creature of my dreams on a flight through the ethereal night—further and further down the path of shimmering reflections.

An hour flew by in an instant. Suddenly Edgar Terekhin's voice broke the spell. "All right, that's enough. Let others have their fun too."

• • •

Back to reality and below deck, I found Skip surrounded by our navigator Sergey Akatyev and boat technician Eugene Platon, all listening to the radio. Skip gestured to me to keep quiet and waved me over. Through bursts of static I could recognize the British accent of a

BBC news announcer, "After violent riots in Bucharest, crowds have stormed and captured the government palace. Romanian dictator Nicolae Ceausescu has fled with his family. Their whereabouts are unknown." Eugene was listening with utmost attention. He was originally from Moldavia, the small Soviet republic that borders Romania and in ancient times had been a part of it. I knew Eugene was a strong supporter of reunification of Moldavia and Romania. The radio voice went on to other news, which included a speech in the Soviet parliament by the most prominent dissident Andrei Sakharov, who had been released from political exile just a few months before. Then the news returned to the riots, this time in the Soviet Baltic republics struggling for their independence.

Most of the news those days was on the crumbling Soviet Bloc. In the few days that followed, the radio brought us announcement of Ceausescu's capture and another round of violence in Romania. And then came the chilling announcement, "... according to unofficial sources, Ceausescu and his family have apparently been executed..." That was quick. The "new democrats" seem to have adopted "red terror" methods as perfected by the Bolsheviks to get rid of their opponents — no trial, no jury, fast and effective — scary.

The whole communist system was falling apart right within earshot. The changes sweeping Eastern Europe were mind-boggling. Germany was celebrating the fall of the Berlin wall, "Velvet Revolution" had prevailed in Czechoslovakia, and Hungary had opened its border with Austria. That was great news, except, of course, for the killing of that poor bastard Ceausescu. But in times of massive change like this, it seems men tend to start with blood and destruction. Hopefully, I thought, the people will calm down, begin thinking rationally, and then start rebuilding. Well, sometimes they do, sometimes they don't. However it works out, we knew we'd be returning to a totally different world than the one we sailed away from.

Actually, we've been a part of these changes ourselves. FAZISI was the first boat from the USSR to ever enter the Whitbread Round the World Race, one of the toughest and most expensive sporting events of the Western world. We were just a bunch of sailors who, without any sanctioning from the Soviet government, had gone ahead on our own and built a magnificent racing yacht, found sponsorship from one of the first Soviet private enterprises formed under perestroika and sailed away into the open ocean. All of this would have been unheard of just a few years ago — totally impossible — yet it had happened. The endeavor changed us. Hopefully, it also helped to change some people around us. In a small sense, our free enterprise had hammered another nail into the coffin of the communist past, and we were proud of this.

Well, perhaps we really had achieved something important and as FAZISI's designer and project manager, I had every reason to be happy. After all, this was my dream come true. The boat that had taken more than three years of my life to become a reality had turned out great, on par with the world's finest yachts. And yes, sometimes I felt proud and happy. Yet the reality of our dramatic situation never eased its grip. The future looked grim. We were battling a stormy ocean that could crush our boat at any moment. But that was the easy part; our other troubles were much more serious.

We had sailed away with an improperly tuned mast that was so terribly skewed to port it threatened to crumble overboard at any moment. The brewing crew conflict was ready to erupt, and we were financially broke. Our Soviet sponsor *Sovmestnoye Predpriyatiye* (joint venture) Fazis SP, one of the first private enterprises formed under the Gorbachev reforms, was not doing well and struggling to survive the turmoil of perestroika. It had already spent far more than it could afford just to bring our boat to the start. Then, only a few days before the race began, we lost our main hope, support of Pepsi International. Their vague explanation came down to fear of negative reaction in America for funding a Soviet boat while potential American Whitbread entries dropped out for lack of sponsors.

How's that for fulfillment of the dream?

The next night on the weather rail, while seated between Dale Tremain and Yuri Doroshenko, I allowed my thoughts to slide back into the past, through the last year—it had been a long, long one. It seemed like a whole lifetime ago we were building this boat at the Poti Shipyard in the Republic of Georgia, yet it was only last winter. Then sailing in the Whitbread was just a distant dream for all of us, and, as we were losing the race against time, that dream seemed to be slipping away. But now it had become a reality all around me, a reality that was not even close to what I had imagined. It was both much better and much worse. What a cliché indeed, but life sometimes presents them.

The sky above us was clear, filled with billions of stars. A cliché again, but this was the reality of that night far away at sea. Those stars were totally different from the ones I'd been used to seeing all of my life. Instead of the North Star, the Southern Cross was overhead. I remember my surprise when I saw its four tiny stars for the first time. How small they appeared compared to the great multitude of feelings they stir in the souls of sailors! Who of us hasn't dreamed of such a night on a boat under the Southern Cross? I kept looking at the twinkling lights until they became blurry — or maybe it was just a sudden moistness in my eyes.

The dream had become a reality, but it brought so much trouble that I wasn't sure any longer whether the effort was worth it. Almost three months had passed since the death of Alexey Grischenko in Punta del Este, but I still wasn't able to cope with its final reality. I just tried to suppress it deeper into my mind, hoping that I would be able to face it later. He was not a very close friend, but that didn't seem to make the loss less painful. He was a good man. We had started this project together and had dreamed together about the race. And now I was on our boat in the ocean and where was he?

Through the mist covering my eyes I saw weak rays of light coming from the southern quarter. They were like distant searchlights scanning the horizon. The light was getting brighter and more visible, changing shape all the time. Then it turned into a fluorescent veil trembling in the wind. It faded for a moment and then, again, its gentle fire lighted half of the sky. I couldn't believe my eyes. Was this really Aurora Australis? We were only at 45 degrees latitude. I never imagined it could be visible this far from the Pole. But it was no mistake and all of the crew now were watching in amazement. As the waves of light ran down from space, I realized this was another blessing that answered my unspoken questions. Still in a web of doubts, I was receiving signs one way or another that kept my hopes alive.

• • •

My thoughts flew further back to when it all had started. The dream had been with me long before it had become a decision three years ago, in December of 1986.

It was a cold and rainy evening, with a northerly wind that could chill you to the bone. I was in Tallinn, Estonia, visiting my mother. She was very lonely and lost since my father's passing away earlier that summer. We spent the weekend together, bittersweet and sad, both still recovering from the loss.

Now I was on my way to the railroad station to catch an overnight express back to Moscow. With 45 minutes left till departure, I paid the taxi driver at the entrance to the Old Town and walked the rest of the way through its maze of narrow streets. On the corner of *Ratusha* (town hall) square was my favorite *bookinist*, the best used-book store in Tallinn. I had bought a few good books there before and now walked along the shelves in anticipation. Rummaging through a pile of old Russian sailing magazines left there on consignment, I suddenly spotted the glossy cover of SAIL magazine. What a stroke of luck!

Foreign magazines were banned in Russia. Who knows what kinds of ideas people might get wandering through seductive pages and comparing the lustrous images with the surrounding drab reality. You could find foreign literature in only a few libraries, that is if you were lucky enough to obtain a special-access permit. Estonia was different; it was almost Europe and life there was less restrictive. Tallinn was a big port, and sailors returning home smuggled plenty of contraband. For those looking for American jeans, French perfume, and exotic booze — or sailing magazines, for that matter — Tallinn provided a better chance than most places in the Soviet Union to find it all.

I didn't even look to see how old the magazine was. I just grabbed it and rushed to the counter. Almost running through the rest of the Old Town, I completely ignored the best spots where under normal circumstances, I would have paused to admire the rugged beauty of the ancient fortress. I couldn't wait to be aboard the train and alone with my treasure.

I probably should explain at this point that I was a total sailing freak, and everything related to sailing was almost like an addictive drug to me. I am sure I could have survived for a couple weeks just on reading sailing magazines and making sketches of boats. Certainly not a good passion for a Russian to have. Actually I am Ukrainian. As a citizen of the Soviet Union, technically speaking, I should have called myself and most of my shipmates Soviets. Sometimes in the following pages of this book I will; however, I'll do it with lots of reservation. I hate the word as much as I hated the system. Russia existed long before the Soviet Union, and the Ukraine was always a part of it. Or rather it was one country long ago called Kiev Russ. So I don't see any problem in calling myself Russian. Sometimes, for simplicity's sake, I will call my fellow sailors Russians as well, although they'd probably disagree, as most of them came from different republics of the former Soviet Union.

● ● ●

I walked through the railroad station, went out to the platform and stepped onto the train. Russian long-distance trains were in fact pretty good. The sleeping cars were divided into spacious compartments — larger than Amtrak's — for two or four passengers each. In the evening and early in the morning, tea and coffee were served right in the compartments. If you wished to have dinner or breakfast, there was a decent restaurant car in the middle of the train.

Being in these close quarters encouraged strangers to become acquainted quickly. By the time the train departed people would usually be well into conversations about the weather (for the beginning), about the other's destination (with polite interest), about politics (very cautiously) and about sports (passionately). Jokes and anecdotes helped the time go by. Soon someone would reach for a bottle of vodka or brandy to share with his companions. Everyone would relax and feel like old friends for a while, and the journey would transform from a mere movement between points A and B to a pleasant ride through time and space.

But now I was in no mood for trivial conversation. After initial greetings, while trying not to be rude, I excused myself saying I was tired and climbed into my upper bunk. I quickly opened SAIL and rushed through its pages. In another stroke of luck the entire issue was devoted to the previous Whitbread Round the World Race. It was thicker than usual and packed with information about the race routes, the boats, the sailors, the sponsors, and the budgets. The Whitbread had been my burning desire for many, many years, and I had dreamed about the race hopelessly, knowing that I would never be able to do it. The iron curtain around Russia, which had stood firm for more than 60 years, was absolutely impenetrable for anybody or anything, let alone a boat and a sailor seeking to escape into the freedom of the open ocean. It was just an impossible dream—nothing more.

Oddly enough, some information about the Whitbread race was available in Russia. I tried to find and read everything I could about it. Now, having Sail magazine in my hands appeared like an omen. What were the odds that I would be in Tallinn and walk into that bookinist store right at the time when someone had left on consignment what might have been the only copy of SAIL in all of Estonia? And that this particular issue would be crammed full of detail about the Whitbread? Come on, in no way was it a coincidence. I shivered from excitement and nervous anticipation, feeling as if I was on the threshold of my destiny.

Whatever. Was I kidding myself?

For the next hours — who knows how many as I never looked at my watch — I was immersed in the magazine. My companions were long since sound asleep while the train sped through the night, wallowing slightly on the turns. As I read on, one thing that grew clearer and clearer was a realization of the extraordinary hardship the Whitbread skippers and team leaders went through. It was not from the ocean, whose challenge was obvious, but rather from the enormous hazards before the race even started, during the preparations. This came as a total surprise — and inspiration — to me.

Let me explain.

For many years, Soviet propaganda tried too hard to convince us how terrible life was in the capitalistic jungles, but I didn't buy it. Newspapers, magazines and Soviet TV were full of pictures of desperate homeless people digging into garbage cans for food leftovers on some dark and slimy street. "A typical city scene in New York," the caption would read. And the other, "An endless line of unemployed, patiently waiting for a free bowl of soup." Or a picture of the Brooklyn Bridge with the words, "The favorite place of suicides, where people unable to cope with capitalistic reality take their last desperate leap." And of course there were always photos of disasters, airplane crashes, smashed cars and trains — all in attempt to convince us that bad things happen only in the West. They had overdone it and the effect (at least on me) couldn't have been more contrary. I didn't believe a word of it and was absolutely sure that Western reality was directly opposite of what Soviet information intended us to think.

It almost looked like paradise when you glimpsed at it through the narrow, barred gaps from the Soviet side of the iron curtain. Compared to the reality of life in Russia, it probably was a paradise. Occasionally I would be lucky enough to hear Voice of America breaking through the interference and suppression of the Russian military radio stations, or get a glimpse of a Western magazine, or watch an American movie. How beautiful THAT life appeared on the magic screen! Over time, in my imagination, I naively painted a rosy picture of Western life, which was perhaps as far from reality as the dark image produced by the Soviet propaganda. I grew more and more to believe that hardship, tribulations, and failures belonged only to the system that I lived in.

It was almost a revelation now to find that those Whitbread guys went through all kinds of problems and challenges and managed to overcome them. I realized that for most of them at the beginning it had been nothing else but an impossible dream. Just as it was for me.

I had already completed a few sailing projects, a very difficult thing to pull off in Russia. I felt quite confident of my abilities. But those previous projects were all amateurish and in no way comparable to the scope of the Whitbread. It loomed at an unreachable height, like Mount Everest, to which it's often compared, dwarfing everything I had achieved before. It made me nervous to even think about it, yet the temptation was irresistible. Deep inside, my confidence began to grow that however huge the Whitbread project appeared, it was doable, as other people before me had proved. If they had done it, why not me?

It's a big undertaking, true. Yet, in a sense, it's just like any other goal. You make your decision, develop a plan of action and move persistently forward until you reach it. If I recall correctly, the Confucian saying goes something like this, "No matter how high the mountain is and how small your steps are, if they lead in the right direction, eventually you'll get there."

It takes 12 hours for the express train to make its trip, plenty of time to have a good night's sleep. It arrives in Moscow before 8 a.m., just in time for the beginning of the business day. That night I barely slept for two hours. After reading the entire magazine, I thought for a while about what kind of boat I would design for the race. The idea of such a dream boat was not new to me; in fact, I had played with it many times in the past and even made numerous sketches. It was different now. For the first time it was not just an abstract idea that I knew would never materialize. Something had radically changed in my mind in the last few hours. Now I was not dreaming about a Whitbread boat anymore. I was designing her.

I pictured a long and sleek, no-nonsense racing machine, very light, much lighter than any boat ever sailed in Whitbread. She would surf like a light dinghy in the prevailing following seas. She wouldn't need a lot of sail area, as the winds are usually strong in the Southern Ocean, and she wouldn't have the bulk that heavier boats carry. Less sail area meant she would be easier to sail. Her bow will be sharp, the waterline narrow, and she would cut effortlessly through the waves. She will sail fast not due to the power of enormous sail area, but because of the efficiency of her elegant, slippery hull. Well, this had been my design philosophy for a long time; still it was amazing how quickly the distinctive features of a Whitbread boat began crystallizing in my mind now.

But no matter how much I enjoyed thinking about the future boat's design, I knew that this would be the easiest part of the project, and it would never happen without two more important factors: organization and financing. So I pushed the boat's image out of my mind and started thinking about these essentials. My thoughts were so clear at that moment that in the next couple hours I had developed a complete plan for the Whitbread campaign; it would take me three years to carry it out. It was a sketchy plan, but that didn't bother me. I knew the missing pieces would be found later.

•••

Upon arriving home, I put all my night thoughts on paper. Now I had a brief action plan with a schedule and a budget. I knew the numbers would change later, who cares. At least it was a starting point. Then I carefully cut out from the SAIL magazine all the pages dedicated to the Whitbread and glued them to a poster board. The display was huge and all there: the colorful map of the world with the race route marked on it, line drawings and technical information on the racers of previous Whitbreads, portraits of the skippers and, of course, alluring images of sailing in the Southern Ocean. My wife Tatiana observed my activities with seeming disapproval but didn't say a word. She didn't share my fascination with sailing and would have rather seen my energy funneled into something closer to the mainstream, like making a decent career. But she was tired of complaining. She knew it would lead nowhere and just erode our relationship more.

I placed my Whitbread poster in the living room. It covered almost an entire wall. Now it would motivate me every time I came into the room, and there simply would be no way of changing my mind. Of course, to a large extent, it still was a game. But the more I toyed with the idea, the more it became evident that deep inside I'd already made a commitment, and there was no way to back out. Yes, I still was slightly irresolute and confused, perhaps even slightly scared of my decision, but with a little bit of encouragement I'd be unstoppable.

2

THE RACE

Once every four years, with the sound of the gun fired by the British Royal Navy, a fleet of the world's top ocean racers sets off down The Solent. As it rushes to exit the strait that separates the British mainland from the Isle of Wight, this magnificent fleet of blue-water raceboats embarks on a nine-month-long marathon around the world. The goal of these racers is not only to return safely after crossing the Earth's most treacherous waters, but to be the first back. For they are racing in the Whitbread Round the World Race, the ultimate circumnavigation.

It first takes the fleet south, down the Atlantic Ocean all the way to the Roaring 40s and Furious 50s, named for the ferocity of winds in the southern latitudes around Antarctica. The racers then turn east, leaving Africa, Australia, and South America to port in this eastbound circling. Finally, they climb north up the Atlantic Ocean and back to England to the finish—a voyage of more than 30,000 miles. Sailors participating in this longest marathon in the world must endure all variety of extremes: from the baking heat of the equator to the dead calms of the doldrums, from the fury of the winds of the Southern Ocean to its monstrous, boat-engulfing seas. They must put up with the cold and the snowstorms of the high latitudes and must course unflinchingly amid the icebergs. In short, they must take whatever the world's oceans may toss their way.

The first Whitbread took place in 1973-74. It marked the birth of the phenomenon of extreme sports, though it would be another two decades before the term would come into popular use. Nine months after the start the sailors returned from the inaugural globe-girdling race, battered but triumphant. The publicity was tremendous, and with the race becoming such a success, it was obvious, it needed a sequel. It followed four years later in 1977-78. And then again four years after that, gradually elevating the Whitbread into the toughest and most prestigious endurance race of the sailing world.

For some strange reason, the Whitbread even received decent media coverage in the Soviet Union. Yes, the race was a bad, big-money, vanity-capitalistic game, but it was also a pure and romantic adventure that pitted brave sunburned sailors against the dangerous oceans of the world. Even the haughtiest of Soviet censors (of course, all information in Russia was checked and double-checked before being published) couldn't deep-six this story about a wholesome human challenge set on the high seas. Russians have always been hopeless romantics. Nearly landlocked, we Russians carry an unanswerable yearning for the far-away horizons and the alluring expanse of the sea — for the promise of freedom. There was good reason why "The Ruby Sails," a sentimental saga of love, dreams, and sailing by the Russian writer Alexander Green, had become such a popular book among Soviet youth. The very term "ruby sails" had evolved into a Russian symbol of the ultimate dream, which, if one only wanted it badly enough, could become reality.

Of course, information appearing in the Soviet press on the Whitbread was as far from reality as any dream is. Here's an example: "Publicity becomes a major prize for companies whose names cover raceboat hulls and spinnakers. In shameless advertising and self-promotion, these companies exploit the pure devotion to the sport, the courage, and the high professional skills of the sailors. And because they receive global exposure, the industrialists, *commersants* and financiers are ready and willing to spend enormous amounts of money." Isn't it great, I thought as I read *Katera i Yachty*, the only Russian sailing magazine, that the world is full of shameless industrialists and financiers eager to spend big money for the opportunity of getting their names on Whitbread boats. If it were my boat, that's exploitation I wouldn't mind.

Actually, when the Whitbread began in 1973, most of its sailors were not professionals at all. True, the racers were devoted and courageous, but they were mainly just passionate amateur sailors. With little organization and regulation, racing around the world in 1973 was still at an embryo stage. This kind of racing stood for an ultimate freedom, and it attracted dedicated cohorts of brave and adventurous free spirits. Who knows what lured generation after generation of sailors to leave the safety and security of land for new horizons – among them Magellan, Vasco da Gama, Columbus, Captain Cook? Of course, they were looking for reward and glory. But I'd bet that even if told they would gain nothing at the end (and that was what most of them did indeed receive — nothing but suffering and untimely death), that would not have stopped them. Some people simply have an implanted bug for adventure and discovery that is just plain irresistible. They are born to find what new land lies behind that faraway mist, to find if the earth really rests on three giant whales, as the ancient books taught. To find if there is a limit to the universe, a limit to their own abilities. Some people are born explorers, born to try and test.

Following the era of great geographic discoveries and centuries of empire building around the world, sailing ships dominated transportation. They were the backbone of commerce, trade, military expansion, and progress -- the backbone of human communication. By the mid-nineteenth century, sailing vessels reached their pinnacle with fleets of square-riggers rushing around the world, delivering exotic goods from the far Pacific to European ports. Time was money — as it always has been. So, inevitably, every clippership's passage became a race to be the first back to Europe in order to get the best prices in the market. In its 1869-70 passage, the British clipper PATRIARCH sailed the London-Sydney-London route completing the eastbound loop around the world in only 136 days. It was a record time that stood for more than 100 years. Another record, the fastest 24-hour run, was set by the American clipper CHAMPION OF THE SEAS, sailing an incredible 465 miles with an average speed of 19.4 knots!

That's how ocean racing was born.

The first man to sail alone around the world was an American, Captain Joshua Slocum in 1895-98. Not only a great sailor but also an accomplished storyteller, Slocum described his three-year voyage in his book "Sailing Alone Around the World," one of the best adventure stories ever written. What one man could do others could too, and Slocum spurred many followers to cross the world's oceans in tiny, vulnerable craft. There might have been many more of them had it not been for the dramatic events of the first half of the twentieth century, which pushed sailing deeply into the background. The world became obsessed with fighting instead. The two bloodiest World Wars followed each other with only 20 years of intervening peace. At the end, Europe laid in ruins. It was not until the mid-1950s that offshore sailing returned to the scene again.

The event that marked the beginning of long-distance ocean racing came in 1960 when five small yachts from England and France, each singlehanded, set out to race across the Atlantic. The first to finish was Sir Francis Chichester on his 40-foot GYPSY MOTH III. Encouraged, six years later Chichester attempted to break the clippership round-the-world record on a modern, specially designed sailboat. Chichester came very close to accomplishing his goal, but, more importantly, he made a very fast solo passage around the world. It was an achievement previously thought impossible.

That done, it wasn't long until the Golden Globe Race was founded in 1968. It was conceived as the ultimate race for the fastest solo non-stop circumnavigation. But it turned into a disaster. Of eight boats starting, only one, SUHAILI, skippered by Sir Robin Knox-Johnson, finished. By attrition, Knox-Johnson had won and became the first person to singlehandedly sail non-stop around the world. The rest of the fleet had fallen away, with some boats capsizing and some racers simply giving up. One sailor, unable to cope with the pressure and the loneliness of the solo race, committed suicide.

Apparently, the human race was not ready yet for this level of adventure. Enthusiasm for transoceanic racing fizzled until a new, less-extreme around-the-world race was proposed. In a way it seemed a sort of retreat to common sense and safety. A new race was proposed as a fully-crewed competition that would follow the traditional clippership routes and include three stopovers, Cape Town, Sydney, and Rio de Janeiro. To ensure proper organization and safety measures, the British Royal Naval Sailing Association helped establish and maintain the rules and safety guidelines for the race. Shortly after, the English brewery Whitbread PLC agreed to be the title sponsor and picked up the tab for the cost of running the race. At the time it was a bold and brave move. Such a big endorsement was unheard of, but it paid off handsomely for the Whitbread Company, helping to establish its worldwide brand identity. Since the most recent Whitbread of 1997-98 Volvo purchased the rights to the race. The next race, set to start September, 2001, will be known under the new name of the Volvo Ocean Race 2001-2002.

The first Whitbread was a well-thought-out, thoroughly organized event, with greater emphasis on safety. Still it took its tragic toll. Three sailors were lost at sea. They didn't perish in vain. Lessons were learned, and new developments in survival gear and the next generation of racing boats, designed to stricter safety regulations, made subsequent races less treacherous. Still, oceans remain oceans. Any ship that leaves the shore is never ensured of reaching its destination.

Through the years the Whitbread has developed into a highly professional sporting event with multimillion-dollar budgets, paid crews, and corporate sponsors that cover hulls and sails with their logos. In that, the article in *Katera i Yachty* magazine was right. Except, it wasn't the companies that were looking for raceboats to sponsor, emblazon with their graphics, and shower with cash. In fact, the truth was just the opposite. And at the time we unfortunately had no way of knowing otherwise. It was the sailors who were seeking, fighting, and competing for sponsors in order to bring their dream of crossing the oceans to fruition.

By the time I bought that Sail magazine and read it in the express train Tallinn-Moscow, preparation for the fifth Whitbread Round the World Race, scheduled to run in 1989-90, was already in full swing. There was no doubt that this Whitbread would be the greatest one yet — possibly even the greatest sailboat race of the century. Pierre Feldmann from Switzerland, who had finished first in the previous race on his UNION BANK OF SWITZERLAND, would be back, this time supported by Merit Tobacco. Ludde Ingvall, another Whitbread veteran, had announced a multimillion-dollar sponsorship from Union Bank of Finland. American Skip Novak, after sailing three previous races as the skipper for other syndicates, the last time on DRUM, which belonged to the singer Simon LeBon of the rock group Duran-Duran, had started his own campaign. And, of course, the most experienced of them all, New Zealander Peter Blake, veteran of all four previous Whitbread Races, would be back with a vengeance, determined to win this time.

Would I dare to join them?

3

WIND OF CHANGES

My full name is Vladislav Valentinovich Murnikov, but friends simply call me Vlad. I was born in 1951 in Cherkassy, a small provincial town some 120 miles south of the Ukrainian capital Kiev. Only a few blocks from our house, down a steep bank, was the mighty Dnipro River, spread out as far as the eye could see. It was actually a huge reservoir or "an artificial sea" as it was called, more than a hundred miles long and about 15 miles wide, created with the building of a hydroelectric dam down stream. For me, as a child, it was truly like living near a huge sea where I spent all my summers in play. During those long vacations, I became an excellent swimmer and rowed kayaks at the Youth Sports School *Vodnik* (Mariner), but I was always dreaming of sailboats. Only occasionally I had a chance to sail for there were few sailboats around. Sailing was not a popular sport in the Soviet Union, and my first real opportunity to sail didn't come until much later in life, in the mid-70s when I was living in Moscow.

I was a smart kid and went through school easily. At the age of 14, after performing very well in a regional mathematics competition, I was invited to attend the exclusive high school at Kiev University, the Ukrainian School of Mathematics and Science. Being very close to my parents, I left home with great reluctance and cried under my blanket during those first lonely nights in the dorm. But slowly acclimatizing to my new status, I eventually came to find school life quite exciting and enjoyed being independent at such a young age. Two years later I graduated with the Medal of Honor. But instead of going to a university to continue on the academic path, studying science and mathematics, I followed my other passion and went into design and architecture.

I spent the next five years at the Moscow Engineering Institute, learning architecture and civil engineering. These were wonderful years but unfortunately they flashed by far too quickly. I was a good student, though I had never worked too hard and was always able to find enough time for reading my favorite books, go to the theatre, as well as for wild parties, rock music, and girls. Beautiful, sweet Russian girls...

My friends and I took up a hippie dress and wore long hair, all the while under a constant threat of getting thrown out of the college — a threat that fortunately never materialized. The late 1960s was a time when the young generation rebelled, not only in the West, in my world too. Most of my fellow rebels calmed down — as well as I did to a certain degree, I guess. But deep in my soul, I never did completely.

The college years flashed by. I successfully defended my thesis on studies of American skyscrapers, and suddenly my youth was gone. I received an assignment to work in one of the enormous architectural firms in Moscow. (I didn't need to look for a job after graduation in the Soviet Union. For a mandatory three years, everyone worked wherever the government considered it appropriate and necessary. The law of "a-guaranteed-job-for-all" in action.)

From the very beginning of my career, I had decided that I would not build career at all, would not climb the standard steps of the professional ladder. Going up that ladder came at a hefty price in the Soviet Union. At some point if you wanted to move up, you would have to become a member of the Communist Party. Non-members were not allowed into the top positions. Some people, looking for the small perks membership promised, joined the party happily. Others -- only reluctantly, saying in justification that they simply had no other choice, that there simply was no other way to get a better, wealthier life.

In fact, they did have a choice. There were two methods of payment for work in Soviet Union. The traditional one, chosen by the majority, was based on the time spent on the work premises. The other one – based on performance and result compensation — was determined by the actual amount of work completed, or projects accomplished. This was a far less popular option, but the one that I chose. Instead of receiving a flat salary, you were paid for the actual job done and so, with efficiency, you could earn much more. On this track, however, there was no moving up in the hierarchy of the Soviet society, and one had to give up all ambitions and remain indefinitely at the lower step of a career ladder. But, at least money-wise, one could be better off than his party-joining peers, without having to make compromises and conform to the system.

Being out of college with very little life experience, I had only sketchy knowledge of how bad the system was. But I had already made one important resolution to myself and would stick to it: I would do whatever it took to not compromise with its rules.

It was my father— though he probably never realized it—who taught me a very important lesson that shaped my entire life. He was a very talented engineer, a workaholic at that, spending literally days and nights at his office. He progressed upward quickly in his profession and before the age of 35 was offered the position of chief engineer at a large construction company. Obviously, it came with the condition that he would join the party. I remember clearly the torturous doubts he had. He discussed the matter with my mother and also with my sister and me, even though we were still just kids and didn't really understand the situation. He wanted us to realize and remember that he was doing this only so that he could provide a better, more prosperous future for us.

After the decision he gradually changed. He was still the same loving father, who cherished those rare moments spent with us away from work, but he was never as open and free-spirited again. Torn between his beliefs and loyalty to the system, which he had finally accepted, he lost that spark of independence, which I had so admired in him before.

In fact, it was my father who triggered my insatiable thirst for freedom and independence. He grew up in the 1930s in a country choked by Stalin's repression. At that time everyone was supposed to be like everyone else, just small gears in the huge mechanism of the communist empire. My father would have probably grown up to become an ordinary, obedient Russian citizen, as had the millions around him, were it not for World War II. When, after a blitzkrieg, Hitler's army had occupied Ukraine, my father, age 15, was detained and, together with thousands of other boys, sent to a labor camp in Germany for more than three years. In the winter of 1945 as the front line approached bringing chaos to Germany, my father managed to escape from his master. After two months of wandering around occupied Europe, meeting Germans and also American, French, and British POWs, he finally crossed the front line, joining the Soviet army in eastern Prussia.

By a stroke of luck, he escaped being sent to the *gulag*, where most of the POWs or slave laborers liberated by the Soviet army ended up. But, perhaps even worse, my father was instead sent to the front line. Without having any training, it was like a death sentence. He had been fighting for less than a month when the German bullet came piercing his chest, wreaking havoc in his lungs and nearly killing him. After a year of numerous surgeries, he was finally discharged from the hospital. The doctors said he would be lucky to live another year. Yet my father survived.

However terrible it had been to be indentured as a 15-year-old to slave labor, in a paradoxical way it had provided my father with an opportunity to see life in Europe and compare it to Soviet Union reality. He made his conclusion, after which he never again bought the lies of communist ideology so successfully fed to his countryman.

From my early childhood with the usual fairytales replaced by my father's stories of his wandering, I grew up very aware of the big and intriguing world outside the Iron Curtain.

• • •

Up until 1986, for almost 70 years, the Soviet Union had stood virtually unchanged, a decaying yet still strong bastion of communism. Then Michael Gorbachev, who had come to power the year before, began making some pretty strange moves. Even years later this man still remains a mystery to me. He came to power in the way that most rulers in the Soviet Union do, upon the death of his predecessor, in his case Leonid Bresznev. Of course, there were no elections of any kind. Actually, preceding Gorbachev were two other heads of state, Andropov and Kirilenko, but their stints at the helm of the USSR were brief and unmemorable.

When Michael Gorbachev became the head of the Soviet Empire in April 1985 no one could have ever imagined that what began as a typical exchange of power would turn into one of the most extraordinary events of modern political history. Yes, I truly believe that what Gorbachev did for Russia bears no analogy to the past. There were plenty of tyrants who usurped power, but as far as I know, there was no other dictator who by his own will would hand his absolute power to the people.

Julius Caesar turned the Roman republic into his own empire. The same trick was performed by Napoleon Bonaparte with the French Republic. Among others were Hitler, Mussolini, and General Pinochet, to name a few. Vladimir Lenin certainly deserved to be on the same list, though technically he didn't end a democracy by seizing power in Russia in 1917. There simply was no democracy in Russia's past. In all fairness, it has to be said that Lenin had in fact allowed some pluralism and elements of marketing economy. It was Joseph Stalin who killed it all in the early 1930s.

By his position as ruler of the Soviet Union, Gorbachev was destined to follow the footsteps of his predecessors and occupy, unchallenged, the throne of the General Secretary of the Communist Party as long as he lived. But there was definitely something that distanced this man from all previous Russian rulers — something in the way he looked, talked, and acted. First of all, by Russian leadership standards, he was a young man. He was also able to make speeches without having to refer constantly to the written text in front of him. True, his speeches were generally too long and boring, but unlike Bresznev, who was barely capable of reading what others had written for him, Gorbachev spoke for himself.

At first not many people listened. Soviets had never paid much attention to the dull bullshit their leaders mumbled from stately podiums. But now it was different. And those who started to listen to what Gorbachev was trying to communicate became more and more puzzled. It all began with subtle nuances. For example, while referring to Russia's chronic food shortages, he suddenly stopped using the term "food programs," as his predecessors had, and instead clearly said, "food problems." This was a change of only one word, but it was an indication to me that this man was not going to feed us the usual lies.

I started listening more attentively to him.

Then the Chernobyl reactor exploded in 1986, and for the first time in Soviet history, the state media told us about the tragedy. It was not immediately, information came a couple days after the explosion, and it was only sketchy, but for the first time we had learned tragic news from the official information sources, not through rumors.

The new term *glasnost* turned up and soon became a part of the Russian vocabulary. Its meaning of "openness," or "desire to tell the truth" was unheard of and foreign to Russia.

It is impossible to read another person's mind and I have no idea what motives were behind his actions. The only reasonable explanation I could find was that Gorbachev was probably just an honest leader, the first one in the entire Soviet history, who simply wanted good for his country. As a product of the system, he seemed initially unsure of what to do. But then, seeing such a huge, resource-rich country — potentially the richest in the world — inhabited by poor, unhappy, and oppressed people, he wanted to improve it.

He began with a mistake. His first decree, just a couple weeks after coming to power, was alcohol prohibition. It was not a complete one, just a significant reduction in production accompanied by the closing of about half of the state-run liquor stores. It seemed like a good idea at the time. Russians were definitely drinking too much, alcoholism had become a tremendous national problem affecting all aspects of life, and Gorbachev probably reasoned that if people drank less, they'd probably work more — maybe even start thinking more clearly.

He should have remembered the history of American prohibition. Not surprisingly, Russians didn't quit drinking. Instead, they busied themselves brewing moonshine or wasting their time waiting in the enormous lines at the liquor stores. The even stricter laws that followed brought no change.

For more than a year Gorbachev tried other things, dashing from one extreme to another, like tightening discipline at work places and introducing steeper punishment for petty crimes. Luckily, he was a clever man and learned quickly from these missteps.

Soon, in a real stroke of genius, he introduced a decree called the Law of the Individual Labor Activities. In plain language, it meant that people were no longer obligated to work only for the state, but if chose, they could become independent individual laborers. Then under another law that soon followed, workers were permitted to form labor cooperatives. Still, there were plenty of restrictions, and by Western standards, it was not a lot. Yet for Russia, allowing even small-scale private businesses was nothing short of a revolution.

At the same time Gorbachev was gradually easing up on censorship. Soon people could openly read once-banned newspapers and learn what they had formerly only known through rumors. The words perestroika and glasnost were becoming more and more common in the media. But Soviet citizens weren't jumping with euphoria at all these changes, or rushing to start their own businesses. They simply couldn't believe the changes were real.

Russians are a strong bunch, not easily impressed. They observed Gorbachev's actions with grim disbelief. The memory of Lenin's New Economic Policy, which permitted relative business freedom, was still vivid, even though it dated all the way back to the early 1920s. Its goal was to pull the country out of the economic chaos it had sunk into after the October Revolution. It worked. Russia was on its way to recovery when, ten years later, Stalin ended NEP and sent most of the new businessmen to the gulags. Those, who were more fortunate, escaped abroad.

How could people believe now in Gorbachev's good intentions? Besides, not many people were really looking for change. For the conformists life was good in the USSR. Education and medical care were free; housing was virtually free with marginal monthly rents that equaled the price of a bottle of vodka. There were no rich nor poor, everyone was getting pretty much the same salary, and nobody was pushed to work hard. Best of all, after Gorbachev's short prohibition, vodka had become readily available again. What's to change?

• • •

I was not a conformist. I wasn't happy performing small duties I had been assigned to in the state-owned design firm. It took me awhile to recognize that what I loved the most was designing and building sailboats. I tried to pursue my passion for boating by any means possible. To the extent that I had built my first boat in the late 1970s, long before Gorbachev's perestroika started, in my one-bedroom, second-floor apartment, section by section, then lowered down through the window and assembled it outside. At 25 feet long, it was not a small boat to build in a tiny Moscow flat. Sounds like a crazy idea, but for me there was simply no other way to do it. Only a few amateurs were building boats then, and one needed to be very well connected to get a building space in a yacht club's shed.

So, instead, I engineered my design in a way that the boat could be built as a composite of prefabricated sections. Each part was small enough to fit easily even into my small apartment. Once all the sections were finished, the entire boat could be assembled outside in just a matter of days, and a construction shed would not be required.

With the design completed and a little bit of money saved, I was ready to start my Big Project. Only then did I recognize that my wife Tatiana was not at all thrilled at the idea of turning our cozy flat into a boatyard. The evenings after dinner, when most Russians were relaxing in front of the TV, became tense times for our family. I tried hard to keep construction noise down, but my attempts to mask the sound of the handsaw and hammer with loud rock music were never completely successful. No matter how frequently I vacuumed the room, it always had that dusty workshop look.

Well after midnight, with three to four hours of work completed daily, I would clean up the mess, neatly array the parts and pieces of my future boat on the floor and cover them with a couple of 4-by-8-foot sheets of plywood. Then I would lay a rug strategically over the components on the floor, and my workshop would be transformed back into a typical Russian living room. No one wandering in realized what lain under his or her feet. We even invited guests, had parties, and danced (on the improvised stage above the boat sections – until of course the pile grew too high to climb on top of it) on those rare evenings when I wanted to take a break from my labors.

Initially Tatiana, expecting it would wind down soon, had a relaxed attitude toward my moonlight boatbuilding. But as the construction progressed, she grew more and more alarmed. At first gentle and then more and more firm, her attempts to dissuade me from continuing on the project had quite the opposite effect and strengthened my resolve to build the boat no matter what. The completion of this project became crucial to my integrity. At that point I was convinced that only my strong attitude and persistence can shape my life in a different, more meaningful way than the drab and boring existence all the people around me were comfortable with.

The whole country was in a deep lethargy, which under Gorbachev was called *stagnation*. In all walks of life, socially, politically, and privately, people were just floating aimlessly, following the current, unable to get a grip on their destinies. There was a feeling of hopelessness, realization that any path they may choose would only lead to a dead end.

No one was happy—with anything, with the political system, with their jobs, with their salaries, with their wives or husbands. In the endless *razgovorach* —talks over a cup of tea or, more often, over a glass of vodka around a kitchen table—it was the Russian convention to complain about life that was slipping away into a hopeless day-to-day boredom. And yet few ever tried to change their lives, and those who did dare an attempt never went further than the first line of hurdles.

The same was true of Soviet political life. Wave after wave, political initiatives sent down from that red brick fortress with ruby red stars on top of its watchtowers -- the Kremlin -- were sweeping the country. By the time those waves reached the far corners of Russia, some 7,000 miles away, they were nothing more than mere ripples on the surface of stagnant, murky water. The Grand Five-Year Plans followed each other, setting new goals for prosperity. Goals, which, not surprisingly, were never achieved. Maybe that was for the better. Those goals had no real meaning and led nowhere anyway. The Russian people were perhaps smarter than their bosses realized. They may have simply sabotaged those empty initiatives sent down from the Kremlin.

I was completely fed up with all the laziness, with all the apathy hexing an entire country into a sleeping kingdom of some fairytale gone awry. I wanted action. I wanted to be free to do what I wanted. And as my first step, I was committed to finishing my boat regardless of any obstacles.

When Tatiana finally recognized the scale of my resolution, she became frightened. Although she eventually gave in to my determination, she didn't really embrace my passion. This put a scar on our relations. Besides being an annoying nuisance to a normal family life, my venture completely drained our resources. The materials were expensive and difficult to find. It took me almost two years to build that boat. The construction progressed painstakingly slowly, moving forward one tiny step at a time, as I was able to find the necessary supplies and save enough money to buy them.

Finally the day had come when I funneled all the components out of our window, lowering them to the ground below, all the while creating a small stir among the neighbors. Then with the help of friends, in a matter of just a few days we were able to put the boat together. The concept worked beautifully.

But it took me another two years to outfit the boat, again using our limited funds and endlessly searching for the right supplies and equipment. It took a total of four years without vacation or even weekends off — four years of hard labor, conflicts, and misunderstandings — but I did build the boat. I called her CHAMPION. She turned out to be a reasonably good performer in competitions, which I entered with a crew of friends. We had very little sailing experience and learned everything by ourselves, sometimes the hard way. But we also had a lot of fun and felt tremendously proud that we didn't need to depend on anyone. I sent CHAMPION's drawings to the only Soviet sailing magazine *Katera i Yachty*, which published them. And over time, other people built sailboats the same way I had built CHAMPION.

The first triumph had almost ended my marriage. But that was not the only problem coming from my innocent passion. Considered an unnecessary luxury in the Soviet Union, sailing, save for the small elitist group of Olympic sailors, was practically excluded from the public. In doing what I wanted, I was a rebel and a threat to the system, and I always felt like I was walking a thin line.

• • •

Gradually I designed more sailboats, and over time the hobby grew into a second profession.

In 1981 a group of Russian yachtsmen led by Michael Tzariov invited me to design a raceboat for the One Ton Class. From the Russian perspective, used to fleets of sailboats 20 to 30-feet in length, the almost

40-foot overall One Tonners were huge racing machines. The One Ton Cup, at the time one of the most prestigious sailing trophies coming out of the International Offshore Rule (IOR) handicap system, attracted strong international competition. Tsariov's idea was that if we could design and build a competitive One Tonner, we might stand a chance of getting government support. That would lead to being permitted to sail outside the country and even enter an international sailing events.

Regardless of how closed the Soviet Union was and how stern its officials were in not allowing any sailboats to wander outside the country, if there was a chance to show off Soviet superiority by winning in sailing competition, its rulers might look favorably upon our idea. Unable to prove the advantages of socialism elsewhere, they were zealous to promote sports and arts abroad. That's why the Olympic athletes were such darlings of the Soviet government and enjoyed a very special status, unlimited resources and caring attention of Big Brother. Just bring more medals back to the Motherland as a validation, if you will, of the superiority of communism over the decadent West.

Michael Tzariov was a unique man, one of those rare Russian entrepreneurial souls eager to pursue the dream despite all the obstacles. His dream, like mine, was sailing. And like mine, his path into sailing was totally unconventional, though in a different way. I don't know how he managed to do this, but at some point he had actually convinced high-ranking bureaucrats in the Soviet space program to buy a sailboat for performing scientific experiments and training the cosmonauts. Those experiments looked more like torture, a kind of cruel and unusual punishment. As soon as the weather would get rough enough, Michael and a small crew would take future cosmonauts out on to stormy Onega Lake, a fairly large body of water where conditions could get pretty nasty. Taking one at a time, they'd confine the poor cosmonaut, covered with medical sensors, to the small cabin for two to three days, where he would bounce around, all the while struggling with nausea and throwing up frequently.

Of course, it was a messy job to clean up the boat after each experiment, but it was worth it, for they had full use of the boat until the next storm and the new victim. The boat was a 30-foot Half Tonner, built in Poland under license from the American designer Dick Carter. It was a good, seaworthy boat, but, heavy and slow, it was not a serious competitor. Michael came up with the idea to build a true performance One Tonner.

He teamed up with one of his sailing buddies who was a *profsoius* (trade union) boss for a major industrial enterprise in Moscow. Together they developed an elaborate scheme to build this boat. According to the plan, Michael and his team would do the actual construction. In addition to being good sailors, they, like most Russians, were also handymen. They would contribute their time while the trade union would provide the construction site and pay for the materials. At the end, the boat would be owned by the trade union and used mostly by its members. But Michael would have permission to race the boat at least a few times during the season. I agreed to design the boat in exchange for a position in the racing crew. Barter was always the primary way of doing business in Russia.

For more than a year the boat progressed well, gradually taking shape. Tzariov put together a great team of eight guys who dedicated practically all of their free time to the project. Soon the hull was completed and work on the deck began. Eager to see my best and most sophisticated design thus far come to fruition, I joined the construction team, putting in as much time as I could. Besides, I enjoyed working with such terrific fellows.

And then it happened. Upon arriving at the production shed one Saturday morning, we found its door sealed and posted with the warning not to open under penalty of law. Alarmed, Michael ran to a nearby phone booth and called his trade-union friend. In a short time he returned with bad news. Apparently, one member of the union for which we were building the boat had sent an anonymous letter to the Soviet economical police. The OBHSS (loosely translated as The Department Against Stealing Soviet Property) was the state's watchdog, a fearsome organization, even more notorious than its political counterpart, the KGB, that made sure no one dared to enter into any sort of private business. The OBHSS was largely a corrupt organization, typically bankrolled by black-market bosses and turning a blind eye to their activities. But it was always eager to punish the smaller fish. While real crooks seldom ended up in jail, even the slightest misstep of an ordinary citizen often cost dearly.

As we later learned, the anonymous letter had hinted that there had to be something wrong with this project if a bunch of folk were volunteering their free time without any compensation. There had to be a hidden meaning to this all, it said, and it certainly deserved an investigation. Anonymous letters were the darlings of the OBHSS as well as the KGB. During the repression of the 1930s and 1950s, Soviet citizens were encouraged to spy and rat on each other. It was considered a civic duty, as Stalin tried to transform Russia into a nation of informants. Neighbor was preying on neighbor, sometimes because he really believed he was helping the system to eliminate enemies — other times because of some more earthly motivations. Thousands of people vanished on trumped up charges only because their next-door neighbor wanted their dwelling or wife or possessions. At stake could be anything, and all it took was an anonymous letter to the KGB for a person to disappear.

Luckily, my generation didn't experience the repression of the Stalin era, but we all grew up hearing stories about the relatives taken at night by the "black crows," the notorious KGB's covered wagons, never to be seen again. By the early 1980s the evil power of the Soviet system had become largely rotted away, as it grew softer and softer. Nonetheless, it could still be scary at times. The outcomes of inquiries always remained unknown.

Michael and his trade-union friend went through lengthy interrogations. Some members of the team were also called in for testimony. Finally, almost a year later — a really tense time for all of us — Tzariov received an official note informing him that the investigation was completed, no wrongdoing was discovered, and the case was closed. Seals were taken off the shed's doors, but none of us rushed to resume the boat's construction. Everyone was still frightened. The energy that had once propelled the project was all but gone. Maybe that had been the ultimate goal of the investigation after all.

For some time the project kept inching agonizingly forward, as Michael struggled to restore his team's enthusiasm. But after a few months, he too gave up. The boat was never completed.

• • •

By the time I was in my late thirties, I had tried many times to pull together various projects, only to encounter over and over again more sticky, swamping resistance. I was fed up with going nowhere, wasting my life like millions of my Soviet compatriots before me. When the idea of perestroika was introduced, I didn't reflect on whether it was for real. At the very least, it offered a chance and I grabbed it. I wondered whether it had been some crazy stroke of fate that all of this happened to coincide with my seminal night-train journey with SAIL magazine and my decision to start the Whitbread project.

One thing was clear to me from the start: in order to get the idea rolling, I had to find supporters. When I first started talking up my ambitious Whitbread plan, most of my friends found the idea monumentally stupid.

"At best you'd fail, turning into a miserable loser," they told me. "But it also could lead you into much more serious trouble. It's just crazy, impossible, better forget about it."

That was pretty much the reaction I had expected. But, surprisingly, a few others showed encouragement, if not commitment quite yet. Had I come up with such an idea just a couple of years earlier, no one would have even listened to me. There was definitely something in the air, brought by a strange fresh wind that started blowing over the Russia. People's attitudes were beginning to show signs of change.

Three people who helped me to push the project from a standstill were Nadja Ovsjannikova, Igor Pronin, and Vladimir Gladishev.

First I shared my idea with Nadja.

She was a close friend, a mysterious psychologist, and a beautiful woman. She came into my life when my relationship with Tatiana seemed to have reached a dead end, and we were contemplating a divorce. It was a time when I was coming to the disturbing conclusion that my best years were slipping by, as I had not achieved much success and satisfaction in either my professional or private life. It made me restless. To some extent that explains the urgency with which I latched onto the Whitbread idea. In attempt to escape the unsettled reality, I without hesitation jumped deep into its dream world.

Nadja was 5'6" tall with a stature of a model, raven-black hair and hazel eyes. By trade she was a certified psychologist, working for a special semi-secret laboratory in the Research Institute for Physical Culture. It was responsible for the mindset of the leading Soviet athletes, including the victorious national ice-hockey team. Nadja liked maintaining a veil of a mystery about her job, hinting with a smile even some sort of benevolent witchcraft. In a word, she was irresistible. At that, she was also a good friend who understood my every word. She knew how the hidden politics of Soviet sport worked and I eagerly sought her opinion on my Whitbread idea and her assessment of the chances to succeed. At first it came as a huge relief when she enthusiastically embraced it. But then she added, "You know, I will always support any of your ideas." Nice thing to hear, but it didn't add objective confidence to my understanding if the project was really any good.

In a short time Nadja became a volunteer manager for the project, helping to carry it through the most difficult time, the beginning. She came up with the concept of competitive crew selection. In the process, a candidate would first submit a resume and description of his ideas on how to win the Whitbread, then go through series of tests, both medical and psychological, which would be performed by the Research Insti-

31

tute for Physical Culture. The selected would join the boat's construction crew, for we wanted each crewmember to be not only a great sailor but also an excellent technical specialist. Whitbread racers for the most part are alone at sea, so having a crew that not only knows how to make the boat go fast but also knows how to repair everything on the boat would be the key to a successful campaign. And finally, each crewmember would go through a rigorous fitness program. By working and training together they would become a real team, strong enough to overcome any future obstacles. It all sounded great, at least in theory.

It wasn't only Nadja's hands-on management talent that made her so vital to the program. Even of higher value was the encouragement that she gave me, assuring me of my decision. She taught me how to communicate my ideas in a way that enabled people to accept them, and how to overcome my doubts and fears. She taught me how to become strong enough to carry the responsibility for the project. If there were a single person of the entire Whitbread project without whom it would have stood no chance of ever happening, that person was Nadja Ovsjannikova.

Now I was ready to talk to Igor Pronin, the chief technical inspector for the Soviet Sailing Federation, where I had been a volunteer for many years. Igor was a well-established scientist working for one of the secret research institutes, which was often loosely referred to as "defense-industry" work. There was nothing unusual in that; all the science institutions in Russia at one time or another had something to do with defense. A composed man who could be stern, Pronin had a sharp mind and was quick to recognize innovative ideas. He had often supported my ideas, perhaps viewed as revolutionary to the Technical Committee of the Sailing Federation, such as my recent attempt to introduce the asymmetrical spinnaker to the racing rules.

By definition the spinnaker is a large symmetrical chute used to sail downwind. It is a cumbersome sail that can be tricky to handle. In cutting it asymmetrically and redistributing its shape, it was possible to make it easier to fly and boost sailing speed as well. I hadn't invented the asymmetrical spinnaker; in fact, it was widely used all over the world. I just wanted to introduce it to Soviet sailing.

But crotchety old comrades in the Sailing Federation stood unmoved.

"It's nonsense. Read the rules. The spinnaker has to be a symmetrical sail, period. Don't you get it?"

"Why don't we change the rules if they prohibit a thing that is so obviously advantageous?" I countered.

"Can you imagine what would happen if we start changing the rules?"

Despite Pronin's strong support, my motion failed and Soviet spinnakers remained symmetrical... for the time being.

My new idea was much crazier than the fight about sail shape, yet Pronin liked it and stood behind it without hesitation. This was extremely important. His authority and respect among sailors instantly added some sort of legitimacy to my Whitbread project.

And then Vladimir Gladishev, my immediate boss and also a friend, came aboard. In all, there weren't many entrepreneurial people in the bad old Soviet Union, but somehow I had been fortunate to meet a good number of them. Vladimir was one such entrepreneur who not only tried to find innovative ways to run the department he was in charge of, but also was open to the fresh ideas outside of his direct business world. Though not a sailor, he, nonetheless, found the whole Whitbread project extremely fascinating. It was Vladimir who helped me get in touch with the Whitbread Round the World Race headquarters in Southampton, England. Of course I could have written them myself, but it was still a time in Russia when any contact with foreigners — whether individuals or organizations — was risky, as it would inevitably attract unwanted official attention. At some point I would need to establish direct communication with the West, but it was wise to put it off for a while until my project gained some recognition and support.

Vladimir suggested using our work department as the medium, thus covering me for the time being. Together we drafted a letter to the race office, asking for a full information package, including the rules, conditions of entry, and a media kit. The heavy envelope came a month later, which, considering the weak links between Russia and the outside world, was actually relatively speedy. I remember it was a Saturday when the package arrived. For some reason Vladimir happened to stop at the office that day, and there it was! Scrapping his plans for the weekend, he drove across the city and knocked at my door. For the next few hours, we giddily rushed through the pages, stretching our poor English in an attempt to make sense of the contents.

From that moment on I felt as if I were somehow physically attached to the race. With every new step the project was increasingly becoming a reality.

• • •

Shortly after, using an opportunity provided by the new

Gorbachev laws, two other designers from Leningrad (since renamed St. Petersburg) and I had formed the Mobile design cooperative. Still with very little hope that it would ever become a reality, we began to make sketches of the Whitbread boat. The dream was gradually taking shape.

By the mid-1980s sailing and especially yacht design had already become my main interest. My paycheck was still coming from a state company where I did various design and engineering projects, but I always wanted to be elsewhere, "messing around in boats," as Maurice Griffith put it. Now suddenly I saw an opportunity to start a design studio and do what I enjoyed the most as my main occupation. I shared the idea with two other yacht designers, Alexander Struzilin and Oleg Larionov, who both lived in Leningrad. After short negotiations we formed the design cooperative, the first of its kind in the Soviet Union. Its name Mobile meant motion, movement forward, perfectly reflecting our mindset at a time.

Prior to joining the cooperative, Alexander was a Chief Engineer of the Leningrad Yard for Sports Boats Construction. The imposing sound of his position didn't exactly reflect its modest scale. True, the yard was the second largest in the entire Soviet Union, but there were only two facilities where sailboats where built then. The other, in Tallinn, Estonia, was slightly larger and more modern than the yard where Alexander worked.

Oleg, a few years younger than Alexander and I, was teaching in the Leningrad Shipbuilding Institute where he also ran a student design workshop. He was a talented designer and I liked his radical ideas and concepts, which were somehow close to my own. We both figured this would help us find common ground and establish a truly creative cooperation. Struzilin, on the other hand, was much more conservative, careful and meticulous, which would definitely complement our bold style. He was actually more of an engineer than a designer. Where Oleg and I were big on concepts and ideas, he was into details. It seemed like a pretty good combination.

Later Oleg Larionov suggested we include input from a few of his most talented students. This sounded like a great idea. They would benefit from the experience gained in the cooperative, and we would have a few extra brains and hands involved. It was still a time when computers and CAD software had only begun to penetrate design offices — in the West that is. In Russia all design work was still performed by pencil, ruler, and handheld calculator. Sure, extra people would help.

I shared my Whitbread dream with my new design partners,

and we started making some preliminary sketches and calculations for the future Maxi. As it turned out, Oleg already had some preliminary ideas on big boats as well, so we had enough to start with. We didn't rush, as the whole Whitbread thing was still nothing more than a dream. Certainly, there was no money for the design, much less for funding construction. And up to that point I had no idea of how to get the money. As an alternative we considered the possibility of selling the Maxi design to one of the merchant marine academies, making the necessary modifications so that it could be a training vessel. Maybe we could convince them to enter the Whitbread as well?

Everything seemed to be going well in our new cooperative and my visits to Leningrad were becoming more and more frequent until, after a few months, I received a phone call from Larionov:

"Vlad, I want to inform you that we voted Alexander out."

"Meaning...?"

"It means exactly what I said. We had a vote and unanimously removed him from Mobile ... Well, we had some arguments here ... You know, his ideas are too old-fashioned and I don't think he's contributed enough to our cooperative anyway."

The alarm that went off inside of my head wasn't all that disturbing. I didn't like what had happened, but sometimes I too felt that Alexander's methodical approach had become a restraint on our flight of creativity. Annoyed that they had voted him out without even bothering to seek my opinion, I asked Oleg:

"Unanimously? What about my vote?"

"Well, I meant by the majority. All my guys had agreed with me. Don't you think that he really didn't fit in? Besides, to me his attitude had always appeared arrogant. He acted like a chief engineer or something, just like on his previous job."

"Look, Oleg, there were three of us who formed Mobile, three main partners. My understanding was that you invited your students sort of as interns or have I taken this all wrong? So the vote, as I see it, was you against Alexander and I wasn't even involved."

Larionov paused for a moment and then threw his last argument, "I think he is forming his own cooperative anyway. You could ask him yourself. So it's no big deal actually... he would have probably quit soon anyway."

I hung up and dialed Alexander's number. All the lines to Leningrad were busy and it took more than 15 minutes, listening to the annoying, short beeps, before I got through.

"It's okay," Alexander replied, "I knew it was coming. There was too much tension and I didn't like Larionov's style from the begin-ning. He doesn't want to be a real partner. He wants to be a boss. That's why he brought in all those guys to support him. Sooner or later they'll vote you out as well." He laughed wearily, "Yeah, I'm starting my own design office. Want to join?"

"Well, thank you, I'll stick with Mobile for now."

It dawned on me that starting a business was not going to be an easy proposition after all—even now, after Gorbachev's new laws no longer prohibited it.

4

CAST OF CHARACTERS

In the spring of 1987, I went to Leningrad to build a set of sails for one of the boats I had designed earlier, the radical, ultralight Mini Tonner M-23. The M stood for my name, the 23 — for the length overall in feet. When I say "build the sails," I mean it literally. There were just a half dozen small sailmaking lofts in all of the Soviet Union at that time, most of them run as underground operations. If it was not a black market, it was certainly a gray one. Were you to simply place an order for sails and then wait for them to be delivered, you'd probably be better off not ordering them at all. The only way to get the sails that you needed, was to be there, helping and pushing the process. Those who were most persistent moved to the head of the line.

I happened to meet Oleg Gulinsky in the sail loft of Strelnya Yacht Club, where he was also building sails for his boat. Of course it wasn't his own boat, he was just a captain of the sailboat belonging to the yacht club. But if he wanted to sail the boat, it was up to him to take care of the sails. That serendipitous encounter on the sail loft floor was to have far-reaching consequences. Oleg was from Moscow as well. He was older than I and better connected and had many sailing friends. I decided to try out my Whitbread ideas on him to see what his reaction would be and whether he could be of any help. Anyway, we were both bound to spend a lot of time together before our sets of sails would be finished, and there was only one topic of conversation of interest to me then.

Oleg became very intrigued with my Whitbread venture but, careful man that he was, he thought it was too risky and held little chance of succeeding. He pointed out that everything in any way associated with the outside world was still unsafe in the Soviet Union, and even the simplest contact with a foreigner could ruin one's entire life.

"I don't think the time has come for such a project," said Oleg, remaining skeptical at first. "I don't believe in all this perestroika stuff anyway. I'm not sure this isn't just another trick. They eased the reins a bit so the naïve people like you would surface, and they would instantly know who's who. Then they would be able to pick out easily all those hot new entrepreneurs who so foolishly exposed themselves and send them off to where they belong … some cold, faraway place, like Siberia. Have you ever thought about such a prospect?" He winced and laughed almost cheerfully.

Like many other Soviet people, Oleg referred to the *vlasty*, or government, as *they*, distancing himself from the bosses at the top. In a big-picture perspective, Russia was divided into *them* and *us*. But there were also other subdivisions of course -- social, ethnic, regional, and even professional to make the actual picture very complicated.

Gulinsky continued, "Take a good look at Russian history. Chilling winds always blow much stronger after a short thaw. What's happening now is just another NEP. Remember? And how did that end?"

"I don't care. And I don't think history ever repeats itself, anyway," I said defensively.

"Well, you'd better wait and see. Pretty soon you'll probably find out it's not such a good idea… "

"That's precisely why I want to go ahead now. Even if this is a short thaw, at least I might get a chance. Moreover, if it's not going to last, it's best to grab it immediately… who knows how much time I've got."

Gulinsky waited for a while to respond and then continued with a cunning smile, "Well, even if there is a chance and even if we assume that you'd be able to achieve something, which I truly believe is impossible, at the end you'd still get nothing for it. Don't you understand that as soon as the guys in the Sport Committee realize that there might be something to your project they'll kick you out and just take over? It happens all the time, on a smaller scale of course … so why bother?"

"To tell you the truth, I wouldn't care if they kicked me out as long as the project were carried through. Listen, all I want is to build my boat and have a chance to sail a leg or two in the Whitbread. Merely accomplishing that much would be like a dream came true. So what if someone else emerged as the leader of the project or even if some Sport Committee boss in the end grabbed all the credit? Well, fine with me."

"That's how you think now. But imagine two or three years from now when you're somewhere down the road on the project, the boat is built and ready to go, and then someone just takes her and sails away as you're left behind watching her disappear."

Neither Oleg nor I could have ever imagined that the scene described so rhetorically would turn into what actually did happen. I
would be left behind bouncing around in a tiny inflatable tender on the
rough Solent, watching my boat sail farther and farther away, diminishing into the pale, hazy mist under her largest spinnaker, emblazoned
with the huge Pepsi logo. However, the Sport Committee would have
nothing to do with that.

Anyway, we talked and talked about the range of possibilities
and outcomes. Gradually out of those discussions the shape of the whole
thing formed in my mind. The seed of the idea sowed on the Tallinn-
Moscow night express was becoming more defined and detailed.

• • •

I was already taking care of the design of the boat, and it was
progressing just fine. We weren't in a hurry because there still was no
certainty that she would ever be built. But if she were, one thing was for
sure: she would be the best there ever was. The boat's design was the
easy part. The project needed a few more important things at this point,
in order to become a reality. It needed money — and lots of it — a proper
organization, and finally, a captain. Money was the most difficult part,
and I wasn't prepared to face this challenge just yet. I figured, let's just
put that aside for now and proceed one step at a time. The next step
certainly would be the search for a captain. I myself couldn't be the
captain. I was a good designer but just an average sailor at best. The
problem was exacerbated by the fact that, because practically nobody
had ever been allowed to sail outside of the country, simply no one in
the whole Soviet Union had any ocean-racing experience.

There were just two major annual offshore races, one each on
the Black Sea and Baltic Sea, unimaginatively called the Black Sea Cup
and the Baltic Sea Cup. Sailors wishing to participate in either of these
races had to start their preparations well in advance — not for physical
and mental training, but getting ready to overcome all the bureaucratic
hassles. One had to fill out numerous forms and receive the necessary
permissions from the authorities, the first and foremost of them, the
KGB. All of this usually took the major part of a year.

The races were run under the close surveillance of the Navy and
Pogranichnaya Sluzba, the Soviet equivalent of the Coast Guard. I don't
know of any attempts to defect during either of these races. But once,
on a foggy stormy night on the Baltic while on a leg from Leningrad to

Tallinn, one of the raceboats mistakenly wandered into Finnish waters. The skipper quickly got the boat out of the forbidden area, but the accident brought far-reaching consequences. The sailor was prohibited from ever skippering again and the captains of the two navy-patrol vessels, which were in the vicinity of the accident and supposed to prevent any yacht from escaping, were punished as well. The following year's race was cancelled and a year later, when it was again permitted, the security measures doubled.

Little wonder that most of the sailing in Russia had taken place on inland waters: rivers, lakes, and reservoirs, with Moscow being the prime sailing center. This was in part because these waters are so far from any borders, and officials didn't give a whit if anyone sailed on the small lakes surrounding the Soviet capital because there was no place to escape to. The other simple reason for the high concentration of the yachts on small lakes around the capital was because most sailboats distributed among the country's few yacht clubs by the Sport Committee, ended up — no surprise — in the hands of the same sport authorities or their close buddies, predominantly in Moscow clubs.

Anyway, whatever the reason, the plain truth was that nobody in the Soviet Union had any real ocean experience, except for a few sailors in the far-east region, in the area around Vladivostok. But they were so far away, some 7,000 miles, and I knew almost no one from there.

Then of course there were the Soviet's very own sailing rock stars from the National sailing team. They sailed the Olympic class boats, the biggest being almost 30 feet overall. With all their racing being the round-the-buoys variety on well-protected waters, they had no offshore experience either. True, they were great sailors, winners of many Olympic medals as well as numerous international championships in their respective one-designs classes. Still, for several reasons, I wasn't at all thrilled with the prospect of getting them involved.

First of all, having become aware of some of the internal conflicts within the Olympic team, I perceived these guys to have big egos. These were pampered sailors sponsored by the government. They lived in much better conditions than the ordinary Russian folks and depended heavily on the support of the Sport Committee. It was no surprise that some of them had become quite capricious and spoiled — definitely not the qualities I wished to introduce into a team preparing to sail the world's oceans. Additionally, being a self-taught sailor, I had very little in common with those sailors, and they surely wouldn't respect me as someone outside their highly institutionalized sailing clique.

So I had agreed with an idea from Oleg Gulinsky, who over time had become more and more enthusiastic and involved, throwing away his initial fears and doubts about the project, to split up the search area for potential crewmembers and more importantly, the skipper. Gulinsky would look for sailors out of Leningrad where he had a lot of contacts, as well as from the rock-star group of the Olympic team. I would search elsewhere.

Looking for the best skipper wasn't easy, because there was more to it than just finding the right person to run the boat. In the spirit of perestroika, I wanted to structure the campaign so it would be run democratically, giving a wide group of sailors equal opportunity to participate, an idea not typical of high-profile sailing competitions. At the same time, this would bring us a broader selection of candidates and the best chance for a strong and competitive crew — as it had been in accordance to Nadja's first concept.

So we contacted the best sailors we knew from the Baltic and the Black Sea region and, of course, from Moscow, and invited them to try out for the crew slots. In keeping with our selection plan, each would present his thoughts and theories on how to win the race – we could certainly use as many fresh ideas as we can get. Then every candidate would go through a set of rigorous tests, with the final selection coming from a series of real-life offshore races.

In the end, the best sailor would emerge as the captain, while the whole project would benefit, drawing from a collective pool of energy and creativity. It sounded like a good idea and it worked — sort of. What I didn't count on was that along with his crewing and creative talents every candidate would also bring long-steeping ambitions. This created a supercharged field with its inevitable squalls and bolts of lightning. My Whitbread project, in fact, had provided the very first outlet for people's unused energy that had accumulated for years, and now, for better or worse, I had to figure out how to deal with it.

• • •

One of the first sailors whom I contacted was Alexey Grischenko.

To this day I am still tormented by the thought of what would have prevailed had I never talked to him. But it's not in our power to change the past. We can only face it and make peace with it.

Alexey was a self-taught sailor who became one of the best amateur boatbuilders in the Soviet Union. Together with his friends, he had built a few boats, the latest of which was the 35-foot Three-Quarter

Tonner GONTA, loosely based on Dick Carter's design. It was a real masterpiece. Alexey was one of the key people in Kiev Yacht Club, well-known for its strong boatbuilding program. In fact, most of the club's fleet consisted of boats crafted by the members themselves. Some of those sailboats were true jewels of design and execution. Frankly, if I saw them now, after having seen so many great yachts around the world, I might change my mind. But back then I knew that at least some of these amateur-built boats were better than those coming out of the Soviet professional yards.

Every May the Kiev Yacht Club hosted a design forum. It was a very informal one, with seminars mixed in with sailing on the Dnipro River followed by big parties continuing late into the night. I never missed an opportunity to attend, particularly because Kiev was absolutely stunning at that time of year with the chestnut trees just starting to bloom. Beautifully situated on the hilly banks of the Dnipro, Kiev had been my favorite city since my high school years spent there, and I took advantage of every opportunity to return there.

When I shared my Whitbread dream with Alexey his reaction surprised me.

"You know when you called and told me you were coming and wanted to talk, I was expecting something like this. In fact, for some time I had been thinking to myself that it was about time to start something big like this. To build the boat that would become a statement... and sail her into the ocean... "

He smiled his usual open smile, "Maybe I'm just getting older and starting to realize that life is short, and if we are to leave any legacy, we should do it now... we might possibly get our chance today. Things are definitely beginning to change."

I had never heard him speak so solemnly, almost compassionately. He had usually approached life with a healthy dose of humor, in a semi-mocking way. Yes, there was still a touch of irony in the tone of his voice, as if he didn't want to appear too serious. But beyond that I felt certain that he took my idea very seriously indeed.

Encouraged, I went on, "I've already told you about the cooperative Mobile," the Soviet sailing world was very small, and everyone knew what everyone else was up to, "We have already started designing the boat."

I had some sketches with me and pulled them out for Alexey to see. I was glad to observe how impressed he was.

"Looks like a bloody surfboard with that flat bottom and banana-like shape. And displacement... wow, only 16 tons. That's less than half of the standard Maxi displacement ... a bit too unusual for my eye, but looks like a great concept."

"And that's exactly what it is now, just a concept. The project is still in its embryo stage. And what I am doing now is trying to put together a team to carry it through... "

"Count me in," Alexey said even before I had finished. "I could never pass up a chance like this!"

In the few hours that followed, I explained the whole plan to him in detail. Alexey agreed with most of it, adding his thoughts as I went along.

I continued, "I see you not only as a one of the potential skippers. First, we need to build the boat, and you will supervise her construction. I can't think of anyone better than you for the job."

"Any particular idea on where she might be built, the building materials, and such?"

"Not yet. No one has ever built anything like this in Russia ... but we'll figure it out in due time. Now, the first thing is to put together a core team."

After a short pondering, Alexey asked, "Who else from the South have you contacted thus far? I don't know much about the sailors from Leningrad but I could certainly give you my advice on who's the best on the Black Sea."

"I've talked briefly to Valery Alexeev from Sochi and I'll be going to see him and talk details. He's another candidate for skipper position."

Alexey nodded approvingly, then interjected, "Stop by to see Victor Yazykov as well while you are in Sochi... "

"I thought he was in Vladivostok. I know he's sailed in the Pacific Ocean as far as Kamchatka."

"That's correct," Alexey replied, "And that's why you might want to invite him. Victor is one of the few people in the entire country who has really done some ocean sailing. He recently moved to Sochi, so you might be able to meet him and Valery on the same trip."

Then he continued, "Looks like there will be a lot of traveling in your future ... you aren't going to go broke before this whole thing even gets started, are you?"

We both laughed, and Alexey asked, "Have you thought about Anatoly Verba?"

"Don't know the man really... heard of him. We may have met a few times, but that's it... "

"He's a sailing coach for the Merchant Naval Academy in Odessa.

He runs a pretty neat program, all tight control and good order. His team performed pretty well in the last two Black Sea Cups. It would surely be worth giving him a call."

• • •

The stars were definitely starting to line up for us. Shortly after returning from my meeting with Grischenko, I received a call that would ultimately shape the whole of the Whitbread-Round-the-World adventure. It came from Alexander Manenko, a slick executive from the huge state monopoly *Vneshtorg*, which controlled all foreign trade.

"Vlad, I have a very interesting man who wants to speak to you about your Whitbread project. How about tomorrow night at my place? Seven's fine?"

I had known Alexander for about a year after first being introduced to him by Vladimir Gladishev. It had been just another one of those capricious meetings to which we don't usually pay much attention when they happen. But now it seemed that destiny was, as ever, weaving its path through a web of seemingly insignificant events, each with the potential of becoming critical to the project. We had gotten together with Manenko a few times since, and once over dinner I had casually mentioned my sailing. I did it without much thought, maybe just to impress him a bit. We were definitely of different ranks: he was close to the top of the society ladder, while I was just an ordinary engineer. So I thought it was probably okay to show off a little and brag about my sailing.

Alexander was a classy man who loved fancy clothes, French champagne, good cars, and having a good time. He had a sharp mind and a great sense of humor, though it was usually more sarcastic than ironic. He was always clean-shaven, so perfectly in fact, I figured he must shave a few times every day. Having had a beard for a few years now, I even began to wonder what a good shave might feel like, slightly envious of his polished look.

Anyway, we talked a little about sailing during that dinner. Recently, as Russia had been slowly turning toward the West, sailing had been gaining an aura of something exotic and desirable, while still remaining a rare activity. Everything luxurious, which at least officially was once considered bad by the Proletariat State, now started to become acceptable, even chic. Soon the pendulum would swing all the way, with Russian *nuevoriches* overshadowing even the glamorous extravaganza of the long-gone monarchy.

Alexander asked me if I could take him out sailing. Sure, why not. A few short day-sails certainly wouldn't turn him into a sailor, but he simply liked being on a sailboat and enjoyed every sailing opportunity offered. Eventually I told him about my project and he responded with a great deal of interest.

"Why would any company want to sponsor a Whitbread yacht?" Alexander asked.

"Because it's a huge floating billboard, which moves around the world for nine months. The exposure is enormous."

"And how much does a sponsor normally pay for this?"

"I don't know any exact figures but a campaign budgeting five or even seven million dollars would not be an unusual thing."

"Wow, it sure sounds like serious stuff ..."

The meeting to which Alexander had invited me in November 1997 was with Victor Tikhov, an executive from the Republic of Georgia. As soon as Alexander introduced us, I felt respect for this bold, bulky man. Heavily built with an undeniable air of substance and importance, he emanated power. But his appearance was a far cry from that of the typical heavy posture of the Soviet boss, as he spoke and moved swiftly and energetically.

"We are now working at starting a new business. It will be a private enterprise, a joint venture between a few Soviet and Western companies," he said, looking straight at me with his sharp eyes. "It will be a totally new kind of enterprise. There are only a few forming now to become a benchmark for future economic changes in the entire Soviet Union."

Needless to say, I was impressed and anxiously anticipated what would follow.

Alexander Manenko took it from there:

"All the paperwork for the new company has been filed, and we have received most of the necessary permissions from the government. We are thinking about ways to promote it worldwide and are considering the possibility of making your Whitbread project sort of our business card."

At that moment I knew that I had just found my first sponsor.

The stage was set, all the major players had taken their positions and the curtain was about to rise.

5

THE LEGEND

Once upon a time on a hot summer day, a tall young man came to the capital city of a small Greek kingdom. His steps were firm, his eyes looked forward with challenge and resolution. The stranger was stunningly handsome, and girls passing by couldn't keep their eyes off him. His tunic, made of a rugged cloth, was well worn and dusty after a long journey. Oddly, he was wearing only one sandal; his other foot was bare. Despite his humble garb, there was something in the way he carried himself that revealed his noble origin.

The local king was told about the strange newcomer and paled with fear on hearing about the missing shoe. Many years ago a fortuneteller predicted that the king would have to give up his throne and power to the son of his older deceased brother. The prince would arrive to claim the kingdom wearing just one sandal. After learning his fortune, the king tried to get rid of baby Jason, but there was no way to fight the will of the gods. They saved the little boy and he grew up in the wilderness in a small shepherd's shack. After he had learned the truth about his origin, Jason decided to go back to his native kingdom and on the way, crossing a roaring brook, lost one sandal.

Appearing before the king, the brave young man claimed his right to the throne, and declared that he would accept any challenge and overcome all the obstacles to show his courage and strength, to prove that he deserved to rule the kingdom. In Jason's proposal, the devious king saw a chance to rid himself of the threatening competitor for a long time, maybe even forever. He would just need to think of a task most dangerous and improbable and then, who knows...

Well, what challenge could be more appropriate for a future king than to bring back the Golden Fleece? Everyone knew that in faraway Kolhida on the shores of the river Fazisi stood an old oak tree with the

Golden Fleece hidden high in its crown. A long time ago it had belonged to the kingdom and symbolized glory and prosperity, but then it was lost. "Bring it back, oh brave Jason, and make our kingdom powerful and undefeatable again, and then who, if not you, would deserve the throne?"

Jason accepted the challenge eagerly.

The trap was laid and the young man jumped into it without hesitation. He didn't know then that the Golden Fleece represented more than a glorious challenge. Over time it had become a symbol of the impossible goal, of an adventure doomed for failure. Many brave men had paid with their lives trying to recover the precious treasure. It was guarded closely by the ferocious king of Kolhida, and the way to it was long and filled with hazard. But Jason cared not, for he was ready to face any danger. He already saw himself on the ship returning to his kingdom's shores with the glittering skin of the golden ram covering his shoulders; he already heard the celebration of the crowd, cheering their new hero and king. He was ready to sail, no, to fly to that distant Kolhida; he was not afraid of the challenges; he would overcome any obstacles.

Well, good luck to you, Jason. Your endeavor is not as senseless as it seems. After all, even impossible goals can be reached if your desire is strong enough. You came into this world for battles, not for holidays. With every step you must perform an act of bravery, and every step should lead toward your noble goal. Don't even think about turning back.

Go for it!

And so Jason gathered the bravest and strongest from all over the kingdom. Among them were fearless Hercules, the healer Aesculapius, and sweet-voiced singer Orpheus. Every one of them had already earned a name and fame, and every one was ready to join Jason and follow him to the very end. They were ready to take any risk; for these heroes confronting and overcoming danger was the only acceptable way of living.

They set off on their journey on the ARGO, a ship most beautiful, strong, and durable, built by the best shipbuilder in Greece. Its sides were covered with the hardest and smoothest planks and an entire oak trunk formed its keel. ARGO was crafted without one single nail, of only the best, carefully selected wood, and it had no equal. Its mast pointed proudly skyward; its line of oars swept like great undulating wings from the rowing ports, 20 oars on each side, with two oarsman on each oar, four mighty arms rhythmically stroking in perfect cadence.

Unstoppable, ARGO cut through the water in near-silent magnificence, propelled by the strength of 80 oarsmen. And when the sea was stirred by a following breeze, they'd pull the oars off the water and as its great sail unfurled, ARGO would fly forward. With a cheerful song, the brave Argonauts hastened on their way, looking straight into the unknown without hesitation. And when the sun slid below the distant horizon and its last reflection on the water faded away, Orpheus would pick up his lyre and spellbound Argonauts listened to the sweet voice, full of hope, urging them to continue into the unknown future.

Day in and day out they sailed toward their goal, and it seemed there was no end to their journey. New dangers ambushed them at every turn along the way.

One day a furious storm tossed ARGO around like a toy, with dark steep waves breaking over the deck, trying to wash the sailors away. Nature was furious and the black sky was torn apart by the arrows of thunderbolts. What if this was the gods' rage? What if they were angry at Jason's endeavor?

The previous day, beautiful sirens had tried to seduce the voyagers with their magical, enchanting songs, wanting to make them forget the purpose of the journey, to lure them into the sweet nets, and enslave them by numbing their will and mind.

They fought off the beautiful Amazons, women-warriors, and the ugly beast Cyclops with only one eye in the middle of his forehead. He was so huge he could lift the ship with just two fingers.

They lost many friends along the journey. After the mourning time, they continued sailing, with sorrow in their souls and courage in their hearts. They went through periods of despair when it seemed that there was no way to go on, when the oars would fall out of their aching hands, and the cries would tear the heart apart—when they could only hope for the mercy of the gods.

The voyage continued until the heroes found their way barred by two notorious crashing rocks, called Simplegards. At certain times these massive stones would move apart to open a narrow gap, dark and almost invisible, but if a voyager hesitated for a moment, they could crash together again and close the passage. No ship had ever been able to pass through the rocks. The risk was enormous, but Jason had no choice. Only by overcoming fear and doubts could they move forward.

Early in the morning, waiting for the predawn mist to clear, the Argonauts prepared for their desperate attempt. Gradually, as they sailed closer, the fateful rocks, in all their evil majesty, seemed to grow larger and larger in front of them. White water roared around, the crashing sounds were nearly deafened the brave heroes. How tempting it was to turn back, to leave all the horror behind. But Jason had already sent forward a white dove to show the way. If the bird was able to pass between the rocks, then ARGO's turn would come. All eyes were glued to the white wings flickering against the dark-gray sky as the dove darted forward, then through, and finally broke free.

Like an arrow, ARGO shot toward the watery gap, all the Argonauts rowing like madmen fighting for their very lives. The rocks crashed together again, closing the passage with such terrible force that the sparks brightened the surrounding darkness. But it was too late. ARGO was all but safe on the other side, just its rudder had been crushed, broken into many pieces. The Argonauts, releasing their breaths in a single triumphal sigh of relief, kept on rowing furiously to pull well clear of the danger astern. They may have lost their rudder but they had made it through, and they began to banter with each other in great excitement, celebrating their good fortune and grateful that the loss was so small.

They quickly fell silent however, looking back to watch in amazement as the massive rocks pulled far apart and stood frozen at a distance, while the turbulent waters slowly calmed. Now the passage would be open forever because they, the Argonauts, had pleased the gods with their bravery and courage, because they had proved that there is a way through any seemingly hopeless venture. Even when eyes see only a narrow gap; even when it seems at times that there is no way through, having faith that the passage exists will open eyes, and allow the vision of what is hidden beyond, providing the strength to go further.

And in the end, no matter how long and rough the way, the goal can be reached.

• • •

And so finally our voyagers, led by the fearless Jason, stepped onto the shores of Kolhida. But that wasn't the end of the struggle. Greek legends don't let their heroes off the hook that easily, do they? Jason and his friends would have to perform many more acts of bravery before they finally took possession of the alluring Golden Fleece. But in the end it didn't bring them the peace and happiness they seemed to have earned. True, Jason did return home a hero and finally got his throne and kingdom, but after that it was all blood and tears and horror over and over again.

Wouldn't it be great if life were fair and simple? Then reaching even the loftiest goal would only require determination, hard work, and courage. But it's not that simple. Sometimes fulfilling a dream can be a disappointment. But then there are other times when the outcome by far surpasses even our wildest expectations.

We are all in God's hands.

6

BUILDING THE ARK

The coastal road from Sukhumi airport to the industrial town of Poti was flooded by winter rains. Tikhov had sent his executive Volga, a luxury car by Russian standards, to pick me up at the terminal. It was pouring so hard the car seemed to be struggling forward against sheets of water, its windshield wipers unable to keep up with the torrent from the opened skies. But the driver, unmoved by the conditions, was paying little attention to the calamity outside, entertaining me with local anecdotes as we sped on our way.

I had decided on the trip on very short notice. Alexander Manenko had called me only two days before to say that the joint venture he was forming with Tikhov had finally been registered.

"It's called Fazis SP and has been titled as a private enterprise number 31 in the Soviet Union," he said enthusiastically. "We are among the very first!"

"What kind of SP?" I asked, knowing SP stood for *Sovmestnoje Predprijatie,* or joint venture. The new term had become a buzzword in the Soviet media, but I hadn't heard the first part of the company name clearly.

"Fazis SP. F-A-Z-I-S. If you remember anything from your Greek mythology in school, you know that Fazis, or Fazisi in Georgia, was the river where the Argonauts found the Golden Fleece."

History had been one of my favorite subjects at school. Of course I remembered the legend. The name made perfect sense. The town of Poti (pronounced POAT-yee) is located at the mouth of the Fazisi River (though today it's called the Rioni). It was held that Poti was the place where in the legend Jason and his brave cohorts had landed at the towering oak tree, which held the skin of the Golden Ram high in its crown. The little Republic of Georgia had taken great pride in being a part of the legend of the heroic seamen Jason and the Argonauts. In fact, it had become a sort of theme of the area and the local attractions, and its many small cafes had names associated with the legend. So for this first Georgian joint venture, the name Fazis SP was perfectly appropriate.

But the Fazis historical roots notwithstanding, the main office of the enterprise was to be in Moscow. It was much easier to communicate and to do business being in the Soviet capital. The joint venture consisted of a group of enterprises from the Poti industrial region of Western Georgia and the German import-export company Wilfred Post Gmbh.

"Part of the Fazis SP joint venture is a shipyard, which among other things builds highly advanced aluminum hydrofoil ferries," Alexander had said on the phone. "Many of these are sold to Greece and other Mediterranean countries. We want to significantly increase exports and that's where your project would come into play. We'll build your Whitbread boat there and from the exposure it'll bring to the yard, I have no doubt, a flood of new business will follow. Tikhov wants you to go and talk to the people at the yard. So if you want this whole thing to start rolling, don't waste any time, jump on a plane now. They're expecting you."

I hung up and called Aeroflot to book a seat on the next available flight to Georgia. Now, with the car trundling down the road through this portion of Georgia, I was looking forward to seeing the place where my boat would be born.

While the state is largely mountainous, its western part, called Kolhida, forms a triangle of lowlands with each side approximately 70 miles long. Two of the sides are rimmed by steep ridges of the Caucasus, Europe's tallest mountains. They form a perfect shield from chilly northern winds. The third side on the southwest is open to warm air from Anatolia and the Mediterranean. The result is a humid, lush, and almost tropical climate. During warm, wet winters temperatures never drop below freezing and it rains three days out of four. Summers are hot and humid. Heavy vapors from the swamps, which cover a large portion of Kolhida, usually fill the air with a hazy mist. But on those days when a fresh breeze blows from the sea, one is usually rewarded with a magnificent vista of the towering snow-capped peaks off in the distance. Cutting right through the middle of Kolhida, like a highway's median strip, is the fast, stout river that flows to the Black Sea. It's called the Rioni on today's maps, but many people still refer to it by its legendary name, Fazisi.

This initial visit was to make the acquaintance of Fazis SP chairman Victor Tikhov. Since he didn't know anything about sailing or the Whitbread, he had asked Juki Tsomaya, Poti's local celebrity and one of the best Georgian sailors, to join him. When introduced, I vaguely remembered meeting him once before. Was it during a regatta or maybe at a Sailing Federation convention? A consummate athlete with broad shoulders and huge arms, Juki moved his 6-foot-3-inch frame with a grace and elegance. He had broken his nose (among other things) in a horrible car crash a few years ago. The twisted bump gave him a look of a street fighter that somehow seemed to add to his irresistible charm. Juki was a director of the local yacht club, a position that allowed him to get a deep suntan in the summers and plenty of opportunities to sail.

He had won his fair share of local and national sailing competitions but that wasn't the only reason for his local popularity. A couple of years earlier he had been selected as a member of the international crew for a high-profile expedition designed around the Argonauts legend. Led by well-known British explorer Tim Severin, it was a reenactment of the legend. A replica of ARGO — as far as the ship's design could be postulated — had been constructed in Greece. Juki had been invited as the representative of Georgia.

I spent the next days with Juki as he practiced the fine Soviet art of probing, testing my character and ideas. People in the Soviet Union were open and candid on the personal level, but in business nobody trusted each other. Before committing to anything together, it was necessary and important to play the probing game. The usual trial rituals included major parties with plenty of drinks, countless toasts, and much loose talk. Behind the process was the adage, "what the sober has on his mind, the drunk has on his tongue." True to this custom, Juki and I spent a couple of grand evenings in Poti's restaurants. I enjoyed them immensely. Who wouldn't? The Georgian cuisine is among the best in the world.

Tikhov must have liked what Juki learned about me for our relationship gradually became more open and trusting.

• • •

It was a time for beginnings. My Whitbread project was advancing as Fazis SP grew and the free-market economy struggled painfully to emerge in Russia. No one had the slightest clue on how to conduct business, what was right, what was wrong, how far you could go without overstretching your luck. The fear was ever present that all of this perestroika stuff was just a short, strange episode in Russian history that might end up at any time in a wave of prosecution, like the NEP many years ago. Those few who were willing to take the risk were brave and ruthless, ready for anything. And yet initially, among them were many idealistic souls who honestly tried to bring change to Russia, whose enthusiasm made those early days of perestroika so incredibly exciting—so filled with hope.

At first fortunes were made almost foolishly easily. Of course you'd have to overcome that barrier of inertia and fear, but once you dared to start, the rest was simple. The playground was virtually empty; competition was non-existent. In the summer of 1988 the motto was "sell computers, get rich." A few years prior, still in pre-perestroika times, the government had launched a huge program called *Computerization*. It was yet another one of the many gigantic undertakings that would periodically sweep over Russia with definitive and frightening frequency. It all began with Lenin's *Electrification*, then *Industrialization* and *Collectivization* followed. Khruschev brought *Chemization*. At best, none of them worked. At worst, they created social and ecological disasters. During *Collectivization* thousands of the farmers were chased away from their lands, many of them ending up in gulags. Later during Khruschev's era, millions and millions of tons of chemical fertilizers were dumped over the Russian farmland in a futile attempt to increase its productivity. As usual, every zealous local official, trying to over-achieve the state-plan goals, took up the cause, which led to over saturating the soils with nutrients, turning fertile land into desert.

Now the time had come for *Computerization*. Strangely enough, this one seemed a pretty smart idea. It was obvious to everybody, even to the government officials, that the Soviet Union was lagging behind the rest of the world technologically and growing ever more inefficient. A computer at every workplace, all of them connected to one huge state-wide network, seemed like a panacea. This surely would work, making the Soviet Union strong and undefeatable again, the true "Leader of the entire Progressive World." Only one tiny obstacle stood in the way of achieving this noble goal: no modern compact computers were made in Russia. True, there were some ancient gigantic machines, but these were generations away from PC technology. No problem; they could be bought abroad. With a special government decree, an enormous budget was appropriated for this purpose, and huge sums of money were assigned to state enterprises throughout the country specifically to buy computers. Shortly after perestroika started, the first joint ventures came to life and all this computer money was simply up for grabs.

The scheme was so simple, almost silly, but open only to a few lucky SPs – joint ventures with special government licenses. Borrow rubles from the state bank, change them into hard currency at the "official" favorable rate, way below the black market or real life values. Then buy computers abroad and sell them to Russian companies at astronomic prices caused by demand, pocketing in the process a 10- to 20-fold profit. The whole thing was brilliant. One didn't even need any cash to get started. The office of Fazis SP was so jam-packed with boxes and boxes of computers that at times it was simply impossible to walk through.

Eventually it was discovered that computers didn't necessarily improve efficiency in the workplace. Fazis SP employees spent more and more time in the office playing computer games, as they discovered that the computers shipped from the West couldn't do much else. A ban on selling any of the serious computer software to the Soviet Union was in effect, though the games were readily and abundantly available.

But who cares? Business was booming nevertheless. There was no competition among sellers, those rare and lucky few with import-export licenses and permits for the official hard-currency exchange rate. At the time of its registration, Fazis SP was only the 31st enterprise in all of the Soviet Union. Imagine a market with only 31 companies and thousands of impatient buyers with millions in computer budgets, which they needed to spend by government decree. It wasn't a market; it was a paradise.

Granted, it couldn't last long. More and more joint ventures were gradually appearing and starting to claim their share. Eventually competition came into the marketplace, and with competition came Kalashnikovs, car bombs, and hired killers. The shady black-market figures that had cautiously emerged into daylight with the dawn of perestroika, now quickly rose into dominant roles, using their old connections in the corrupted Russian society and simple brute force. In just a few short years, what started as an enthusiastic and idealistic drive for change would turn into a wild, unruly battlefield for money and power. And when the smoke cleared, the hopes for Russia were lying in ruins again.

But back then, in the summer of 1988, it was just beginning, a strange and wonderful time when everything seemed possible, and the air was filled with expectations.

• • •

Upon my return from Poti, Alexander Manenko introduced me to two other major partners within the Fazis SP.

"Alexander Kedishvili is a director of our Moscow operations and will work closely on the financial side of the Whitbread project. He went through the school of Vneshtorg and then worked as a diplomat in the Georgian Consulate in Moscow." With a smile, Manenko cheerfully patted the shoulder of the impeccably dressed, well-mannered, and somewhat reserved man in his mid-thirties. Then added with a sly wink, "He is also a descendant of a very old and most noble Georgian family, real royal blood."

"I don't know about that," Kedishvili's smile was shy and apologetic, "but I'm surely looking forward to working together with you on your exciting Whitbread project." There was something about Alexander that immediately appealed to me. Luckily, it wasn't just a first impression and over time he became a great supporter of the project, sharing with me not only the good times but all the troubles as well, and I'm infinitely grateful to him.

The other person was Wilfred Post himself, the German partner of Fazis SP. A skinny fellow with a head of curly hair *a-la* Kurt Vonnegut, he looked more like an immigrant from the Middle East than a citizen of the Bundesrepublik. Not very large by any standards, his import-export company had annual sales of around 70 million dollars (nobody would reveal exact figures those days); nevertheless, it was the biggest German trading company active in the Soviet Union. Wilfred's manner was correct, if not cold, and extremely businesslike. It was clear that he didn't share the popular enthusiasm toward the Whitbread adventure.

"Don't lose focus, my friends. We are in business to make money, not just to have fun. I've got a buyer in Germany for five railroad cars full of pigskin. We need to find a supplier pronto. Then there is a customer for Russian stainless steel, lots of it. As you know, it's considered a strategic material by your government and therefore prohibited from export ... Well, there are always ways around that. Let's find instead a manufacturer of hammers or axes or something like that, and order a couple million of them made of stainless steel. It still would be a great deal with enough profit. Now, back to business, my friends. "

As a gesture of friendship and a token of everlasting relationship, Wilfred presented Fazis SP with a Mercedes Benz. Being the boss and the person with the best driving record, Manenko became its sole user. Actually Alexander even picked the color himself from the catalog. "Wet asphalt" it was called, though it looked more like a prosaic dark gray. The Mercedes was a small one, series 190, but it was among the first ones in the Soviet Union and therefore unique and precious. Time when only a Mercedes 600 would count was still a few years away.

Fazis SP's commitment as an initial sponsor was substantial: build the boat and provide management for the project. All this could be done in rubles. But then we'd need to outfit the yacht and buy the hardware, rigging, and electronics. It must all come from the West, as such things simply weren't made in Russia. Like everyone else in the Soviet Union — like the Soviet Union itself — Fazis' management was short of hard currency. We needed to organize a fundraising campaign in the West and to find a co-sponsor with deep hard-currency pockets.

Russians were using this new word "fundraising" more and more. Everyone understood fairly well what the "fund" part of it meant. But no one had a clue on how to raise them. It was obvious that we needed to approach foreign companies for the hard currency, but how? The Soviet Union was still essentially closed to international business. It would be two more years before the Berlin Wall would fall, and there were very few offices of well-known Western companies in Moscow, all small, obscure, and idling. Still under close surveillance by the KGB, they were not easily approachable. And even if you could get in touch with a representative, you'd probably be talking to a low-ranking clerk, sent to Russia as some sort of punishment, who had absolutely no decision-making authority. In addition, it was commonly thought that most of the Westerners in Moscow were intelligence officers and contact with them could easily get you into trouble.

Russia was just becoming a new frontier and along with the honest and idealistic Westerners who had recently wandered in, there were also plenty of shady characters, adventurers looking for a lucky strike. They would show you flashy business cards proclaiming executive representation of major Western corporations, but they had that undeniable air of fake around them. You would not buy a used car from guys like that. From time to time, one of them would cut a huge deal with some powerful Soviet ministry to be its exclusive representative in the West, only to find later that their competitors had struck the same exclusive deal with the very same ministry. Just as it was supposed to be on the wild frontier, everyone was fooling everyone else.

It was a murky world of middlemen and mediators, but at the time it was really the only way to get in touch with the Western companies. Well, there was also a direct route; just send a fax or a letter to the corporate headquarters. But who would expect some global giant to negotiate directly with an unknown, newborn Russian company? Anyway, with only a few operating fax machines in all of Moscow and all of them still controlled by the KGB, with every message censored before being released, which usually took weeks — well, just forget it.

• • •

Michael Tsivin was another Fazis SP employee. He was sort of a Moscow playboy, always perfectly shaved and smelling of expensive men's cologne. He wore elegant clothes from French and Italian designers as casual attire. His wife was a movie actress. Michael knew everyone worth knowing in Moscow and his connections were probably the prime reason why Manenko had hired him.

In 1988, as even to larger extent now, connections were an extremely valuable commodity in Moscow. In our search for sponsorship these contacts, found through Michael or as we called him — Misha, led us to numerous initial contacts — and many meetings followed. One of these contacts was a shady black-market figure who at one point had served time in jail, but with the arrival of perestroika had been reborn as a legitimate businessman. Through his connections at the top, he'd cut an exclusive contract for one thing or another and in a few short years, he'd grown into a multimillionaire.

Another contact was Babek Serush, a Syrian businessman of substantial influence in Moscow. The highly energetic Babek was very short and broad, somewhere in Danny DeVito's size range, with sharp, smart eyes and a charming smile. By any standards, Babek was not a handsome man, yet it was easy to like him. In 1988 his business was quite modest, but he had a great talent for putting on a show, and could be generous. As a result in Russia Babek was considered as rich as Oriental Shah. He became a sponsor of the very first Moscow beauty pageants and, by no coincidence, shortly after married a beautiful Russian girl.

There were many other businessmen like Babek. Some would become very rich, but not all were lucky enough to survive the turmoil of perestroika. They were blown to pieces in their Mercedes 600s on Moscow streets, killed in their Renaissance Mediterranean villas, sacrificed in the no-compromise struggle for power and wealth.

Alexander Kedishvili was not at all thrilled with the direction of the sponsorship search. Through his friends in various departments of Vneshtorg, he tried to steer it toward more official channels. Manenko brought out all his contacts as well. Initially, it was agreed that I would just be the liaison between Mobile and Fazis SP, concentrating mainly on the technical aspects of the project, while both Alexanders would carry on the sponsorship search. But it soon became evident that it required a good deal of knowledge about the Whitbread Race and sailing in general, so I became more and more involved in their negotiations. Finally, a few months later, Manenko offered me a position in Fazis with the imposing title of Chief Specialist to handle the Whitbread project.

All in all, during the late summer and fall of '88, we went through literally hundreds of business meetings. At that time my appointment book looked as if it belonged to an executive of an international corporation rather than to a humble Russian engineer (well, by that time , I must admit, I had already been elevated to a "Chief Specialist" level):

August 1988

> Simenco Finance – Mattie Grunland
> Union Bank of Finland (already a sponsor of one Whitbread boat)
> Mosfilm (to discuss movie-documentary rights)
> Daimler-Benz (prepare proposal for Herzog Eberhard in Stuttgart)
> Satra (they had publicity rights for Moscow Olympics in 1980) – access to PepsiCo and American Express
> Nisso Boeki
> Dresdner Bank (at Babek Serush's office)
> Aeroflot/PanAm
> Vsevolod Kukushkin (chief of sports department of the Telegraph Agency of the Soviet Union)
> Meeting at CNN Center (Vladimir Posner)
> Italian-Soviet Chamber of Commerce
> ICI (Great Britain)
> Movie Cooperative Fora

September 1988

> Deutscher Bank
> FKB (marketing and advertising agency, joint venture with Vneshtorg)
> Team BBDO (has some interest in sponsoring us for a Dutch textile company)
> Sudoimport
> Cooperative Actioner
> Satra (contacts to North Sails and Hood Sails)
> Young and Rubicam
> Yamaha

October 1988
>Moskovsky Narodny Bank (bank in London,
>owned by the USSR government)
>Autoexport (import-export car-trading
>company)
>Lada-Poch (French company selling Russian Ladas,
>sponsor of an ocean-racing trimaran)
>ISL, Switzerland.

And so on.

We made a huge list of every company that could potentially become a sponsor and every media outlet that could provide publicity, and of every person who could lead to a valuable contact. We were determined to not leave any stone unturned and went through the list methodically. Less than one year remained until the start of the race and most of the other syndicates already had their sponsorship lined up. Some, with their boats already built, had even begun boat trials with on-the-water training.

• • •

Immediately after receiving the first support from the Fazis SP, I drafted an agreement between Mobile and Fazis for designing the boat for the Whitbread. From now on, the design process received somewhat official status, but, according to the peculiar Soviet regulations, Mobile was not allowed to be paid for the job. Like every new enterprise, our design cooperative was struggling to survive in a twilight zone of discarded old rules and new ones that were yet to be written. Although Soviet lawmakers may have given in slightly to Gorbachev's ideas on opening up individual entrepreneurial spirit, in no way were they going to make life easy for these new "wannabe" capitalists. Besides, the old system was just too strong, too self-sufficient, and too all-encompassing. It was like a living organism, a parasite that penetrated everywhere and covered everything. It simply wasn't going to yield without a fight to any change that endangered its existence.

The new laws regulating cooperatives' activities limited them to providing services and selling goods only to private individuals, not to organizations. That forced them to keep low profiles. And the problem was exacerbated by the fact that people in Russia in general didn't have much money and consequently business was weak.

"Just make sure those capitalists don't grow too fast," was the bureaucrat's refrain. Later a special decree was issued that outlined more clearly the relationship between different types of enterprises in the Soviet Union. If a cooperative wanted to do business with a company, as in our situation with Mobile being hired to design for Fazis SP, there had to be mediators. They went under the title Association for Scientific and Technical Creativity of Youth, established at the local Communist Party committees.

So I met with them, making my best, most convincing presentation—I had to make it appealing, because they wouldn't take just any project. The young communists seemed impressed and fed me a lot of flattering jabber on how my project would serve the glory of Mother Russia and how much they cherished the initiative of the guys like me. Finally, the time came to discuss the terms of our mutual agreement.

"We'll provide your Mobile cooperative with all the legal support you may need to organize the proper relationship with Fazis SP. This is a totally gray area and a potentially dangerous one as the joint venture is connected to the West. There may be complications... but don't worry, we have the means to take care of such things. We will open a special bank account on Mobile's behalf, where Fazis SP will deposit payments for the design services, and then, after withholding our commission, we will pay your cooperative. This way you won't be dealing with any company directly, and the law will be properly observed. Your project is very special and will probably require more work... Nonetheless, we are ready to give you our usual deal. Our standard commission is 80 percent."

"Fuck you!" I thought, but politely said good-bye, I'd be in touch, and walked away. Those communist bastards were going to make sure that, even if capitalism ever prevailed in Russia, they would be in the right position to grab the juiciest pieces of the pie. It's no wonder that the first generation of new bankers, industrialists and media monopolists to eventually emerge a few years later was mainly made up of the very same communist rank and file.

As for us, we went on with the design, working without pay till the law was changed six months later. The Mobile studio was located in a dark and wet cellar of an old dilapidated building just a few steps behind the beautiful facades of St. Petersburg's palaces. Despite the miserable working conditions, the dream kept our spirits high—for a while, at least. Everyone was after big money now and the lure was so tempting. More and more time the guys would spend daydreaming instead of drafting. They were dreaming about huge houses on the waterfront or yachts tied to private docks, and most often about dark bottle-green Jaguars, exactly like Margaret Thatcher's. How the hell did they know what color Margaret Thatcher's Jag was, or even that she had one?

As our sponsorship search advanced, conversations in the design office centered more and more around money. The project's kitty was still empty, but the anxiety was rising higher and higher on how the money would be divided when it finally started pouring in.

"Vladislav, we don't want Fazis SP to grab all the benefits and all the sponsorship money, while paying us only peanuts for the design. Our role is much bigger, and we deserve more. After all, we started this project when there was no Fazis whatsoever." We were sitting in Oleg Larionov's small office that adjoined the main design studio, drinking tea. It was lunchtime but the room was almost dark with ominous black clouds covering a tiny piece of the sky visible through the basement window. A serious thunderstorm was brewing.

"I think you'd agree," continued Oleg, "that Mobile should be a major player, totally informed of what is going on with the right to participate in the decision making. I don't trust Tikhov, so consider yourself our man in their camp.

"Come on, what's this nonsense about camps? We're not competing with Fazis SP, are we? I really hope that we can find a way to work together as a team, otherwise this whole thing will go nowhere."

The first rumble of thunder was so loud and close Oleg flinched and spilled his tea. The next second it was pouring outside and became even darker in the office.

"Why don't you turn on the lights? We're sitting here like a bunch of conspirators plotting against Fazis. What have they done wrong?" I said with a smile, trying to relax the atmosphere.

"Nothing so far," replied Oleg, "but the day is not over yet. And I'm not plotting. I just want us to agree on the strategy so we don't miss what we're entitled to... Tell me how much sponsorship money Fazis expects to receive."

"Come on, Oleg, it's too early to talk about it. Nobody has any idea yet of how much we could get, if any. It's like dividing up the skin of a bear that hasn't been hunted yet."

"When Fazis gets the money, it'll be too late to discuss how to divide it. We need to put down our conditions now." And then he added, almost like a threat, "And you must decide whose side you're on, Mobile's or Fazis'."

The first cracks had begun to appear in our relations but still, I couldn't imagine that in just a few months our design cooperative would crumble, putting the entire venture in jeopardy.

• • •

Regardless of what might have been going on inside the Mobile cooperative, the design of the boat was speeding along. We had already finalized its basic characteristics and had started working on the hull shape and the deck layout. Because no one in the Soviet Union had ever done any ocean racing, there was no experience to draw from and plenty of guesswork involved. We went through exhaustive brainstorming sessions that were filled with brilliant ideas, arguments, and ingenious solutions. In fact, it was, perhaps the most fun I'd ever had. Unfortunately, the more the project progressed, the more I got into things like management and fundraising, and spent less and less time at Mobile. I was painfully learning how to sacrifice fun for the chance at success.

By early summer of 1988, all of the conceptual design had been completed and the beautiful, sleek, low-slung racer on the drafting boards was looking at us impatiently. It seemed that she couldn't wait to materialize out of shiny aluminum and be set free into her element. The yacht looked strikingly different; she would be something the sailing world had never seen before. While we were completely confident in our design concept, there were, of course, many details that we would like to compare to other Whitbread raceboats—just to make sure that our ideas were better. Granted, to create an extremely radical, revolutionary yacht it's good in a way to be totally isolated from the world. But it's also a tremendous, as well as sometimes silly, undertaking to reinvent things that man had already thought of and created long time ago.

If only we could see other Maxis—just get a quick glance.

Well, the lucky opportunity presented itself soon enough in July 1988, when Ludde Ingvall, skipper of Finnish entry UNION BANK OF FINLAND, decided to bring his boat to Leningrad as a part of a promotional European tour. He ran an excellent, well-organized campaign, backed by the powerful bank, and with his brand-new racer already launched and sailing, was involved in an extensive, year-long program of boat-tuning and optimization, and crew-training. Ludde figured that he'd ride the perestroika wave. Being one of the first foreign yachts to ever sail into Russian waters, his UBF would enjoy enormous celebrity status and deliver plenty of publicity to her sponsor. Not so fast my friend when you're dealing with Soviet reality. The Red Coast Guard allowed the Finnish boat into Russian waters but put her on the quarantine dock in the most remote corner of the huge commercial port of

Leningrad, closing off any public access to her. So much for exposure and publicity.

I had learned about the visit by chance and arrived from Moscow armed with VIP invitations, procured from the Moscow office of the UBF, for the whole of the Mobile design team. But the guards around the yacht stood firm, not even bothering to look at our invitations. "*Nyet*! No, nobody's allowed, no exceptions." Had this happened just a couple of years earlier, the guard wouldn't have even talked to us and have us instantly detained on the spot for attempted unlawful contact with the foreigners. Perestroika and glasnost, however, were flourishing all around and the atmosphere was filled with—I can't even find the definition—something new and exciting. I breathed these fresh fumes and, encouraged—or perhaps simply intoxicated—headed for the office of the border guard that was located there in the port.

The colonel in charge listened to my plea with a cold, remote face. He wasn't the least bit softened by my argument that a visit to the Finnish yacht was absolutely critical to the future of Soviet yachting and even more, to the whole of international prestige of the Motherland.

"I hear you but I simply have no authority to allow anyone on board the foreign vessel."

"Then could you tell me, please, who has the authority?" For the first time I noticed a spark of human interest in his eyes, caused by my persistence. The guy certainly wasn't used to a situation where someone would continue arguing after being told *nyet*.

"Only the commander-in-chief of the whole northwestern military district," he proclaimed with the utmost self-importance, indicating that at this point the conversation was clearly over.

"Okay, how can I get in touch with him?"

"Are you crazy? He is a General major, you can't talk to him directly. You must go through the chain of command." The tone of the colonel's voice was stern, leaving no doubt that it would be a big mistake to attempt to go through the chain of command. He looked at me as if to say, "The chain ends here."

And just to make sure, he threw in the last argument.

"It's Sunday anyway and you couldn't find him even if you tried. He is probably at his private *dacha* someplace and no one has a phone number there, except for his close assistants."

"Look," I gathered all my persuading powers, "the boat we're now designing ... the whole project ... it's all being done for the first time. It might bring Soviet sport into a new level." I honestly believed in what I was telling him and it probably was my determination that finally broke through to him.

He held a very long pause, looking me straight in the eyes and then squeezed out, "Okay, let's try to find him, but beware if you get me into trouble."

Almost an hour later, after countless calls, we finally got the General's number and, my fingers trembling, I dialed it. Luckily he was at his dacha but at first was extremely annoyed at being disturbed. He almost hung up on me. Yet somehow I was able to catch his attention for just one crucial moment, then told him, as briefly as possible, the whole story, feeling that gradually the man of power was becoming more and more relaxed and attentive. He threw a few pointed questions and then finally asked me to pass the phone to the chief of the border patrol.

Listening, the colonel stood straight at attention as if the general were right there in front of him.

"Yes... yes, comrade General. Glad to follow your orders."

He put the phone down looking dumbstruck.

"He told me you may go there ... I can't believe this. Do you understand there is a borderline between this Finnish boat and us? This is the borderline of the Soviet Union. It is sealed, period. No one could penetrate it. And yet, the comrade General told me that you may go through."

Still shocked, he was slowly regaining his composure and getting stern again.

"Okay, only for half an hour. And only the three of you. The rest will stay here." His voice was firm now. "And remember if you're trying to play some sort of trick here, I'll lose my head but you'll lose yours first."

Trying to get there before the colonel changed his mind again, we virtually ran to UBF secured behind the chain of border guards, who reluctantly stepped aside and let us through. There was definitely something in the air in Russia that was starting to turn everything upside down. Nothing was sacred any longer, including the sealed borderline.

At first Ludde Ingvall wasn't happy about our visit, fearing that we would spy on his secrets or, much worse, even copy the design of his boat. Come on, mate, your boat is a yesterday compared to our innovative beauty. We looked around getting more and more excited. Yes, yes, and yes! There was no doubt that our baby's design was head and shoulders ahead. I couldn't wait till she would be racing, demonstrating what she was capable of.

Gradually Ludde melted slightly, especially after I showed him, as a token of trust, the drawings of our boat, which I had with me. He invited us to a press conference and reception in the lavish *Intuorist Hotel Pribaltiyskaya*, which I gladly accepted, having no idea that this press conference would eventually lead to the break up of Mobile.

• • •

Larionov and the whole Mobile gang were extremely grateful for a tour of UBF, but when I returned to Leningrad a few weeks later, something had radically changed. I was met with such open hostility it was almost frightening. At first they avoided answering my questions about what was going on and for awhile we tried to proceed with the business as usual. But the atmosphere was so gloomy I could not take it any longer.

"Come on guys, tell me what's happened."

"You want to know what's happened? Then look at this," snapped Oleg, throwing the magazine he was holding at me. It flew across the room but didn't reach me, landing on the floor between us. Puzzled, I picked it up and leafed through its pages, quickly spotting a picture of Ludde Ingvall and me during the UBF press conference. The article that followed was in Finnish and I couldn't make out a word of it.

"Okay, so what's wrong? Did you read the article?"

"It's irrelevant what this article is about," he said— surely Oleg knew Finnish no better than I —"Just count how many times your name is mentioned in it versus that of Mobile's."

Wandering through the jumble of unfamiliar words, I did my counting and was surprised to find my name mentioned three times, while Mobile was mentioned only once. Now I knew I was getting to the heart of the matter.

"It's clear to all of us here that Mobile means nothing to you," Oleg's eyes sparkled with hate as he hissed, "The only thing you care about is self-promotion! It's disgusting!"

The crime was evident and ashamed, I had nothing to say in my defense but I was puzzled indeed. I remembered talking a lot about Mobile and our design during the press conference but certainly couldn't recall ever even mentioning my own name, except when I was introduced at the beginning.

Needless to say, the first thing I did upon my return to Moscow was to visit the Union Bank of Finland, where I asked Mattie Grunland, my brief acquaintance in the bank, to translate the damn article. Actually, the article turned out to be a pretty good one, with nice words about the Mobile cooperative, the innovative FAZISI design, and so on, but nothing about me.

"Nothing? How's that, nothing? What about this and this and this? Isn't my name mentioned here three times?"

"Oh, that... the journalist just says, 'I asked Mr. Murnikov... Murnikov answered... and Murnikov had told me...' That's it."

"That's it?" Such a stupid thing had put a huge rift in my relationship with Oleg Larionov, making me an enemy of the rest of Mobile. I called them immediately and explained what the article was about. They seemed to calm down a bit, but our relations never returned to friendly and trusting terms again. It all went downhill after that article.

•••

Meantime in Poti the boat's construction had started, slowly at first but accelerating swiftly. As had been earlier decided, the crew began gathering at the shipyard to help in the building and to begin preparations for the race. Tikhov arranged for a dormitory right there on the plant premises, complete with a canteen and fitness center. First to arrive were Alexey Grischenko and his friend Igor Mironenko from Kiev. Soon Anatoly Verba joined with his team. All Odessits came complete with nicknames. Sergey Stanetsky, well-muscled, with broad shoulders and long, blond hair that gave him pretty wild look, preferred to be called "Elephant". Navigator Gennady Korolkov, nicknamed "Crocodile" was followed by Vladimir "Kuli" Kulinichenko, whom Verba introduced as the best helmsman.

According to Nadja Ovsjannikova's plan, each potential crewmember presented a resume and made a presentation of his ideas on how to make the campaign successful. We all learned a lot from this. Everything proceeded in orderly fashion for a while but then a flood of those wanting to crew began to inundate us. In just two months we had received more than 70 applications for 16 crew positions. People were calling me, writing letters, or sometimes just showing up in Poti.

"I've heard about your project, it's the most exciting thing I can imagine. I have experience, have raced long distance. Here's my resume. I do not ask for any specific position, I just want to be involved. My name is Vladimir Musatov."

The handshake was firm, the smile was compassionate and enthusiastic, and I simply had no heart to turn him down after he'd made such a long trip and offered so openly to help.

Rami Leibovich flew from Riga, Latvia, and didn't ask for anything either. He just changed into working clothes and joined the construction crew.

But not all of them were this way. Soon ambitions started surfacing and I didn't even notice how the whole atmosphere became supercharged with competition. This was a selection process, all right: survival of the fittest. Anatoly Verba was becoming more and more relentless in his desire to become the skipper at any cost. But the more he wanted to succeed, the less convincing he looked as the candidate for the captain's role. The crew didn't like his style — much too authoritarian — and eventually they went on strike, probably the first one ever in the Soviet Union.

Tikhov called me in panic and the next day I was in Poti. Walking toward the construction shop, I saw Alexey Grischenko and was glad that I could get the news from him first.

"What's going on? Mutiny aboard the ship?" I only half-joked, seriously concerned with the unexpected turn of events.

"Well, maybe just a little bit," he smiled wearily. "It's all calmed down already and everyone's back to work. But the problem is serious. You know Anatoly was an instructor at the Merchant Academy in Odessa where he was used to dealing with kids, sometimes undisciplined. Then a dose of authority was probably appropriate... But now he's treating grown men like kids. He addresses everyone not by their names but just 'Hey, boy.' Who'd like that?"

"And that's all?"

"Well actually it's more serious. He's already managed to divide the crew into two camps, the Odessits and the rest. He makes it perfectly clear that if he's the captain, the sailing crew should consist predominantly of his bunch. Whenever he talks he refers to the Odessits as 'the sailors,' and to the rest, as 'the builders.' Obviously, it makes everybody extremely anxious, thus morale has taken a nosedive to the bottom."

"I don't get it... how could someone do such a stupid thing? You told me he was a good captain, a leader, and now... this? Not only is it bad for the whole project, he's also destroying his own chances, as his guys are in the minority. I really don't understand how he could be so blind."

"Yes, it's strange. I've always respected him and would have never anticipated such foolish behavior. Anyway, last night we had a meeting and I was able to somehow sort things out. Everyone has returned to work. But now most of the men want him out and want me as a captain."

He looked uncomfortable saying this.

"Now, that's exactly what I've been thinking for quite a while. As far as I can see you are certainly more qualified than Verba."

We had barely touched on this issue since our first conversation at the Kiev Yacht Club long ago. But watching the construction process in Poti, I saw more and more clearly that Alexey was a natural-born leader who knew how to be stern and demanding, yet remained an easy and friendly man, who could motivate people and bring out the best in them.

"You're already the leader of the team. It's not surprising that they want to see you as their captain. Besides, you're certainly as good a sailor as Verba."

For a while he was silent, then spoke slowly, carefully weighing every word. "I've been thinking a lot about this. And I am still not sure if my experience will be sufficient. This whole campaign is totally different from anything we've done before. I've built a few boats and consider myself a good boatbuilder but this time it is so different, it's just another level. The size does matter and this is, after all, the Maxi Class… I've never even been to an ocean and I just don't know whether I'd be able to rise to the challenge."

"You can count on the fingers of one hand all the people in this country who've been to an ocean before," I said. "Everything at some point has to be done for the first time. I'm doing a lot of things that I never thought I'd be capable of doing in my life. Do you want me to tell you all my troubles?"

"No, thank you, you may keep them to yourself," Alexey said smiling cheerfully. I'd always admired his ability to shrug off problems and replenish his optimism from some bottomless pit of energy. His voice was much more confident when he spoke again.

"I am sure you understand how much I want to be the captain. I'm just not ready yet to take over the responsibility. Let's come back to this later, we still have time. As for the problem at hand now, maybe you could send Verba on a vacation or something. I need him out of here to calm things down."

"He already had a vacation last month… And I know, I couldn't get rid of him completely. For some reason Tikhov definitely wants to keep him around, probably to have a system of checks and balances in place in accordance with the old politician's law: Divide and Rule. Maybe he feels more comfortable keeping some opposition to my ideas and actions. I could understand this."

I thought for a moment.

"Oh, I know what I'll do. I'm finishing the specifications of the boat's gear and equipment and could use an extra hand. Verba knows some English so he could go with me to Moscow to look through the marine catalogs. That should occupy him for a week or two. Would that be sufficient time?"

"It'll do. And don't worry, we'll pull it through somehow."

• • •

Alexey was heading for the storage warehouse and I joined him to check out the shipment of aluminum plating that had just arrived. Those were the sheets, four millimeters thick that would be used for the boat's topsides. The Soviet State's industrial standards allowed pretty broad tolerances so the actual thickness of aluminum sheets varied from 3.7 to 4.3 millimeters. With growing alarm, I watched Alexey picking up the thicker sheets after carefully checking them with his caliper.

"Hey, wait a moment. You're not supposed to do that."

He looked at me, smiling slyly, "You don't want me to use the thinner ones, do you? All the guys in the crew are already afraid that the boat is too light to hold together in the ocean. They're building her for themselves and want to be certain she's strong enough to survive."

Shit, I hadn't thought about it from that perspective. Another problem to worry about, and a serious one.

"Come on, Alexey, you know better than anyone that the boat needs to be built as precisely as possible. That concerns not only dimensions but weight as well. She must be measured later exactly as designed to receive the required rating. It doesn't help at all to use materials almost ten percent thicker."

"Well, I'll do my best, but you could measure the whole pile and wouldn't find two sheets of exactly four millimeters thickness. It's either less or more. Which ones do you want me to pick? And that's not all. When I order materials, the wait is sometimes too long and I simply have to use what's on hand or else we'd never get this boat built."

Indeed, it was a very serious problem. But there were so many of them — all sorts of them. Logistics had become a nightmare. Materials, tools, everything was in huge demand and short supply.

My visits to Poti grew more and more frequent and still there wasn't enough time to take care of everything.

• • •

No matter how confident I might have appeared to the others, deep inside I was fraught with doubts. The whole thing was becoming more and more real and I was in charge of it. It was a very exciting yet scary position. Dreaming was so safe and easy. But now I had fears similar to the ones that tormented Alexey Grischenko. I was finally recognizing the overwhelming scale of responsibility I was about to take on. Actually I wasn't just about to take on. I hadn't even noticed how and when it happened, but everything now was moving inexorably forward and I had no choice but to carry through with the plan. I was well beyond the point of no-return.

In mountain climbing, one of the most crucial aspects of survival is the proper timing of return, regardless of whether the summit has been reached or not. High in the death zone that surrounds Mount Everest, where the air is thinned to only 30 percent of its density at sea level and temperatures at night can easily match those at the Poles, a person can survive for only a short time. It becomes a matter of life or death to have enough time not only to reach the summit but also to descend to lower altitude as soon as possible, while one is still alive.

Depending on the weather conditions, smart and disciplined climbers turn back at the exact time that they set for themselves, even if they are only a mere hundred feet short of reaching the goal. The defeat seems to be devastating at the moment but then there might be another opportunity in the future, a more successful one. Many of those who have failed to observe their own turn-back time and continued to the summit out of the last drop of energy have had their brief moment of victory on the top of the world, but lost ultimately. Their frozen corpses high on the flanks of the mountain are a reminder of the importance of the choices we all make.

Unfortunately, being very much aware by the end of 1988 that our project had been falling more and more behind schedule, with the obstacles ahead seeming unsurmountable, I didn't have the freedom to turn back. Like a heavy freight train that initially requires enormous power to overcome its inertia and start rolling, the whole thing was on the move now and charging forward. After gaining momentum, it had become unstoppable, despite the fact that construction of the boat was proceeding painfully slowly, despite the serious design flaws that I had discovered, and despite my final break-up with Mobile, which coincided with all of this.

We had gradually drifted apart after that interview published in the Finish sailing magazine. The break-up had become only logical so I wasn't a bit disappointed when Larionov announced one day that they had a meeting and had unanimously voted me out. Struzilin's predictions had come true. Fine. Creative cooperation is an extremely sensitive thing, more so even than a marriage. If it doesn't work just make peace with it and let it go. "But don't worry," continued Larionov, "We'll finish our design work for Fazis SP and would never do anything to breach our agreement."

Like hell they wouldn't. During my next visit to Poti, a frustrated Alexey handed me the set of drawings that had just arrived from Mobile.

"I don't believe it, they specified a deck thickness of only 1.5 millimeters. It's insane."

I looked at the drawing myself. No, it couldn't be. Very quick calculations confirmed what I knew right away. If built according to Mobile's drawings, the deck would collapse and the boat would fold in two as soon as she hit the first big wave. Either those guys had gone absolutely mad and forgotten everything they'd ever learned about boat design, or it was some sort of a desperate attempt of sabotage. Hard to say. But after having worked with them for a while, I knew that they were, of course, capable of correct calculations and were in fact pretty smart designers. So madness was out of question. Well, at that point it really didn't matter whatever drive was behind their actions. There simply was no time to reflect on this.

Later I heard some rumors that Larionov and his gang kept working on the boat's design after our split up, trying to put together their own Whitbread campaign. I didn't pay much attention to it, and only briefly wondered if they had ever corrected their mistakes. It would be fun to watch THEIR boat breaking in two. That would certainly make my day.

Now the choice was simple: either quit or to take over the design process myself in addition to all the other duties I was already performing. That would be definitely too much to pull off. The voice of reason was screaming in my head, "It is all too late. Just face the reality and drop the whole thing. There is no chance you'll be able to sort out all this mess." To tell the truth, I was really frightened. But even if I did decide to, I knew it was simply beyond my power to stop everything at this stage.

The project was already living a life of its own. Too many people were involved now; too much human energy, too many ambitions and desires were invested in it, not to mention all the material things and money. We all had made a commitment a long time ago. This was the opportunity we had been waiting for all our lives, and for better or worse we had made a decision to stick with it. Besides, we simply didn't believe that we would ever have another opportunity. The situation in Russia was absolutely uncertain. The rising flood of changes sweeping all around might bring a cathartic cleansing to the society, but it could also wash it away into total chaos and anarchy.

It was now, or never.

7

THE BOAT. PART 1

It's time now for a short technical interlude to present my boat in some detail.

The fact that a Maxi racer had never been designed and built in Russia before provided a strange and significant advantage for us. Not affected by momentum that causes designers of more extensive experience to follow their usual, often conservative approach, we began with a clean sheet of paper. Obviously having never done a Maxi before, we couldn't design just another evolutionary boat. Then, why not go all the way and create a totally revolutionary one? In a sense, the lack of boat building in Russia and the fact that most of our previous designs still remained only on paper were both a blessing, allowing us unlimited creative freedom and helping our unleashed imaginations to soar.

For this very reason, even before starting Mobile, all three of us, Larionov, Struzilin, and I, had already come up with radical designs. Many of these were never built and our combined practical experience remained admittedly slim. Yet from a theory standpoint, our work was impressive. In addition, Struzilin had done a lot of tank testing as a part of his graduate studies at the Leningrad Shipbuilding Institute's facility. And now we had this wealth of data to draw from for our concept of an offshore racer.

The biggest challenge was not so much to design a fast boat, but one which would outperform the others within the International Offshore Rule, IOR for short, the handicapping system used for the Whitbread. The IOR defined a tight framework of the boat's principal dimensions affecting its performance, such as hull size, shape, displacement, and sail area. If a designer wanted a faster boat by increasing sail area, he would need to shorten the length of the waterline or increase the weight, or do both. The idea of the rule was to keep a fair balance.

For every gain made in one area, another area was penalized.

The obvious temptation was to optimize the boat's design around more sail area. This, after all, is a sailboat's source of power, like the car's engine. But taking this straightforward approach presented plenty of drawbacks, like higher loads on the rig and the hull, which could lead to fatigue and breakage. More sail area would also require more stability, resulting in increased lead ballast to prevent the yacht from excessive heeling, and so on.

An alternative was to design a more efficient hull shape with less resistance and drag, which could move easily through the water even with less sail area. Power versus efficiency — we chose the latter. We designed our yacht to be long and sleek, with a narrow waterline and minimal wetted surface. Even if we needed to give up some sail area with this approach, it still promised superior speed advantage.

A lightweight displacement was not only an important factor in the boat's performance; it made the loads on the hull and rig smaller too, which thereby allowed for a lighter structure of better durability. The load on the crew would also be reduced, as the yacht would be lighter and simpler to handle. Our crew, who'd be having their first ocean experience on a Maxi, would certainly appreciate this. Furthermore, the boat could be sailed with a smaller crew, and the amount of provisions and drinking water aboard could be reduced as well. It was like a chain reaction with one advantage leading to another.

There was more.

Less sail area meant fewer sails in the inventory, each of them smaller and cheaper. With limited resources, we were going for efficiency, and our design, at least theoretically, promised the best performance.

• • •

Certainly, light easily driven boats existed before this. In fact, there is even a special class of them called the ULDBs, which have sustained, though limited, popularity in the US. The acronym ULDB stands for Ultra Light Displacement Boat. The idea for these boats goes back to the late-1960s in the California resort town of Santa Cruz, home of a small enclave of talented yacht designers. Their mantra was "Fast is fun!" and "(Rating) Rules be damned!" With surfing waves a feature of this part of the California coastline, the light and long boats could ride them on a plane. It seemed a natural evolution for the area.

George Olson, a founder of the ULDB movement, described how

the ULDB concept was formulated, "If you take a boat and stretch its waterline length 25 percent but keep everything else the same — the beam, displacement, and sail area — the boat will become faster. It's obvious. What came as a total surprise when we performed the conversion, the top speed didn't increase just 25 percent. It doubled!"

In 1976 ULDB designer Bill Lee rose to fame. Lee, nicknamed "The Wizard" both creative in boat design as well as in life style, was wont to show up at the launchings of his boats dressed in a star-spangled robe and looking like the wizard Merlin himself. Maybe he would even tap the yacht with his magic wand. One ULDB by Lee indeed sailed with a special karma. It was the 65-foot racer MERLIN weighing only 20,000 pounds, less than half the norm for a boat this size. She established a record in the TransPac Race from Los Angeles to Honolulu that remained unchallenged for over two decades.

Californian sleds were awesome sailing machines but they had one significant weakness. Designed with a total disregard of the IOR, their ratings were terrible. Consequently, they would often take line honors for the fastest time over the race course but almost never they won any major regattas on corrected time.

Our approach was different. We designed our boat to be a no-nonsense ULDB, but we also studied the handicapping system well and found a way to get a reasonable rating to boot. It took us almost two years to come up with the right combination. But in the end we figured we achieved what had never been done before: a sled that was also an IOR boat with a good rating.

• • •

Besides being revolutionary in her concept, our boat was radical in execution as well. The hull was designed with a shape such that in light air its waterline became shorter, allowing for the displacement to concentrate in a compact volume, thus minimizing the wetted surface. The substantial bow and stern overhangs not only added to the yacht's grace but also helped stretch the waterline when the boat heeled and accelerated in a freshening breeze. Its relatively wide, flat transom promoted good planing characteristics.

The bow was sharper than usual so the boat would cut easier through the waves. The sharpness resulted from moving the hull's overall volume more aft to further enhance high-speed planing. The keel (and rig) were also positioned more aft than was the convention. Each detail, however minor, helped bring other improvements. For example, in moving the rig further aft, hull pitching was reduced. It also allowed for locating the headstay some eight feet back from the bow, making it far easier and safer for the bowman to work in heavy conditions.

And so on.

Each of these details was small by itself, but combined they helped to create a well-balanced yacht with all design elements in harmony.

We had chosen aluminum as the construction material primarily out of necessity. By this time most of the Whitbread racers were built of composite laminates of carbon fiber or high-modulus Kevlar fibers and epoxy resin. These materials offered outstanding strength-to-weight ratios but were too expensive for us to seriously consider. Besides, no one in Russia had experience working with composites, especially in constructing a Maxi raceboat. We were well aware of the recent problems one of the New Zealand campaigns had had. Something had gone wrong in the lamination process of FISHER & PAYKEL to the point that the builders had no choice but to scrap the hull and start over again. We simply didn't have the money or the time for that.

After it was decided that the boat would be built at Poti Shipyard, which had extensive experience working with aluminum, the choice of material became obvious. But now we had to deal with the fact that aluminum was significantly heavier than composite.

Part of our radical design solution was to greatly reduce the boat's freeboard — down by about one foot all around the hull, except the bow. This not only reduced the entire surface area as well as the weight by more than 10 percent, but also moved the deck, with all its hardware, a foot closer to the boat's center of gravity, increasing stability. It also gave the boat a distinctive sheerline with a sharply upturned bow – and a reason why she was later frequently nicknamed the "Soviet banana-boat."

To further reduce the hull weight, we developed an extremely elaborate structure with a thin outer skin and an extensive network of supporting frames, longitudinals and stiffener members. The thickness of the plating varied dramatically over the boat's length and height depending on the amount of local load in each particular area. For example, the rear topsides, the least loaded part of hull, were merely 2.5 millimeters (less than 1/8 of inch) thick. Moving forward to the area subjected to the wave slamming, the thickness gradually rose to 4 to 5 millimeters. Down toward the bottom, it increased even more, with the area directly adjoining to the keel built out of plating 8 millimeters (1/3 inch) thick.

Our building specifications called for the exact aluminum thickness necessary to carry the load in each particular area, not even a pound extra. By such rigorous weight control we were able to design an aluminum hull of about the same weight as a composite structure. Frankly, we believed our Maxi was arguably the most advanced aluminum yacht ever designed. But I was afraid that we might have gone a bit too far. Now our super sophisticated design needed sophisticated construction. Could we get it from a yard used to building commercial ships rather than the Soviet Union's first ULDB Maxi?

•••

One of the most interesting features of our yacht was its deck layout. Because of the low freeboard, it had to have a good-sized cabin house to provide adequate inside volume. This was a very unusual feature for Maxis, which normally had flush decks. The elevated cabin house became a shield against the elements, sheltering a cockpit and protecting the crew somewhat from the fury of the ocean. The cockpit, as well as most of the deck gear, was concentrated in the middle of the boat for the best weight distribution.

Twin steering stations on the each side of the boat were located unusually far forward, at the hull's maximum beam — in a style adopted by most of the America's Cup racers ten years later. It provided the helmsman with the best position to see the sails and view the waves and the sea state. When the yacht heeled, the helmsman, located in the windward cockpit, became elevated to the highest point on the deck, some 15 feet above the sea level. The headsail trimmer was two feet forward of the helmsman, and the mainsail trimmer – just behind, a few feet toward the centerline. The combination made for instant communication and coordination in steering and trimming the boat. The entire watch was concentrated in one place in the center of the boat so everyone could feel himself an intrinsic member of the team. It would be essential to create a bond, a sense of togetherness, so important in the desolate stretches of the race on the dangerous Southern Ocean.

Below deck the layout was Spartan at best, just the bare essentials. We were often asked later by the curious onlookers, "How could you live in such cramped conditions?" The answer was simple: our boat was not designed for living in, she was designed for racing on. No one, for example, would expect air-conditioning, leather seats, or any other creature comforts in a Formula One car. In the very same way, our yacht contained only absolutely necessary gear, nothing more. When competing in an ocean race, the deck is the place where you work and live, and it should be as efficient and as safe a place as possible. As for the comfort below deck -- you go there only to sleep for a few hours, grab a bite to eat, and then rush back up on deck again to drive the boat hard; that's it.

Comfortable bunks for each crewmember, a dryer, a decent heater, a small galley (there was not much cooking, as most of the food was freeze-dried, just add boiling water and the meal was ready) located on the centerline to minimize the motion and even equipped with a swivel chair for the cook's comfort (none of the other boats had such luxury), and a well-stuffed navstation were the necessary components. Oh, yes, there needed to be a basic head, of course, as simple as possible for ease of maintenance. Anything more would just add excessive weight.

The fact that the interior volume of our boat was small, less than that on most Whitbread racers, might actually become a blessing in high seas. When the boat is bouncing and slamming around, constantly attempting to catapult you into the air, the smaller the space, the safer it is, the handholds are easier to reach, and the chance of injury is less.

· · ·

The night before the Whitbread start when our boat was docked with the rest of the fleet at the Southampton Town Quay Marina, the late Eric Tabarly came aboard. The most celebrated French sailor and undoubtedly one of the world's best sailors of all time, Tabarly had sailed all previous Whitbread Races. He walked along the deck, checking the equipment, stood at the steering wheel, nodding approvingly at the deck layout, and then went below. Finally, coming out of the hatch, he exclaimed, "*Oui, tres simple, c'est bon!*"

Eric certainly knew a good boat when he saw one.

PART II

TRIUMPH AND TRAGEDY

8

THE PEPSI LETTER

An average Whitbread syndicate's campaign budget in 1989-90 was approximately five million dollars. That included a boat, crew expenses, logistics, repair, travel, communication, everything. Obviously, for a variety of reasons, no one disclosed exact or accurate figures. There were some announcements and some leaks and rumors. Certain syndicates preferred to look more humble, while others instead inflated their figures to appear more powerful and intimidating for poorer competitors. Economic turmoil in the Soviet Union presented us with an advantage of sort. The prices of goods and services were cheap, and in fact kept falling while we were working on the project, thus enabling us to launch our campaign for just a fraction of what it cost the others.

At the beginning I prepared two budgets: a minimal and an optimal. The minimal one was well below one million dollars. In addition to the boat's construction, it included sails and other equipment, which we would need to procure in the West, plus a container with workshop and spare parts that would follow the boat from stopover to stopover. And, of course, there had to be the money to run the project for more than two years.

At that point, I hadn't figured much for crew expenses. They were thrilled just to be involved in the project; pay wasn't an issue. I'd heard, "Hey, Vlad, this is a chance in a lifetime" or, "If I'm lucky to go, who cares about pay? Just to sail around the world, what could be better reward?" I could understand this. I myself felt exactly the same and was committed to do anything just to have this opportunity. But when I discussed the budget with Tikhov for the first time, he immediately dismissed this volunteer attitude. "Come on, you'll all have families to feed while you're goofing around in the Southern Ocean. I'm going to put in a monthly salary of 300 rubles for every crewmember. Plus everyone will become an employee of Fazis SP with all benefits, etc." While 300 rubles a month was a pretty generous pay at that time, compared to an average Soviet salary of about 180 rubles, it still was only about $30 at the black market exchange rate and fit nicely, even into the minimal budget.

An optimal budget, counting on a large corporate sponsorship, included such lavish things as a full sail inventory — just as our competitors had — plus an on-board navigational computer with top-of-the-line software for weather forecasting. It also included a spare mast on standby, ready to be airlifted to any point on the globe in case the original one broke. A shore support team to help the crew repair and maintain the yacht during stopovers was also a part of this package. And there would be funds to fly crewmembers home during the stopovers or fly in their loved ones. I also wanted to pay the crew much more, as a bonus, especially if they performed well. We had heard about professional sailors in the West who supposedly earned huge fees. Wouldn't it be great for our crew to become rich and famous, as well, after the race? But obviously it was not a priority at this point.

My dream budget was full three million dollars.

• • •

We didn't know how much sponsorship we might be able to get from the West, but had no doubt that we would receive some. Breaking out of its communist past, the Soviet Union was a media star and with perestroika on the rise, the sponsor's benefits of being associated with our project would be numerous and obvious. We figured that any corporate executive would have to be blind, or just stupid, not to recognize the great opportunity we offered them. All we needed to do was reach out and show them what we could offer.

As the one most fluent in English of all my Fazis cohorts, I drafted our first press release. Leaving the style and the grammar untouched, I've included it here — not without some reservation. It is funny, but a bit embarrassing too. You'll understand.

"... A Soviet yacht, representing the Golden Fleece Syndicate, will for the first time in the history take part in the prestigious sailboat race.

... The Syndicate, organized by the Phasis firm, the Poti territorial-interindustrial amalgamation, and the Poti Yacht Club, will sail in a

quest to win the prestigious Whitbread Round the World Race. Modern Argonauts are set to overcome any difficulty and dream of finishing first.

The vessel is been built by a most innovative concept and combines high-speed, reliability, and light weight. We have taken into account weather conditions and perspective trends in yacht building to design a yacht that has excellent performance characteristics to ensure the success.

The yachts is being built at the Poti shipyard that is world famous for its hydrofoil passenger vessels of the Kometa and Kolhida type. State-of-the-art technology and high-class specialists help the Poti shipyard build advanced vessels from aluminum alloys.

The crew consists of many world famous Soviet racers, world and Olympic champions. There are winners and finalists of major Soviet cruising competitions such as the Black Sea Cup, the Baltic Sea, and Onega Lake Cup, participants and organizers of cruising voyages in the Pacific Ocean near Sakhalin Islands and Kamchatka. The men were weathered in extreme weather conditions in these areas and are ready to sail the Antarctic waters where the course of the Whitbread Race lays.

International cooperation will help fulfill our plans. We are looking for sponsors, who will grasp the opportunity to advertise their products using our yacht. Our vessel is the first Soviet boat to take part in the Race and it is certain to attract worldwide attention.

For the first time in history we are to field a Soviet yachts in WRTWR. We will try to exert maximum efforts so that the Soviet yachtsmen will leave their mark on the development of sailing, help strengthen international relations and promote perestroyka in our country."

And so on. You get the idea. Armed with such a powerful marketing tool, we felt ready to conquer the Western corporate world. What fools we were!

Our first major sponsorship meeting was held at the British-Soviet Chamber of Commerce. We had high hopes, for this was our access to British companies already quite familiar with the Whitbread and ocean racing. British Airways had sponsored a few offshore boats before. British Oxygen Corporation was the title sponsor for a major singlehanded event, the BOC Round the World Challenge. And then there was Richard Branson, an accomplished adventurer balloonist and sailor, holder of the transatlantic record, which he set on "Virgin Atlantic Challenge."

In addition to all this, he was the owner of a nice fortune in the form of a record company and Virgin Airlines. Wouldn't it be terrific to get him interested and involved? Maybe even join our crew? Imagine the possibilities! Oh, dreams, sweet dreams.

As I walked into the lobby of the Moscow World Trade Center with Alexander Manenko, he asked me: "Could you tell me roughly how much money we need?" A few days before I had given him my budget calculations with detailed explanations. It was obvious now that the folder rested unopened in the bottom of his briefcase.

"I've prepared two budget figures. The smaller one..." I started as we walked into the elevator.

"Give me the bigger one," Alexander interrupted.

"Three million dollars."

"Okay, I'll tell them five," Alexander said as the elevator stopped at the 21st floor and we walked out.

Toward the end of the meeting, after we had presented all the benefits of our project and had had a few coffees and brandies, traditional to all Moscow business meetings, one of the Brits asked in a very polite voice, "Gentlemen, would you tell us please what amount of sponsorship you are looking for?"

"Seven million," replied Alexander without hesitation.

"US dollars, I reckon?"

"Why, pounds sterling, of course." This answer took him a few seconds to perform mentally some simple mathematical calculations involving currency exchange.

"Are you out of your mind, Alexander?" I asked in despair while we were returning to the Fazis office in his Mercedes. "Maximum that we need is three million and that would be total luxury. If we are greedy and ask for too much, we might well end up with nothing."

"You are so naïve in business, Vladislav," he took one hand off the wheel and patted my shoulder. "You have so much to learn. Never start negotiation with what you want. Besides, when you charge more, everyone takes you more seriously. Don't you worry, one thing they taught me well in *Vneshtorg* is how to negotiate. I know how to approach the other side, how to grab them, and hold tight, strangle them until they start to beg you to agree to any conditions."

For a time we drove in silence while I digested the business lesson. Then Alexander continued, "Please also understand clearly -- Fazis SP is getting involved in the whole affair not because we're so thrilled by your prospect of sailing around the world. We want to make money on this. And I have a gut feeling we'll make good money. You calculate how much you need to run this project, I'll decide how much I want to sell it for, and those are two totally different things."

And again after a short pause, "I expect we can make at least two millions on this — and Fazis needs this money. We have a business to grow."

He actually didn't say "millions," he said "lemons." This was the current trendy word in the new-changing Russia. It sort of constituted "millions, lemons — who cares." We were still poor but quickly converting into capitalists, and taking pride in it.

•••

Undoubtedly, the most prominent figure among all foreign businessmen in Russia was Ted Turner. He had just opened the CNN Moscow bureau but that was not the main reason for his frequent visits to the Russian capital. The Goodwill Games was.

By the mid-1980s the whole Olympic movement had ground to a standstill and seemed to be falling apart. In 1980 the city of Moscow and all of Russia made a tremendous human and financial effort to make its Olympics the greatest sporting event in history. But instead, it became a fiasco after the United States and most of the Western countries boycotted the Moscow Games because of the Soviet Union's involvement in the Afghan war. Not surprisingly, in retaliation, the USSR boycotted the next Olympics held in Los Angeles, and all the eastern satellites followed obediently. The L.A. Olympics became a success nevertheless, thanks to its smart organization; still, it lacked almost half of the world's best athletes. The next venue was to be in Seoul, South Korea. The chances that the Soviet Union would boycott the games again looked pretty solid, and that might mean the end of the Olympic movement altogether. The opportunity for athletes from countries around the world to meet and compete regardless of their political systems was in jeopardy.

To the rescue came Ted Turner with his Goodwill Games in 1986. I don't doubt an idealistic notion on his part to create an alternative opportunity for American and Russian athletes to compete — after all they shouldn't be victims of politics. But it was also a shrewd business move, for if the Olympic movement eventually crumbled, Ted Turner would own whatever was left of it in the form of the Goodwill Games. It was sort of a hostile takeover. As it later turned out, by the time of the Seoul Games in 1988, Russia had changed enough not to boycott. As result the Olympics emerged stronger than ever, making the whole

Goodwill affair pretty irrelevant.

In his younger years Ted Turner had been an avid yachtsman chalking up a very impressive record that was crowned by winning the America's Cup in 1977. I had read about his sailing victories; to me he had the aura of a hero. I couldn't even imagine meeting him in the flesh. Yet here I was now, looking for ways to approach this man not only because of his obvious sponsorship potential, but also in a big part due to my genuine interest in him as a sailor and a great achiever.

Ted Turner was quite a celebrity in Moscow and it was rumored that his gatekeeper at the time was Galina Nikolopulos. After some research, I found people who knew her, got her unlisted phone number, and managed to receive an invitation to several events where Big Ted was the guest of honor. Usually those were grand banquets organized by *Goscomsport* bureaucrats in celebration of the Goodwill Games, with plenty of fine wine and stronger, high-quality liquor, and numerous toasts proclaiming international cooperation, spirit of friendship, and sportsmanship. One particular imposing reception of this sort was held at the Prague, a lavish restaurant located at the famous Moscow corner where Arbat Street and Kalininsky Prospect meet Boulevard Ring. The Prague occupied a four-story building with many richly decorated dining halls and intimate banquet facilities. Quiet piano and violin music flowed from a winter garden. Food was delicious and expensive, and drinks plentiful. If I hadn't been invited as a guest to the fancy Prague, a visit there could have easily relieved me of half of my monthly salary.

It was during the course of that evening that I happened to realize how drastically my social status had changed. My Whitbread project had already received decent publicity in the Russian media, and I found myself absolutely unaccustomed to my new fame.   Not that I had become a celebrity; still, I had noticed that people started treating me differently. I couldn't say I was comfortable with my new status, feeling like a total stranger in this elite crowd of high-ranking Soviet bureaucrats and foreign diplomats. The gathering was predominantly male and featured an array of top Sport Committee officials and bosses from the all-Russian trade unions, which controlled leisure and sport activities in the USSR. In accordance with an unwritten protocol of the communist purist ideology, there were few women. It was still a long time before the New Russians with their scandalous lifestyle would came out in the open.

Unlike the Russians, Ted Turner arrived in a company of a tall and strikingly beautiful blonde model from Sweden. At some point I was introduced to her, and I believe she whispered, Ingrid, in response, but now I'm not certain. We chatted casually about sailing for a while, then she said, "Ted would be glad to talk about your boat. He loves sailing. I am sure, after a few vodkas he'd tell you how to steer the boat like a champion."

She stood with her beautiful legs spread wide apart, as if balancing on a gyrating yacht's deck. Her hands gestured with a firm grip on an imagined steering wheel. She laughed and I wanted to pinch myself. Here I was, in the midst of a grand banquet at the Prague, talking to a woman whose beauty could overshadow any Hollywood star, ready to meet Ted Turner himself and to talk to him as if we were equals. My dream in reality was even grander than I could have ever imagined.

After the Russian officials made all the usual speeches and toasts appropriate to the occasion, Ted's turn came. His steps were slightly unsteady when he walked to the podium. He touched only briefly on the subject of international cooperation, friendship, and sportsmanship, and then drew the attention of the respected assembly to his beautiful date. At the end of his little speech, to the slight shock of the assembly, he held up his glass in a toast to her, and reluctantly they all drank. It was getting late, many toasts were proposed and drunk to, and even the crustiest commissars were in a relaxed and mellow mood.

Soon the chance to talk with Ted had come up. As Ingrid predicted, at one point in our conversation he did actually steer the virtual steering wheel of an imagined boat, but was otherwise serious and attentive. He asked detailed questions about the project and in particular about our boat design. And then to my greatest joy he said, "You know, I am really interested. I'll think about it. I'd like to do a couple of short legs on your boat or at least steer at the start. I'll show you how to sail and kick some ass!"

He gave me his business card and invited to a meeting the next morning.

That night, as I rode the last subway train back to my apartment on the outskirts of Moscow, I really wasn't there but rather levitating somewhere near heaven, or at least close to the Southern Ocean. I barely slept that night.

The next morning promptly brought me back down to earth. I knocked at room number 568 in the Continental Hotel, and the Tycoon opened the door himself. He looked all business, dressed impeccably in a three-piece black suit, but the look on his face clearly indicated that the hangover was torturous. The excitement of the previous night was gone and there was very little talk about boats and racing. Instead he spoke about financial problems and the losses associated with the Goodwill Games.

"At this point," Ted concluded, "I cannot commit money to any other project. But I think your idea is interesting and I'd like you to be in touch with my manager. Maybe we could do something in the future."

• • •

While a major hard-currency sponsorship remained elusive, we were able to quickly cut a few small deals, which brought in some cash and/or in-kind sponsorship. The Soviet airlines *Aeroflot* agreed to give us an unlimited supply of tickets and sponsored a spinnaker with their logo. As it turned out this all-purpose spinnaker made by Hood Sails would be our best one. Unfortunately, their routes didn't cover Australia and New Zealand, so we still had to buy tickets for connecting flights; but nevertheless, it was a good deal.

Ingosstrakh, the Soviet national insurance company, supplied in-kind support in the form of the boat's insurance for the entire year of racing, which otherwise would have cost us at least $50,000. And the Soviet shipping company *Sudoimport* offered free use of their maintenance and repair facility in Montevideo, Uruguay.

The first real sponsorship breakthrough came in December of 1988 through Dennis Conner, probably America's most celebrated sailor. For the past 20 years his name has been closely entwined with the America's Cup. It was he who lost the Cup to the Australians in 1983 after America's successful defense of the Cup for 130 years. There were plenty of challengers from different countries, but American sailing dominance seemed unquestionable. The gentlemen of the New York Yacht Club, where the baroque trophy had been grandly on display behind glass in its trophy room, got so used to the victories, they had an expression for those who dared to defend the America's Cup. "The skipper who'd lose the Auld Mug will pay with his head displayed instead."

And it was Dennis Conner, who became the unfortunate skipper. He was defeated by Australian Alan Bond, whose radical, winged-keel boat skippered by John Bertrand came out faster by just a small margin. It was a spectacular battle in which the match was decided only on the last upwind leg of the final seventh race. Overnight Dennis became the most famous sailor in the world, but it was the kind of celebrity status that nobody would care for.

Somehow he had managed to keep his head, and as it turned out, he, in fact, did a big favor to the Cup by losing it. While it remained a highly publicized and still the most prestigious sailing event by the early-1980s, the general interest had certainly been fading away. The outmoded 12-Meter, the Cup's boat of choice, was inherently slow, and the permanent venue off Newport, Rhode Island, in the muggy, windless months of August and September didn't add much to the racing excitement. The endless string of American victories had made Cup racing so predictable with competition never even close.

When the unthinkable had actually happened and the America's Cup moved to the Royal Perth Yacht Club in Western Australia, it received the biggest boost of its history. Numerous American syndicates were created to challenge for the Cup and bring it back. Other countries, realizing that the Cup was indeed obtainable, also challenged. As a result the 1986-87 America's Cup series attracted a great fleet of top level competitors. The spectacular sailing conditions on the windy Indian Ocean off Fremantle made for a display of the best America's Cup racing ever. And Dennis Conner was a star again, this time defeating the Aussies 4 to 1. His dominance had been so strong there was no need to run the last two races of the series.

And now the American hero was about to come to Moscow with a sponsorship check from Pepsi.

Dennis' name had first come up a month earlier during my meeting with Hans Waimer from the German company Speedwave, which would be supplying a keel and rudder for the boat, and John Green from Sparcraft, the mast-making company. They had both done big-boat racing with Dennis and were on friendly terms with him, particularly Hans. So he offered to help us to get in touch with the famous sailor.

Among the major corporations that had supported Conner's America's Cup campaigns were Pepsi, Merrill-Lynch and American Airlines. They had certainly gotten enough publicity to justify their hefty contributions; nevertheless, they had been restrained to the shadows and made to keep their sponsorship involvement low-key. The New York Yacht Club's old guard strained to protect what they viewed as the Corinthian spirit of America's Cup competition, whether it actually existed or not. On the other hand, the Whitbread organizers openly embraced the notion of commercial sponsorship and allowed the companies to get all the benefits they paid for. In contrast to pure classic appearance and proud boat names of the America's Cup like INTREPID, FREEDOM, STARS&STRIPES, TENACIOUS, and AUSTRAIA, the Whitbread yachts flaunted names such as GATORADE (drinks), FORTUNA EXTRA LIGHTS (cigarettes), STEINLAGER (beer),

CHARLES JOURDAN (clothing) and UNION BANK OF FINLAND (money), shamelessly covering their hulls and sails with sponsor's logos.

There could definitely be visibility benefits for Dennis Conner's sponsors, had he decided to get involved, in one way or another, with our project. For Dennis himself, without plans to enter the Whitbread, being associated with our project had personal benefits too. At the very least it would bring him the publicity of being the first American sailor who had ventured into Russia. We agreed that Hans would discuss all this with Dennis. Only a week later a fax signed "Dennis Conner" arrived from California. It read more like a letter of agreement and stated that Dennis would arrange a sponsorship deal with Pepsi International under the following conditions:

-- Fazis SP will organize a major press conference covered by both Soviet and worldwide press.

-- The press conference will be featured on the major Soviet TV channel.

-- There will be guaranteed articles in major Soviet newspapers and information will be sent worldwide via the TASS Agency.

-- All Dennis Conner's expenses while in the USSR will be covered by Fazis SP.

The suggested timetable was only one month away, but the rush was good for us as our anxiety about getting sponsorship was very high. The agenda was ambitious, requiring a lot of organizing, but doable.

One month later I was at the Sheremetyevo II airport awaiting the arrival of the Lufthansa flight from Munich with Dennis Conner and Hans Waimer aboard. The iron curtain still stood firm, but gone was the era of treating every foreigner arriving in Moscow as a potential enemy of the state. No more thorough checks by a squad of Soviet border guards. Formalities had been greatly reduced. Soon I spotted Hans among the passengers going through customs controls. Next to him was a bulky figure completely immersed in a huge fur coat. Dennis Conner arrived well prepared for the ferocity of the Russian winter. I immediately recognized the face seen so often in yachting magazines, even though in person Dennis looked much broader, with double chins sitting firmly atop the enormous fur collar. After the usual greetings, we stepped outside into a warm drizzle and walked to the parking lot. The winter of 1988 in Moscow was unusually mild.

After Dennis and Hans had checked into their hotel, I took them to dinner at one of the restaurants at the Trade Center. Alexander Manenko had a conflicting meeting and was expected to join us later. At first Dennis appeared stiff and uneasy. It seemed to be the usual discomfort of a foreigner newly arrived in Moscow. Later, after a few toasts of vodka and some caviar, he would relax and sit less intensely. Despite his discomfort, I sensed a hidden energy through his misleadingly bulky and soft appearance. His sleepy, half-closed eyes and puffy cheeks gave the impression of a benign and friendly owl; but then, out of nowhere, his look would turn sharp and concentrated as an instant reminder that the owl is a predator after all.

Alexander finally arrived, apologized and took a place at the table across from Dennis. I introduced them. With a big ceremonial air, Dennis reached for the briefcase beside his chair and extracted an envelope bearing a Pepsi logo. Slowly and solemnly he handed it to Alexander. I could hear my heart pounding in the heavy silence that fell over the table. Opening the envelope, Alexander Manenko first pulled out a check, then the letter from Pepsi. We all froze staring at him. He didn't open the letter but just kept looking at the check. Then spoke to me in Russian, his voice clearly disappointed:

"Tell them the sum on the check is one digit too small."

He could speak English a little like everyone in Vneshtorg, but on certain occasions preferred not to and used me as a translator instead. He handed me the letter and the check.

Dennis didn't understand what was going on but sensed that the effect the letter was producing wasn't what he had expected. Embarrassed, I feigned to be deeply engaged in reading the letter. First my eyes just slid over the text again and again, its meaning eluding me. Then the words started to penetrate slowly into my mind, "...we are honored to offer sponsorship... Pepsi International cannot miss such a unique opportunity... become an exclusive sponsor for the pre-start period and depending on results... would consider option to extend... At the start line your boat should carry a spinnaker with the Pepsi logo."

I moved my eyes to the check. The amount was $250,000 US, obviously much less that we'd expected and definitely much less than we needed. At first I felt disappointed like Alexander. Nevertheless, it was a lot of money and it was just a first step. So unlike Alexander, my expectations slowly improved. Besides, Alexander was right, we had different goals. He wanted to make money on this, while I just wanted to organize a successful Whitbread campaign. Frankly, I didn't even understand how he expected to make any money. Even if we found a multimillion-dollar sponsorship, I was pretty sure that the sponsor would require total disclosure of our spending. But then Alexander had far more business experience than I did. He probably knew better.

Tired of waiting for me to translate his phrase, Alexander glanced at his watch and addressed Dennis and Hans in English, "Gentlemen, unfortunately I need to go. Another appointment."

He turned to Dennis, "Thank you for your assistance in our sponsorship search. I hope you'll enjoy your stay in Russia."

Then he added in Russian for me, "I recently heard from Babek Serush. He has a much more serious proposal then this one. Explain you later."

After Alexander was gone we all felt a bit easier. To relax the atmosphere I turned the conversation to sailing and it worked. After all, sailors the world over share the same passion and somewhere deep inside they are all the same. Well, maybe not exactly the same. While I was just an ordinary Soviet guy with nothing more then a big dream, Dennis at this moment was sailor number one in the entire world. And this guy had flown half way around the planet to support my dream. The more I thought about the situation, the more remarkable it seemed as I grew more and more grateful to the guy. I took the Pepsi letter and read it again. An attachment I hadn't noticed before stated that if initial pre-start sponsorship worked out, they would continue advancing fees for every leg of the race for a total of about two million dollars. A payment schedule was enclosed.

"This sounds great," I told Dennis, "but we really need the schedule reversed. More money now to equip the boat and bring her to the start line and less later, after we are on the right track. Could you explain that to them?"

"Look, Vladi," his voice was calm and reassuring, "nobody knows you and you are way behind any reasonable schedule. The chances are you won't even make it to the start. Don't take offense, I'm just being frank with you. That's why they're offering less in the beginning and more later, if you prove you can deliver... "

I listened to his characteristic monotone and confidence started to quietly fill me up as he continued. "Nothing's firm of course. But it is never firm in deals like this. Do a good job before the start and you'll have a chance."

I knew we would be at the starting line. And I knew we would do a damn fantastic job for Pepsi.

• • •

Part of the itinerary prepared for Dennis was a quick visit to Poti prior to the grand press conference. Upon our arrival at Sukhumi airport, I tried to explain to him that now we were far south, deep in the

Soviet subtropics, but he ignored my warnings, as well as the sight of palm trees outside the plane's windows. He put on his fur coat and stepped out into the 75-degree heat. Everyone around was wearing short-sleeved shirts, looking with puzzlement at this strangely dressed for-eigner. But Dennis remained calm and confident — this was the Soviet Union after all, a vast frozen country up north; a furious snowstorm could hit at any moment.

We drove Dennis to the boatyard and showed him the construc-tion, which only had just started. I'm sure it left him unimpressed. There was not much to see, only a few aluminum ribs on a strongback, but he told me that quality appeared to be very good and technology sophisti-cated. I figured he knew what he was talking about as all his previous America's Cup boats were built of aluminum. The only concern he ex-pressed was that we were running out of time with only eight months left before the start of race. How well I knew this; in fact, building a Maxi usually took longer than the time remaining. But then ours was not the usual situation.

Then we drove to the port where three identical Peterson 44s were docked. Fazis SP had chartered them for two weeks in order to run a series of races as a part of the crew selection. All the cream of the crop of Soviet sailing were there, including many sailors from the Olym-pic team. Some of them Dennis already knew, having sailed against them.

A short sail had been organized for Dennis and some local VIP guests that Victor Tikhov had invited. He had one of the boats provi-sioned with a good supply of Georgian cognac and some fine food. Two cameramen with huge Beta cameras joined the party. It was already sunset when we arrived at the dock, and the crew had been waiting for quite a while.

It was obvious at first glance that they had dug in and sampled some of the stashed provisions — mainly the liquid part. Dennis looked at them and hesitated for a moment, then stepped on board. Before Hans Waimer followed him, he turned to me and asked rhetorically, "They are drunk, aren't they?" Well, by Russian standards, technically they weren't. Maybe just a tiny bit. Anyway, what's a couple of glasses of good brandy to a strong sailor? Hans later wrote an article for a Ger-man sailing magazine about that wild sail with the crazy Russians. He colorfully described how they had gotten drunk before casting off and were afraid of nothing and no one. I didn't mind the article.

Our sunset sail did turn wild, true. The water in the harbor was smooth but the wind was blowing offshore at 25 knots and steadily increasing. We set the spinnaker and flew off into the darkening sea. The farther we went from the shore, the higher the seas built. Occasionally the boat would catch a crest of a bigger wave and start surfing in a cloud of spray, accelerating and rolling violently from side to side under the huge masthead spinnaker. On one such roll the vang fitting snapped and the boat spun into a wild crashing broach. For a few long seconds she remained on her side, stalled, shaking violently, sails slapping in the water. The video man who was on the leeward side when the broach happened, found himself in chest-high water struggling to keep his expensive equipment dry.

Dennis was sitting high on the weather rail next to me in relative safety. But when he spoke his voice was shaky, "This is insane, Vladi. I can't swim, no joke. Tell them to turn back. I wouldn't want to make history becoming the first American sailor to drown in the Soviet Union." It seemed to me he was smiling but in the growing dusk I was not sure. Not knowing whether he was serious or just joking, I played it safe and told Valery Alexeev to steer the boat back. And so he did.

As usual, the visit ended with a banquet in Poti's best restaurant. If you haven't noticed yet, Soviet people are used to a lot of partying, which is always accompanied by ample quantities of liquor. It just comes with the territory. And this was especially true in Georgia, where hospitality is a big part of the national culture.

In accordance with old local tradition, the toasts were colorful and long. The guests around the table were drinking Georgian wine (Kinzmarauli was the best) from their glasses, but when your turn came to propose a toast, you were supposed to pick up a spiraled ram's horn, fill it with wine, and drink all of it after your toast. The horn was huge, holding the contents of a full bottle of wine, and richly encrusted with silver and gold. This was sort of a test of manhood as once the horn was filled, you couldn't put it down on the table because it didn't stand up. You just had to drink it all at once. So it was okay if someone didn't want to do this and would just make the toast with a regular glass. But, of course, this would have been perceived as weakness.

When Dennis' turn came to make a toast, he bravely picked up the horn, waited till the waiter poured a whole bottle of Kinzmarauli in it. Then he stood up, and no one at the table could hide a smile. At the beginning of the party Tikhov had presented Dennis with a souvenir of the area, a woolen hat typically worn by mountain shepherds. It had very long knitted earflaps, which the shepherds would wrap around their necks like a scarf when cold winds would blow off the glacier-covered summits. The earflaps were actually so long you could wrap them around your whole torso. Dennis put the souvenir hat on his head and knowing that it looked funny, still wore it with great dignity. He picked up the horn and made an appropriate toast. By its length and content, it was quite on par with Georgian tradition and the local elders at the table were approving, nodding their heads as I translated. Then he drank the whole horn without a break and turned it upside down when he finished. Not a single drop came out. Now he had won the hearts of the Georgians.

By 3 a.m. the dinner was finally over, and Dennis was escorted to the place where he was staying. It was a small mansion called Government's *Dacha*. Even in provincial towns there were such dachas to entertain and accommodate important guests and foreign visitors if they happened to be visiting the area. They usually were comfortable and richly decorated, but the visitor's comfort was not their purpose. Rather it was for the convenience of the KGB agents. It was easier for them to control and monitor every visitor's move that way. A big pool table stood in the hall downstairs, and before we said good night to Dennis, Tikhov suggested they play a game. Tikhov pulled a twenty dollar bill out of his pocket and placed it at the corner of the table. Dennis added his twenty next to it.

They both were skillful players, and while their movements around the table were unsteady (and who could blame them after that many toasts, all made with the horn), their shots were strong and precise. You could easily see that they both really enjoyed the game. They were virtually equal, but in the end it was Dennis who prevailed — or maybe Tikhov was just letting him win in a gesture of hospitality.

"Thank you for the great game," Dennis said as he collected both bills and started upstairs to his bedroom.

"The man sure has balls. I give him that," Tikhov quietly said to me in Russian, the respect evident in his voice, as his eyes followed Dennis approvingly out of the room.

• • •

On our return flight to Moscow, the snowstorm Dennis had been expecting for so long finally hit. The plane was on final approach to Vnukovo Airport when it went into thick clouds hitting strong turbulence. Just a few minutes before touchdown, the engines roared full force again, and the plane banked sharply to the left and started climbing again. The nervous voice of the flight attendant announced, "Due to the meteorological conditions Vnukovo Airport is closed. Strong snowstorms have caused the closing of all the airports in the Moscow area. We are heading to Ulyanovsk for emergency landing."

Ulyanovsk is an obscure provincial town on the Volga River about 500 miles east of Moscow. But it was known everywhere in Russia as the birthplace of Vladimir Ulyanov-Lenin. So with this unplanned addendum to the itinerary, Dennis would be able to see the place where communism was born. Actually there wasn't much to see. The airport was very small and completely buried under a blanket of snow. Inside its terminal, a big red banner, which was draped across the top of the inside wall, read, "Lenin lives on in our achievements." In fact, Lenin had been dead for 64 years.

There was a small waiting room with seating for barely 100 people. Our flight was a Russian jumbo jet IL-86 with a capacity of at least 400 passengers, and it was full. There was no restaurant in the airport, and after a couple of hours spent relentlessly pacing across the floor, hunger became all too evident. To make matters worse, a large group of tourists from India, all dressed in white robes, were much better prepared for this emergency. They pulled out several portable kerosene stoves (how the heck did they sneak them onto the plane?) and started cooking in the corner. The aroma of spicy Indian curry, which immediately filled the small space, was absolutely murderous.

Unable to cope with it any longer, we stormed out, grabbed a taxi , and went into the city in search of a restaurant. Half an hour of a hasty search — we didn't want to miss our flight if the weather cleared up — revealed a grim truth: all the restaurants but one were closed in spite of the fact that it was only 9 p.m. And the one that was open had no food. We had a drink instead. That helped us somewhat to cope with reality.

We went back to the airport, by that time realizing just how foresighted Dennis had been to bring the infamous fur coat. He found an open spot, threw his coat on the floor, and laid down. In a couple of minutes he was sound asleep. Hans, Victor Tikhov and I stood around, envious of his opulent comfort, still struggling with hunger, as the happy Indian gentlemen in the corner enjoyed their meal.

The weather finally cleared up by 4 a.m., and we arrived in Moscow just in time for the early morning press conference. With more than 200 journalists from all over the world, it was a smashing success, and the coverage was much more than we had promised Dennis. I sat next to him at the usual banquet that followed. He was leaving later that afternoon, so this was my last chance to get some more of his wisdom on the subject of sponsorship games.

My question was one of an attentive student, "So, you've seen our project... and you have so much experience in this type of thing, what could you advise me now? What should we do to pull it off?"

"Well, you surely have a huge publicity potential. The main problem is the lack of time. And lack of experience, of course. You need to hire a marketing company to handle all the sponsorship business.

"Be careful though," he continued, "not many of these marketing guys will deliver what they promise. There is always the danger of getting into an exclusive deal, and then the guy will do nothing and still get his commission."

We had already realized earlier the need for marketing professionals and gradually shifted our search in that direction. Now, with the Pepsi letter, this would be much easier. I thanked Dennis again for his involvement. He spent only three days with us in Russia, but I had grown to like him. His whole visit had been a lot of fun, sort of a short break in our hectic schedule of hard work. But fun aside, one thing that was dead serious and clear right now: he had brought us Pepsi sponsorship and, with it, worldwide recognition for our project. It certainly should work now!

• • •

The proposal Alexander Manenko mentioned at the end of his brief meeting with Dennis Conner had come from Klaus Wawer, representative of a sports marketing agency Lintas Worldwide. I had never heard of it, but Alexander certainly considered it a serious player. "Come on, these guys represent all major European athletes, tennis players, hockey players, you name it. They arrange multi-million-dollar deals like a piece of cake. They know all the right doors to the biggest corporations. If they decide to take us that will be our golden chance." The proposal couldn't have come at a more timely moment. There is a Russian saying: "The lucky hunter has game running into him." Klaus Wawer was based in Cologne, and, luckily, in just a couple of weeks Alexander would be going to Germany with Wilfred Post. He would meet with Klaus and discuss the deal in person.

In fact, we had already had a similar proposal from the huge Soviet marketing company *Vneshtorgreklama*. But after some discussions, we'd come to the general consensus that a Western firm, especially a company with such a reputation as Lintas Worldwide, would do a much better job.

Everything went smoothly in Germany, and Alexander returned

with a signed contract.

"Hey, Vladislav, you can celebrate now." Like a magician, he pulled a thin stack of paper from his enormous briefcase. "Here's all you need to make your dream come true."

The contract was written in German, but an English translation was attached. One thing had become immediately evident: the contract was not in fact with Lintas Worldwide but with a company named ASM International. "Oh, that's just a division of Lintas, which will specifically take care of our business," explained Alexander. In a nutshell, ASM International was to raise a total of $5 million dollars in sponsorship money for an average commission of 10 percent. There was, in fact, a flexible commission schedule, but that is of no importance to our story. More important was the fact that Alexander had included in the contract a paragraph that, in exchange for exclusive sponsorship rights, "ASM will guarantee a complete promotion of our project." While in English "promotion" is quite a loose term that can mean a lot or nothing depending on interpretation, in Russian it has a very definite meaning, "to take care of, to carry on, to support entirely."

So while Klaus Wawer had no problem in signing the contract and promising promotion of our campaign which obliged him very little, for us it meant that he guaranteed five million dollars in hard sponsorship cash. That explained Alexander's magician-like gesture when he revealed the contract—as if he were pulling a golden egg out of an empty hat. And that explained why at that moment I felt assured that the financial side of our project was finally set and I could totally concentrate on the boat construction. Everything was falling in place now, and only one problem remained, the race against time to finish the boat construction. But I knew that was something I could handle.

A few days later Klaus Wawer arrived in Moscow to discuss his action plan and the list of sponsors he had already approached. Before we started the meeting with Victor Tikhov, Manenko and Babek Serush, he stopped me for a moment in the hall, "There is one delicate matter I want you to explain to Victor. We cannot use the name Golden Fleece for the boat." He felt uneasy continuing. "You know, in Europe, or at least in Germany, golden fleece means, you know, hair between women's legs. I mean the pubic hair ..."

"So what's wrong?" I teased him, "I have nothing against pubic hair or, pardon me, golden fleece."

"Oh, me neither, believe me," and by the expression on his face, I could certainly believe him, "but I don't think any serious sponsor would want to be associated with a boat of such name."

"Okay, okay, I've got you. No more Golden Fleece."

When I translated our conversation to Tikhov, he didn't hesitate a second.

"Call her Fazisi then. "

9

THE ESCAPE

Spring of 1989 had come and the start of the Whitbread was approaching inexorably. But no matter how hard I tried to speed up the construction schedule to meet the deadline, we just kept falling behind. After the break up with Mobile, I set up an improvised design office right in the shipyard. My ex-partner Struzilin had joined with a couple of designers from Leningrad. I also brought in a large-ship designer and ship's register inspector Leonid Farvarschuk from Odessa, who added valuable expertise as far as the engineering calculations and design details. After going over the boat's structure (and correcting a miscalculation made by Mobile), we had assured ourselves that the boat would be able to take anything thrown its way. FAZISI passed with flying colors the required approval of the American Bureau of Shipping. The ABS inspectors later told me that ours was one of the most comprehensive design packages they had ever reviewed.

The hull was taking its finished form and it looked good. The welding process was so precise and careful that when Alexey Grischenko cut the braces attaching the hull to the construction strongback, the boat didn't move a bit. That was significant because it meant that there was no stress accumulated on the aluminum structure due to the repeated heating and cooling from the welding. FAZISI's measurements matched the design dimensions nearly perfectly. I had been concerned that the boat's ends might torque out under the tremendous loads that the Maxi absorbed during construction. But this wasn't the case.

To a great extent our success could be attributed to the special welding technology developed by the Kiev Paton Institute of Welding, renowned as the most advanced research center of its kind in the world. The Institute brought in its best equipment, its top welder and on-site engineer to constantly monitor the temperature and heat distribution within the hull. A new member of the team, Eugene Platon from Kiev, became instrumental in this process as well.

At first, Alexey wasn't enthusiastic about bringing him in.

"I know one guy, a member of our yacht club in Kiev," Alexey told me. "He's a great engineer, a genius when it comes to all things mechanical. Name's Eugene."

"Why haven't you invited him here before?" I asked.

"I was kind of reluctant for a while. The problem is, I don't really like him personally. He's a very ambitious guy, and after the problems we've had recently with Anatoly... But we could certainly use a specialist like him now. I could put Eugene in charge of the welding, and later let him oversee the installation of all the mechanical systems."

"How's he as a sailor?" I asked.

"About average. But at this point what I need more than a sailor is a good technician. I can't control all the aspects of construction myself."

Another Soviet scientific giant involved in our project was the State Chemical Research Institute. Unfortunately this arrangement wasn't as successful as the one with the welders, but it wasn't the scientists' fault. The Chemical Research Center had formulated for us a special epoxy compound used for fairing the hull. Although FAZISI's welded aluminum hull came out quite smooth, it still required a good deal of fairing to make it absolutely perfect. For a boat to be fast, its surface had to have minimal friction so the water would flow over it absolutely unimpeded by even the slightest, microscopic imperfections. Making the hull absolutely smooth, or fairing it, is a slow and tedious process. First the entire surface is covered in a jelly-like compound, which is allowed to harden. Then that's sanded to a fair, distortion-free finish. This process is repeated numerous times — as long as it takes to arrive at a mirror-smooth surface. That means the entire 1,400 square-foot hull has to have the finish of an expensive imported sports car.

The compound developed for us by the Chemical Institute contained a special component that was intended to make it better than anything else in existence. But in the end, it was this ingredient that instead caused a lot of trouble. The special compound was meant to dry to a hard, but slightly flexible finish. For a hull this large, in extreme conditions under constantly changing loads, with the waves slamming the boat like giant sledgehammers, there had to be some flexibility to the finish. If the fairing compound was too hard, it would inevitably start cracking and eventually peel off.

Barrels of the miracle stuff developed by the Soviet chemists had arrived. While busying himself on the final welding touch-ups on the deck and dealing with the plumbing and electrical systems, Alexey named Anatoly Verba the foreman in charge of the fairing. When I arrived at Poti on my next routine visit, I came upon a frightening reflection of Anatoly's management skills. Instead of putting the guys with past experience on the job, he let everyone to do it. He divided the entire hull surface into equal squares of eight feet by eight feet and assigned one crewman to each section.

Some of the guys actually did a pretty decent job on their lots, but others failed shamefully. In the end the boat came out as a kaleidoscope of multifaceted surfaces with each piece looking entirely different in its own unique way. The worst thing was that while everyone did the best he could on his own little parcel, no one paid any attention to the borders where the patches converged. The end result was an amazing work of art, an 83-foot-long abstract sculpture -- unfortunately not the hull of the sleek racer it was intended to be.

"Hey, Anatoly, did you do this on purpose?" I tried not to sound too sarcastic.

Sensing the mockery, he replied defensively:

"I did it the best way I could. This is a hell of a job, the worst imaginable. Try sanding it yourself, you'll see. The dust is absolute poison. If there's to be suffering, then everyone should suffer equally. Would you do it any other way?" Anatoly seemed to be confident that he'd done it right.

"You're supposed to get a fair hull as a result, not have a fair process." I wondered if it was worth any more explanation. "Look at all these patches. Some are well polished, others — just terrible. Didn't it ever dawn on you that everyone performs differently, everyone is good at something but not at everything?"

I couldn't find anymore words and turned away in despair. I went looking for Alexey.

"Have you seen the results of Anatoly's fairing? All this work is absolutely useless. You should've been on top of this yourself!"

"And who then would take care of all the other things?" Alexey said, not hiding his deep frustration. "I need to delegate, otherwise we'll never complete the construction. Sometimes it works, sometimes it doesn't."

We stood in silence for a few minutes. Finally I spoke, trying to encourage him:

"Well, that's okay. We can probably grind off some of this stuff later, I hope. But the deck came out really great. And I was told the

engine has already been installed?"
"Yes, come inside. I'll show you."

• • •

As time was running out, it became evident that if we waited for all of the rig and hardware ordered abroad to arrive in Poti and then took time to install it, there would be no time left to sail around Europe to Southampton, as planned. Besides, we needed at least a few weeks before the Whitbread start for Pepsi's sponsorship events — not to mention time for the boat tests and preparation.

One more factor suddenly began playing a significant role in our project. Earlier in April, a peaceful demonstration in the Georgian capital of Tbilisi had ended in violence and people were killed. All of Georgia broke out in riots and fighting. The mood in the Republic had become deeply anti-Russian. In Poti the attitude toward our project still remained friendly, but Tikhov was worried that it could change at any moment. The whole thing seemed in jeopardy.

On my next visit to the boatyard, I was stunned to see the destruction that had changed the landscape along both sides of the road that leads from Sukhumi airport to Poti. Just two weeks ago it had been so peaceful, but now windows were broken, the road shimmered with pieces of broken glass, and on every corner, groups of angry men were shouting. I also saw burned overturned cars in the ditches alongside the road.

On the way through one of the normally peaceful and picturesque villages, we were stopped and surrounded by a large mob that started pushing and rocking the car, screaming and shaking their clenched fists. The driver looked nervous but patiently negotiated with them, speaking Georgian for more than five minutes until they reluctantly spread out and let us through. I wonder what would've happened if I had tried to speak to them in Russian.

• • •

It was probably no coincidence that American Skip Novak got involved exactly at this moment. Over the years he had developed a reputation as a sort of Whitbread emergency manager. Actually, his first letter had arrived sometime earlier, in the fall of 1988, shortly after his own Whitbread project had been taken over by his friend Roger Nilson, and Skip was looking for an alternative option. I knew of Novak as he had sailed in three Whitbreads. During the last one aboard DRUM he had became quite famous, sharing celebrity status with the boat's owner, rock star Simon LeBon of the group Duran Duran. Simon sailed a few legs of the race himself and wrote songs inspired by the experience.

But it was during the lead up to the start that this Whitbread project made the headlines. A month before the start, during a training race, DRUM lost her keel and capsized. I read about the dramatic rescue when Skip made sure every one got off safely. I was impressed by his decision to quickly repair the boat and go back to sea. Clearly, he was a brave sailor.

Resolved to have a well-organized, successful entry for the 1989-90 Whitbread Round the World Race, he founded Team Skip Novak. This time everything would be done properly -- no more lost keels. Proper is sort of a magic word for Whitbread sailors. Facing an endless chain of challenges and problems — many monetary — with some projects becoming just mere exercises in survival — every Whitbread skipper and project manager likes to think that there will be another chance, another Whitbread when everything will come into place just right. There will be enough money, the boat will be built without any rush and thoroughly tested, and the best crew will work without conflict. In a sense, the word 'proper' means perfect and therefore unreachable. Something in the realm of pipe dreams.

Skip's fourth Whitbread campaign got off to a good start. Soon he was able to raise enough money to build the boat. But shortly after construction had began, he went on a sailing and climbing expedition in Antarctica for six months. I wondered if he had lost his focus. I could relate to that—an understandable hunger to do more and more. For myself, I could not recall another time in my life when but one thing had so totally taken hold of me.

Anyway, when Skip returned, he found himself forced out of his own Whitbread project. Roger Nilson, a long-time sailing friend who had managed the project in his absence, decided he might as well stay in charge and do it his way.

Skip looked for other projects that might need a skipper, but it was too late in the game. Every team was all set on their crew. He didn't want to be left out of this Whitbread; we were essentially his last hope. Not discouraged that his first letter didn't spark any interest on our part, he sent us a second proposal in the spring of 1989. Now, with our skipper selection still in limbo, the timing couldn't have been better. My long list of possible captains had narrowed down to just Alexey Grischenko. He was a good skipper but he still remained unsure whether he had sufficient experience to do the race well.

So when Skip's second fax arrived, it immediately drew attention. What about having two co-captains, American and Russian? In keeping with our Pepsi sponsorship, the project would become a real joint venture. Besides gaining all the obvious benefits of Skip's experience, this would also make the whole thing a publicity marvel. I sent him an invitation. Surprisingly, all the usual drawn-out formalities of procuring a Soviet visa took only a few days, and soon I was meeting him in Sheremetyevo.

Having seen Skip's picture in yachting magazines, I knew his face well. His long, eagle-like nose and minor resemblance to Frank Zappa made him easy to recognize. And yet, expecting him to dress more like another rich American, a-la Dennis Conner, wearing fancy, expensive clothes — maybe even a little bit of fur — I almost missed Skip among the crowd leaving customs. At first I didn't pay much attention to the humble-looking man in an old, well-worn leather jacket and even more worn jeans. Then just as he was swiftly walking by, I caught a glimpse of his distinct profile and immediately recognized him.

He didn't look like a rich American at all but rather like a vagabond. But in a sense that's exactly what he was, an ocean vagabond with more than 200,000 offshore miles under his belt, having plied the most treacherous waters on the face of the planet. Exactly the man we needed.

I took him to dinner at the Belgrade restaurant, a flashy tourist place with mediocre cuisine. He was staying right there, and I didn't want to waste any time getting to another place. Over dinner I brought Skip up to speed on the essentials of our project and proudly put my idea of co-skippers on the table. For a moment a heavy silence hung between us. It was evident that no matter how great the idea seemed to me, it had one serious flaw: Skip didn't want to be a co-skipper. In a straightforward manner, he let me understand that our late entry, inevitably laced with potential problems, was too risky an adventure for him to be closely associated with. All he wanted was to become a paid consultant for the pre-start period and then just walk away. Certainly, I wasn't looking forward to that.

It was obvious to me during our first meeting, and even long before, that our project had already passed the stage when it needed a consultant, or to put it another way, the stage when a consultant would make any difference. I showed Skip FAZISI's drawings and photographs of her under construction. He seemed visibly impressed to find this sexy looking boat, bold and beautiful. It was certainly not some ugly, unsophisticated—agricultural--design he might have expected to find in the Soviet Union. There wouldn't be much he could advise us design-wise, maybe a few details here and there. He couldn't become a sailing coach either, as there simply wouldn't be enough time for real crew training before the start. Of course, he could contribute some of his experience on FAZISI's equipment and gear that still had to be procured. But that wasn't so crucial. Clearly what we needed most of him was to sail the boat, to co-skipper her with Alexey Grischenko.

In the end, it took Skip two trips to Russia and a visit to Poti to check FAZISI's construction in order to make up his mind, but actually it was a no-brainer—he simply had no choice if he wanted to become involved. We needed a captain, not a consultant.

Alexey Grischenko was happy with this arrangement. He flew to Moscow to meet Skip, to learn how to communicate with him and find some common ground. The biggest challenge to their working together was, of course, language. Alexey's poor English and Skip's total lack of Russian. It didn't seem that the potential communication problem bothered Skip at all, but Alexey was really worried. His knowledge of English was truly minimal, but I found that his conversational abilities were better than those of other crewmembers. His vocabulary was short, but he was capable of understanding much of the specialized sailing jargon. The worst thing was that he felt uncomfortable and shy about speaking English, being overly aware of his shortcomings.

So we decided it would be better to have their first meeting in Moscow in a private atmosphere without the crew around and all the pressure it might impose. Surprisingly, they found a way to communicate quite well. Amazed at watching the creative ways people find to understand each other, I gradually retreated from my initial function as an interpreter.

We discussed in detail how the concept of two captains could work in reality. Skip's position on the boat should be more of a strategist-navigator in charge of making the major sailing decisions. Alexey would manage the crew and actually sail the boat. It would become a bit like a relationship between the CEO and the president of a corporation. As necessary, I would help them communicate. On those legs when I would not be crewing—knowing that there remained plenty of work ashore, I didn't expect to sail the entire Whitbread—Eugene Platon would become the interpreter. His English was at least as good as mine, maybe even better. And then I had hopes that Alexey would eventually pick up more English, Skip a few Russian phrases, and at some point they would become able to communicate without outside assistance.

We also used those few days in Moscow as a short break from the hectic construction schedule and spent a great evening together at my apartment sharing sailing stories and making plans for the future.

The next evening we went to the summer theatre at Gorky Park to watch the musical "Juno and Avos." This play was the big hit in Moscow at the time and tickets were hard to get. JUNO (named after the Roman supreme goddess) and AVOS (a Russian word which can be translated as "good luck," "chance," or sometimes as "hope") were two Russian ships that sailed to California early in the 19th century to establish the first Russian colony there. As with most musicals, it was of course a love story, but also a story about Russian free spirit, entrepreneurship, and craving for new discoveries. For Russians in the midst of perestroika, all these things had a special meaning. We all felt as if our country were going through the most important moment in its history, ready to cast off and sail in search of its new destiny. To Alexey and me, the musical was even more meaningful as it was a story about sailors who went on a journey that had never been done before by Russians. We looked at each other, both barely holding back tears, as the chorus sang the theme song:

"… We are numbered, we're really numbered
And the worst -- we are apart…
But under the Russian sacred flag
Good luck will cancel fears
AVOS will pull us through!"

While we were walking back to a metro station through the dark alleyways of Gorky Park, the refrain was still reverberating in our minds, "… Let Russia's destiny fly on the wings of sails!"

Alexey put his hand on Skip's shoulder, smiled at him, then turned to me and spoke in Russian:

"I like the guy more and more. I am sure we'll make a good team. It won't be easy, but we'll work it out."

But upon our return to Poti, I found that not all of the crew shared Alexey's enthusiasm toward Skip. Anatoly Verba summed up the opposition's opinion: "If we lose, he'll just say it was our fault, the Russians simply can't sail. If we win — he'll grab all the glory."

But this time I couldn't care less about Anatoly's opinion.

The joint venture had been born.

• • •

At the first meeting in Poti with Skip as a part of the team, we brainstormed for ideas on how to get FAZISI to the starting line. I sensed he was impressed by the bold outcome of that meeting. Instead of waiting for the equipment to be delivered from Europe, we came up with the idea of having the boat flown to England and finishing her there. There was a Soviet cargo plane just big enough to swallow FAZISI's hull in its cargo hold. It was the famous ANT –124 "Ruslan," the world's largest transport plane, and it had recently been in the news after bringing in a single flight all 200 tons of equipment for the first-ever Pink Floyd laser show in Moscow.

Victor Tikhov loved the idea. It would solve most of our problems — at the least buy us some time. We also decided to have a symbolic FAZISI christening in Poti, which actually turned into two events. The first one was simply a rehearsal at the boatyard, the other one, the next day in port, very official and ceremonial — what else would you expect in Georgia?

Late into the night we discussed the details of FAZISI's completion and her transportation to England as well as the particulars of the launching ceremony. Tikhov would definitely turn the celebration into a most memorable event for the crew and for the entire town of Poti, which had been our base for almost a year and had become the birthplace of the boat. Despite the explosive political atmosphere, Victor was determined to end this initial stage of FAZISI's journey on an upbeat note.

About midnight when we returned with Alexey to our dormitory, we found the crew in the commons room in the middle of an improvised party. A large table was loaded with snacks of sausages and vegetables and generous amounts of vodka. Our arrival was greeted with loud cheering.

"Hey, guys, where've you been so late? We've been waiting and waiting and then just got started without you."

"What's the celebration all about?"

"Oh, why, we just wanted to mark our victory, the completion of FAZISI's construction. Don't we deserve to celebrate a little after months and months of slave labor? We knew that Fazis SP wouldn't bother commending us, so we decided to do it ourselves. Come on, sit down and relax. Here are your glasses."

With a brief appropriate speech, which I must admit sounded rather somber, I downed my shot of vodka and sat silently in the corner. Yes, those guys did a fantastic job and truly performed an impossible task. I was proud of them, glad that we went so far, and yet I felt strangely bitter at that moment. The crew's attitude had lately grown more and more alarming, a strange mixture of arrogant belief in their superiority and confidence in their special capabilities, which they thought were not properly appreciated by the others. More and more frequently I would hear, "We built this boat. The plant did practically nothing... nobody around here is really working, it all falls on our shoulders... we developed the welding technology, those geeks from that famous Paton Institute had no clue... "

We, we, we—it was a sort of collective egotism. Recently, they had been acting more and more as if they belonged to some elite, exclusive club. Well, this certainly signaled a kind of team spirit, but I didn't know if I liked it. Actually, I grew angrier the more I thought about it, especially considering Tikhov's preparations for the grand celebration, while these guys already went ahead and took care of themselves. They already had their own private party, not giving a damn about Tikhov's preparations. My eyes moved from face to face of my fellow sailors gathered around the table. Everyone looked happy and smug about what they had accomplished, extremely proud. I could see that no one had even the slightest thought that Fazis SP, which they resented now, was in fact the company that was giving them the chance to fulfill their dreams.

"And I am going to sail with these people around the world," I said to myself almost in despair. "Am I out of my mind?"

• • •

FAZISI's farewell was transformed into a huge celebration with thousands of people cheering, bands playing, and folk dancers performing. The crowd was at least 5,000 strong. To increase the media coverage, Tikhov had even chartered a special flight from Moscow to bring in a couple dozen journalists, many of them foreign. Nana Alexandria, the women's world chess champion and Poti's local celebrity, broke the traditional bottle of champagne against FAZISI's bow. Then Alexey and Skip together lifted the broken bottleneck and held it high in the air, like a torch symbolizing the unity of the two FAZISI captains.

The banquet that followed that evening was held in a huge restaurant at the port, the same place where we had had our first dinner with Juki upon my arrival in Poti a year and a half ago. How far we had come since then! We've made it, haven't we? It had been an exhausting marathon—rather more a high-hurdles run. But now it was coming to a conclusion. In a few days we would leave the Soviet Union and then two months later, with all our troubles behind us, we would sail away into the ocean. I felt extremely tired, but very happy.

But in just a few minutes it was all about to change.

I saw Gerd Budzek, the guy whom Klaus Wawer sent over from Germany to help manage FAZISI's public relations campaign, making his way through the crowd toward me.

"Vlad, where's Tikhov? I need to talk to both of you. It's quite important."

I spotted Victor in the opposite corner, surrounded by journalists, talking and laughing loudly.

"What is it? Could it wait till tomorrow?"

"I'd rather have this conversation now and get it over with."

I called Tikhov and the three of us stepped out on to a broad balcony overlooking the dark quiet harbor. Behind us in sharp contrast, the brightly-lit restaurant vibrated with loud music that penetrated through the closed glass door. After the warm coziness of the restaurant, the fresh breeze from the sea made me shiver.

"I don't want to ruin your celebration. But... well... I think I need to warn you that Klaus Wawer is not exactly the man you think he is," started Gerd. "He has nothing to do with the Lintas Worldwide organization now, and, I suspect, they haven't even heard about you. I think there has been some sort of misunderstanding... Yes, he did work for them before but now his company, ASM, is just him and his partner, Michael Winterfeld. That's it... I am working for them only temporarily."

Seeing the alarmed expressions on our faces, he quickly added, "Maybe it's nothing to worry about, really. I am not saying that Klaus can't do a good job for you. I know he is working hard... I just wanted you to understand the real situation."

"Shit. Exactly what we need now, on top of all the problems we have already had," Tikhov said and added to me in Russian, "It's all really strange. Why is he telling us this right now? Maybe he has some hidden agenda? Ask him."

Before I was even able to say a word, Budzek spoke in broken Russian, "*Ya govorju po Russky nemnogo* — I can speak Russian a little bit. But don't worry, I'm not planning to doublecross you. It's much simpler. I like you guys and admire what you've accomplished so far. But I think you're under an illusion as to what really awaits you in the West... and I'm afraid you are bound to be disappointed. I simply want to make it clear, to prepare you to face the reality."

"Well, thank you. But I think it's too late now," Tikhov turned to me and said, "Anyway, we can't stop now or even change a thing. The boat will be flown to England as planned and once there, you'll be playing it by ear."

He walked toward the door, turned and added:

"I hate to say it, but the whole thing is becoming more and more trouble each day. Why did I listen to all that sweet talk from Alexander Manenko and gotten involved in the whole affair in the first place?"

• • •

FAZISI was put on a cradle, taken by barge 75 miles north to Sukhumi airport and loaded into the belly of the Ruslan. It was too risky to use a truck to get her there, as there might have been road-blocks on the way and some crazy nationalists might have wanted to take the boat as ransom. Despite a hasty departure, we left Georgia with deep gratitude and sadness. It was FAZISI's birthplace, a great region with friendly hospitable people whose only flaw was an occasional hot temper. I was heartbroken to learn just a few weeks later that Georgia had sunk into a bloody civil war.

FAZISI had managed to escape at the last possible moment.

10

VICTORY BEFORE THE START

Time passed quickly during our four-hour flight, and then the engine sound changed, becoming lower as the plane descended sharply. The behavior of the Ruslan, essentially a military aircraft, was entirely different from that of a typical passenger airliner. Human comfort was of no big concern with these pilots, and their maneuvers were aggressive and abrupt. The descent from 30,000 feet took us only six minutes instead of the usual 20 — and, of course, without the usual "fasten your seatbelts" or "no smoking" signs.

The passenger cabin, located above the cargo bay, had no sound insulation whatsoever, and all of the plane's sounds, from the roar of its turbines to the creaking of its aluminum skeleton, could be heard. There were more than a hundred seats in the cabin but only two small windows on each side of the fuselage. The entire crew was now gathered around them in tight groups, faces pressed against the Plexiglas, desperately trying to catch a first glimpse of the English countryside rushing toward us. But the layer of clouds was too thick; all we could see were just long strands of white vapor that streaked quickly by.

Finally, at only 600 feet altitude, the clouds thinned to a light mist and then, all of a sudden, we could see green hills, dotted with curious groups of trees, bunched together and braided by the ribbons of roads. We could see houses that from a distance bore a resemblance to small fortresses, looking independent and proud, exactly what we were anticipating the British countryside would look like.

The Ruslan banked hard several times, quickly gliding down, getting closer and closer to the ground until we landed, unexpectedly gently, and then rolled, gradually slowing down, along the tarmac runway of Heathrow Airport.

Before me lay a complete unknown; a strange world that would become my home, at least for the time being. The Soviet Union with all its twisted reality was far away now, and hopefully all our hurdles had been left behind along with it. We've made it to the West, and from now on everything should be okay, shouldn't it? During the short time after our landing, my thoughts jumped hurriedly between hopeful anticipation and dreadful doubts. I really had no idea as to what to expect. The frantic exchange of faxes and phone calls after that late night conversation with Gerd Budzek just before our departure had left me in complete uncertainty.

The only thing that seemed more or less clear was that Jim Saunders, an old friend of Skip's, would meet us at the airport with a crane and a tractor-trailer to transport FAZISI to Hamble Yacht Services. Even this wasn't 100 percent clear to me because I was far from confident that I understood Jim correctly, especially since he spoke with a heavy south-England accent. Talking to him on the phone from Moscow, I had barely managed to pick up a few words from the thick drawl, and then, using my imagination, had pieced together what he probably was telling me.

As for our financial relationship with ASM and the status of the Pepsi sponsorship, I was in total darkness, and this flight to London in a large sense was a jump into the unknown. After the concerns expressed by Gerd Budzek regarding ASM and a flurry of last-minute calls and faxes to Moscow before we took off, nothing was certain. Yet I can't say that doubts overwhelmed my thoughts. I wasn't depressed, just the opposite; I was filled with the joy of challenge, with an excitement of being on the edge, controlling the events and realizing a degree of risk — a piquant mixture of exhilaration and fear that can make life so full and exciting.

The aircraft finally stopped, the door was unsealed, the ramp lowered, and smiling Klaus Wawer, followed by his partner Michael Winterfeld, quickly climbed in carrying giant bags with Pepsi logos on them. They unzipped them and in mere seconds everything was enveloped with Pepsi paraphernalia: banners, slogans, T-shirts, sweaters, etc. The Pepsi generation had just begun.

We quickly changed, and now the Russian team, all freshly attired in Pepsi stuff, was ready to meet the world press, which was already noisily climbing into the plane. Blinded by non-stop camera flashes, confronted by outstretched arms holding mikes and video cameras, we felt cornered, surrounded, and totally overwhelmed by this first tidal wave of publicity. It was all so new and unusual to us, and we tried to hide our uneasy feelings behind the mask of bravado: "We are proud to be Russians! We couldn't care less about all this fuss. We've come here to beat you and win."

While this circus was unfolding, the plane's crew continued on with the work, preparing to unload its massive cargo. The enormous Ruslan nose was slowly swung upwards, revealing the inner bowels of the cargo hold. Powerful hydraulic rams smoothly lowered the plane's belly down until it touched the ground. The ramp was lowered and then everything began to hum, whine, and move, pushing the boat out. Now the guys were torn between helping the plane's crew and satisfying the appetite of a hungry press. But amazingly, in spite of the chaotic scene in and around the aircraft, the unloading proceeded smoothly and quickly.

Completing this picture of frantic activity was Skip himself, seeming to be everywhere all at once. With several cameras hanging from around his neck, he'd shout orders to the crew and briefly join in with the work. Then he'd answer reporters' questions, and take countless pictures of his own. Now I saw Skip in his element. Sponsorship was his way of life, he was like a fish back in water. Amazed, we watched him in action and even tried to pick up on some of his tricks of the trade. With the initial shock already gone, we were quickly becoming more and more comfortable in our newfound celebrity status.

FAZISI's shell was finally out on the concrete apron where a large trailer and crane were waiting. So far so good. I shook hands with Jim Saunders for the first time. He was wearing a flamboyant Hawaiian shirt printed with bright red, blue and yellow flowers, which as I later came to learn, was actually one of his more conservative shirts. Definitely not in keeping with the understated British style, Jim's dress code provided him with boundless opportunities to express his vast individuality. A man who might be called a Renaissance man, Jim is a person of endless abilities and interests. With seemingly equal enthusiasm and aplomb, he could model formal evening attire, drive a race car, manage a risky project, handle any rigging job, or sail off over a distant horizon. In a word, he was exactly the man we needed in our situation. Surprisingly, understanding him in person at that first meeting was even more challenging than over the phone. Perhaps part of this was due to the fact that he'd allowed several pints of beer to slip past his lips while he waited in the airport for our late flight.

Over the course of the next few months, Jim would become an integral part of our project and would vigilantly watch to it that the boat was always shipshape. Later he would sail on FAZISI during the most grueling second leg, and later still, after the end of the race, my family would find a temporary refuge at his home in Hamble. Then we would spend quiet evenings at dinner together and, over a bottle of good port, recall our joint work on FAZISI. We partook of Jim's hospitality along with other sailors from different corners of the world — Australia, France, and Switzerland. And it would be there, in the milieu of those friendly evenings in his warm British home, that I first realized that we had, in fact, accomplished the Whitbread Round the World Race, and in a way had become a part of yachting history.

But now, as I still stood on the tarmac of Heathrow Airport, all that was so far in the future. At this moment we were separated from the finish of the Whitbread — and, for that matter, from the start — by a distance of cosmic dimension. As the clock ticked on, counting down the last weeks before the start, the boat was still a mere aluminum shell.

Only now had I chance to look around the airport. Submerged in a deep twilight and outlined with a velvet-blue sky, it was brimming with controlled activity. Planes were taking off and landing every few seconds. After the provincial sleepiness of Moscow's Sheremetyevo Airport, the comparison was overwhelming. I finally realized: yes, we are finally in the West. We have made it. We have managed to escape.

It felt like we had made it through a narrow, treacherous tunnel and finally broken free into open air. The whole world was ahead of us...

On an adjoining runway the supersonic passenger jet, the Concorde, was taxiing after landing. With its thin-legged landing gear and down-sloping nose, it looked like a modern version of the pre-historic pterodactyl. Then it rolled behind our yacht and lined up with the Ruslan. As if by command, the armada of photographers seemed to trip their shutters en masse — the magnificent sight certainly deserved it. FAZISI's exotic profile having just emerged from the womb of a Russian military plane, the elegant Concorde gliding by in the gentle English twilight, the bright red hammer and sickle insignia marking the Ruslan's tail, the British Airways logo emblazoned on the Concorde's fuselage, and the huge Pepsi logo covering the whole side of FAZISI: all this in one camera frame. What a picture-perfect vista of perestroika!

In less than two hours after our arrival, FAZISI had been safely loaded onto the tractor-trailer and parked for the night at the airport. We left for a late supper at the Sheraton Hotel, where our future management team, gathered by Skip, was awaiting our arrival. Jane Redford had come from Paris, where she was a project manager for the French entry OPERATION CARGO, later renamed CHARLES JOURDAN. Skip thought that having her working simultaneously on two similar

Whitbread projects would save money for both. Her sister Monica Tingay, to whom Skip offered a position of secretary and office manager, accompanied her. And, finally, Michele Suna from New York, with whom Skip had worked on his last project, was also joining our effort. Of course, I had no idea of how good they were and had no choice but to accept Skip's selection of our future personnel.

As it turned out, this team wouldn't last long. Jane had plenty of problems with the French project and left for France only days later. Michelle also disappeared. It happened so quickly, I hardly knew she was there before she was gone. Only Monica stayed, plugged into her job and ended up being with us for a long time. A tiny blonde with confident, if not authoritarian, manners, she had held various jobs in her life as she wandered through many countries. She first met Skip while managing a gay restaurant in South Africa in 1982, when he was skipper of the Whitbread racer ALASKA EAGLE. The Whitbread race was not such a demanding venture during those good old days; sailors had plenty of time to relax and have fun during the stopovers. And at some point during those fun times at the Cape Town pubs and restaurants, Skip acquired the nickname "Eagle," not only because of the name of his boat, but mainly because of his distinct profile. Monica told me he didn't like the nickname and hated it when people called him that. Now she learned the Russian word for eagle, *ory'ol*, and never let a chance go by to use it in a semi-kidding way, with a childish satisfaction that Skip had no clue what it means.

Later during that first long night in England, I also had a meeting with Wawer and Winterfeld, who brought me up to date on the situation regarding the Pepsi sponsorship. But by this time I was completely worn out, and, because of my exhaustion and difficulty understanding English, the conversation passed right over my head. Only one thing seemed important at the moment: as long as they both were here, and everyone in the crew was covered from head to toe in Pepsi logos, everything was okay. Gerd Budzek had just rung a false alarm. With that comforting thought, I fell into bed and immediately dropped asleep. Behind me was a long exhausting day, FAZISI's first day of life in the West. It was a day I would never forget.

• • •

The next step was to deliver FAZISI to Hamble Yacht Services, near Southampton, where we would finish construction and outfit her. Hamble is a very old village with sailors making up a good part of its population. This was Skip's home — his turf — he knew everybody there and suggested it would be the best place to finish FAZISI. The village streets were too narrow for the big truck hauling FAZISI to get through. The solution was to bring the boat first to a big marina a few miles up river where she was launched for the third time in her very short life — this time very quietly, without any hoopla — and then towed down to Hamble.

She was met by an impressive crowd mingling on the dock, everyone commenting on her unusual shape. She certainly looked strange now, floating like a cork on the water, with her canoe body just slightly submerged, as her empty hull with no keel or rig weighed almost nothing. Even to my eye, she looked odd so I could only imagine the first impression she was making on the people on the dock. But, to my surprise, the comments on the dock were mostly positive, though expressed with a good dose of skepticism.

FAZISI had already made a splash in the yachting media and had been awaited with curious anticipation. But with just six short weeks left before the start, everyone doubted that she would ever be finished in time. People would have laughed had they known that our plans actually called for finishing FAZISI in just two weeks. The schedule was absolutely crazy. But in keeping with the Pepsi agreement, we were expected to perform a full month of sponsorship hype, following yet another official launching ceremony. No one short of us believed this would be possible.

Much was said on the dock. Of course, I didn't understand most of the talk but the general sentiment was doubt and disbelief. One of the more skeptical of the group, a bulky man with a pint of beer in one hand, separated himself from the crowd and, after taking a large gulp, turned to me, "Very unusual boat you've got here, mate, I've never seen anything like that. And pretty nice looking at that, I must admit."

He looked at me slyly and took another generous sip from his steamy mug. "I'd love to see how she'd perform in the race. It's rather sad that I won't have such an opportunity."

"What do you mean you won't have the opportunity? What is your problem?" I asked almost rudely, knowing exactly what he meant and not liking it at all.

Not discouraged by my harshness, he continued in the same sly tone: "The problem is not mine, it's yours. To outfit the boat in a condition like this you'd need at least four months, and how much time do you have left before the start, huh?"

What could I reply? I knew that we will finish everything on time, we simply didn't have any other choice. But, in all honesty, I was afraid of the scope of the tasks we had ahead of us, and doubts, no matter how hard I tried to push them away, wouldn't leave me.

After talking to the guy for a few minutes, I realized that my opponent was none other than one of the construction managers for the Town Quay Marina in Southampton. This was the marina that in a few weeks was supposed to become the base for the entire Whitbread fleet before the start. It happened that earlier in the morning I had stumbled onto a short newspaper article about this marina. Just like our boat, the marina was also behind schedule and serious doubt was being raised that it could be completed on time.

I had a sudden idea.

"Okay, I'd like to make a bet for a bottle of champagne. If your marina is completed before we launch FAZISI, you win. I'll buy you a bottle. If it's the other way around, you'll buy me one. And it has to be the best champagne."

He didn't hesitate a second before accepting the bet.

Later when FAZISI joined the rest of the Whitbread fleet at Town Quay Marina, it still looked like a construction site, chaotic and almost neglected.

To this day, I still haven't received my bottle of champagne.

I wasn't discouraged by the dockside skepticism. If they didn't believe, that was their opinion. I had grown accustomed to the fact that most people met my project with disbelief, and by that time I couldn't care less. An enormous amount of work remained ahead of us, but the situation now had changed dramatically. We had made it to England, we had completed the hull, and all the equipment was here, awaiting installation. We had left behind all the bureaucratic obstacles and inefficiencies of the Soviet Union, all the red tape and the formalities, each representing a stumbling block. We were finally free from the grasp of that system and understood clearly that the future was totally in our own hands. What a new feeling!

It was lucky we couldn't see into our future. Who knows, if I had had the slightest hint of what was ahead, I might well have quit right then and there on that dock at Hamble Marina.

• • •

Looking back now, I can't believe that in such a short time we got everything done and FAZISI ready for the start, but then we were unstoppable. I created a detailed flow chart with all the tasks we had to do, the timetables and the deadlines showing how the jobs were inter-connected. In most cases, beginning a new job was impossible without finishing the one before it. I posted the chart on the wall of the trailer we'd rented for our office so everyone could visualize the entire pro-cess and realize his importance in it. Every day I marked our progress. At eight o'clock each morning we'd get together in the office for a few minutes to discuss plans for the day, and every evening we would check to see what had been accomplished.

There were practically no disruptions. I tried to distribute re-sponsibilities in such a way that everyone would be assigned to a job that he knew and could perform best. For the most part it worked. Our two best mechanics, Eugene Platon and Igor Mironenko, were put in charge of installing the deck hardware, steering wheels, and large winches. Yuri Doroshenko was responsible for installing the engine, generator, and water maker, and for assembling the plumbing system. This was a colossal task; he performed it on time. So I couldn't blame him for messing up the plumbing a bit. As it turned out after the start, salt water came out of the fresh-water faucet, hot water came out of the cold-water tap, and so on. As a result it was necessary to totally redo the plumbing system while racing.

But fortunately, such mistakes were rare and few; and in the end the work wasn't all that bad, considering the rush in which it all had been performed. The arrival of the sails added even more work. In the difficult artistry of sailmaking, Vladimir Kulinichenko and Valery Safiullin spent days at the North Sails loft totally immersed in vast seas of Kevlar and Mylar.

The work list filled pages and didn't seem to be getting shorter. As soon as we would solve one problem, a few others would pop up. Some were smaller, like dealing with the lazy local welders. To answer it, Nodari had found a surprisingly elegant solution involving a bottle of excellent Georgian brandy.

While most of the welding work was finished in Poti, there was a little work like welding foundations for some of the gear that still needed to be done. We simply didn't have this equipment back in Poti, and, confident that there would be no problem doing it in England, we had decided to put off this seemingly minor job til later. Skip contracted the local welding company located right there in the yard and requested two of their best welders. They arrived the next day with all their tools, placed them on FAZISI's deck, took a look around, and disappeared. The next morning they reappeared again, spent an hour and a half tink-ering with the welding transformer, and vanished again for the day. On the third day, after they failed to show up altogether, I headed up to the manager's office.

"I saw them earlier this morning. They said they were going to your boat," the manager said, looking embarrassed. Together we went in search of the missing welders and finally found them in a small locker-room drinking tea and deeply engaged in conversation. When their boss reproached them angrily, they quickly stood up and told him they were already on their way to FAZISI.

The entire job shouldn't have taken more than five hours, but when a whole week had passed and nothing was done, I grew seriously concerned. First of all, they were holding up the other work. Until those damn foundations were welded, we couldn't go any further. Apart from that, I wasn't sure what sort of financial arrangement Skip had made with them, but suspected that if they were being paid hourly, that, ultimately, was the reason behind their lack of haste. In the end, they would present us with a giant bill for the time spent drinking tea and discussing global issues. Annoyed, I told Skip to do something. After all it was he who had hired them in the first place. Two more days went by and Skip still hadn't come up with a solution. The once-minor problem had now become a huge one. When I suggested that Skip find a replacement for the welders, he said it was impossible. They were the yard's official subcontractors; outside welders weren't allowed on the premises.

The situation seemed unsolvable until one morning Nodari approached me and in his usual unhurried manner asked: "Vladislav, I understand there's some kind of problem with the welders?"

When I explained the situation to him, he said he knew the way to stimulate the welders and make them work.

"What do you have in mind?"

"Remember those cases of Georgian cognac that Tikhov stashed in our container to celebrate the start of the race? I think if I offer those guys a bottle, that might speed up the process. This method always worked back home when I needed a job done."

"What are you saying," I exclaimed in disbelief, fearing possible international misunderstanding. "Maybe this works at home but we're in England now! And you want to bribe these guys? Besides, don't tell me you think a single bottle of cognac would motivate them. They probably earn more than 2,000 English pounds a month and could buy all the cognac they want for themselves."

"But all the same, I hope you won't object if I try to talk to them. This method has never let me down."

"Well, when everything else failed… we don't have much choice. Why not give it a try… but they get the bottle only after the job is completed."

About midday a cunningly smiling Nodari led me to the boat where, to my astonishment, the entire job was done. While I stood there dumbstruck, the satisfied welders withdrew with their prize into the locker-room to spice up their afternoon tea party.

• • •

But not all the problems were that easily solved. We anticipated that our scarce ability to speak English would be a hurdle to surmount, but I was surprised to find out how serious an obstacle it turned out to be. Prior to our arrival to England, I naively believed that I spoke decent English. After all, I read sailing literature relatively easily, wrote most of the FAZISI press releases myself, and took part in countless negotiations with Westerners in Moscow, all conducted in English. But it was one thing when a foreigner and several Russians met. What one didn't understand, the other would, and an understanding was achieved by combining our knowledge of English. That had created an illusion of fluency. Now, finding myself mainly alone in the midst of English, this illusion disappeared very quickly. It was especially difficult to communicate in situations when I had to take care of crucial matters immediately — and that was almost always the case. There was no time to contemplate. Decisions had to be made instantly, sometimes during a heated argument, when several people would speak at once, loudly trying to out-shout each other. To pick up even the essence of these discussions was tremendously difficult, requiring maximum concentration.

It was tough not only during work hours but every minute of our new Western life. For most of the crew who knew no English at all, even an ordinary visit to the grocery store was a challenge. They would attempt to communicate what they needed through an array of gestures, unintelligible sounds, and all other imaginative ways. Now we realized to the fullest what it meant to be strangers. We were slightly scared but brave. Besides there was nothing we could do about it; we just had to live with it.

But one problem that came as a total surprise to me was a growing misunderstanding with Skip. His well-mannered, even shy, behavior during the courtship time in Russia had now changed dramatically. He became aggressive, sometimes even rude. We were all under a lot of pressure, and sometimes there was no time for good manners, but it was much more than that. At times it seemed to me that Skip just simply tried to take over the project and reshape the whole thing to suit him better. In an effort to subvert an open confrontation, I entered into an endless game of balancing the interests of everyone involved. I was becoming quite a politician.

On a personal level, I was really fascinated with Skip — even before we met. Knowing his previous odysseys, his achievements, and the disasters he had been through, I respected his ability to withstand unlucky turns of fate. Somewhere in my subconscious I probably wanted us to become friends. Remnants of the romanticism I had had at the start of this journey were still in me. That was when I believed that all sailors were members of an international sailing brotherhood, made up of unspoiled and uncorrupted people whose hearts and souls totally belonged to the sea.

I really wanted Skip to understand my dreams and desires, as well as join in sharing the risks necessary to reach our goal. I was desperately yearning for someone who would be willing to take a portion of the burden of responsibility that I had carried alone for so long. Well, it seemed that Skip's priorities were different. Sure, he did a great job for the project; without him we stood no chance of pulling it off. But then, there were many other crucial key people without whom the project wouldn't have survived.

Trying to find a way to reach Skip, I decided to talk to Monica who had known him for a long time. The opportunity came at a party organized by the women of MAIDEN GREAT BRITAIN. The music played loudly and the beer, stuffed in ice-filled barrels, was plentiful. The tables were set up both outside on the porch and inside the house, which the MAIDEN team had rented. Our crew, who by that time had worked for two weeks non-stop, had eagerly looked forward to the party. Interest was especially peaked in light of rumors and jokes circulating around the Hamble waterfront concerning a certain bet the girls had placed among themselves. The first woman to score with a Russian would win a 50-pound kitty. As far as the Russian crew was concerned, they were ready for some excitement and hoping to get lucky. Sure enough, the prize found a lucky winner that night, but respecting privacy, I won't reveal any names.

Monica, far removed from the office routine, looked elegant in her evening dress. She was in good spirits, and I wanted to take advantage of the informal atmosphere to engage her in an intimate conversation. No, no, I didn't have any silly intentions. I just wanted to talk about Skip. After some light chat, I gradually led her to the topic and told her about the frustration that I was experiencing.

Her answer wasn't comforting and she didn't mince any words. "Don't delude yourself," Monica said. "You're never going to get along with him. Skip is used to doing everything himself the way he wants it done. He always surrounds himself with people whom he's selected, and who are ready to obey him. Face it, you're both leaders and doomed to a conflict. You will never become friends. He simply doesn't need any friends."

Her predictions shocked me, but in the end she was right. I think all might have gone differently if Skip had tried to become a true team member and submitted to the interests of the project instead of trying to rearrange it. For a long time the project was living a life of its own, with its own rules, and any attempts to alter it made matters even more complicated.

But then Skip wouldn't have been Skip.

• • •

I was eagerly expecting a meeting with Klaus Wawer and Michael Winterfeld to find out finally where we stood on our sponsorship. The first thing Michael did upon their arrival in Hamble was to show me a signed contract with Pepsi.

"You see," he said, "We are doing our job. You can expect the first payment soon but be aware that delays are possible. Do you have enough money to complete the boat to ensure her presence at the starting line? Remember, this is the key provision of the contract."

"Of course not! That is why we need Pepsi's money — to complete the boat. That's what they offered initially: to bring FAZISI to the start line." I replied, then added in a calmer tone of voice, "I really appreciate what you've done so far. Now, if I understand right, you, the ASM, are responsible for our fundraising, correct? And here you are now, asking me if we have enough money? That's exactly what I would like to hear from you: what is our financial situation? How have your negotiations with Pepsi progressed regarding the sponsorship for the entire race? What other leads have you developed if they choose not to execute the option to continue?" I had too many questions.

"You shouldn't be concerned about Pepsi," said Michael. "Their inclination toward continuation is very favorable, and our talks are proceeding just fine. Oh, by the way, they want to change the boat's name into FAZISI-PEPSI. Don't you think this is a proof of their long-term intentions? I believe, you have nothing against renaming the boat?

"Of course not, if that's so important to them," I answered quickly.

"We also have other potential sponsors that we're working on now. But, of course, we're concentrating our efforts on the Pepsi deal, as it's practically a sure thing. We are doing our best to ensure that you have enough money for the race."

Well, that sounded great, but doing one's best sometimes might not be enough. To me Michael's comments didn't sound exactly like a commitment to pull us through financially, and I decided to point out exactly what we expected from ASM.

"In accordance with the contract between Fazis SP and ASM, you were granted exclusivity in exchange for your guarantee of total financial support of our project."

Michael looked puzzled, "We would never do that, and certainly there is nothing in the agreement that would lead you to believe so."

The meeting that started optimistically was now taking an unexpected turn that alarmed me. I reached for my briefcase and pulled out the contract, which by then I had read so many times I had almost memorized it.

"Here it is, 'ASM will raise US $5 million in sponsorship and guarantee full promotion of the FAZISI project.' Doesn't that mean that you are responsible for taking care of FAZISI's finances?"

Michael now sounded even more puzzled when he said, "Promotion is promotion, nothing more. I want to stress it one more time that we're doing our job as good as we can and the prospects look very good now, but we do not guarantee anything."

Skip, who had kept silent since the beginning of conversation, intervened impatiently. "Come on, guys, don't waste your time on these details. Let's concentrate on more important things, like when you will be able to close on the full Pepsi sponsorship deal."

These were not just small details to me. It dawned on me now that there was some big misunderstanding on how Fazis SP and ASM interpreted the contract. All of us, including Manenko, Tikhov, and myself, were under the impression that ASM had no problem in getting enough sponsorship for the project and was eager to get an exclusive contract. We understood that our task was to bring FAZISI to the West, and then they would take care of the rest. Fazis SP executives believed that the amount of five million dollars was guaranteed, meaning not only plenty of funds to run the FAZISI campaign, but a handsome profit as well. I suspected now that this was not how ASM saw the picture.

Forget Fazis SP with its expectations; it appeared as if nothing was for sure now. We were totally in the hands of ASM.

And after Michael Winterfeld left, I suggested to Skip that we meet an attorney fluent in both English and German who could bring clarity to our understanding of the contract. But as any attorney would do, he just told us that it could be interpreted either way. However it was intended, we now depended entirely on ASM. I had no choice other than to make peace with it, hoping that they would do their job. Besides I had too many things to take care of, the most important one: to bring FAZISI to the starting line.

Before leaving Moscow, we had agreed with Tikhov that upon our arrival to England, all financial matters would be taken over by Valery Chumakov, a 50-year-old former official from the Sport Committee. His introduction to the project sparked lots of rumors and curiosity. One day Valery just walked into the Fazis office in Moscow and said that he was tired of the bureaucratic routine, excited by our project, and wanted to be involved. Although no one knew him, Tikhov and Manenko were surprisingly enthusiastic and supported his candidacy. His previous position in the Sport Committee was a manager responsible for taking Soviet teams abroad into competitions. He would certainly bring good experience of having done business in the West, of which we all lacked.

There was, however, one delicate concern. In the past all government officials, allowed to travel beyond the Soviet borders, were, according to popular belief, KGB agents. I wouldn't have been surprised to find out that the notorious secret police had planted someone in our project. I was even curious as to why they hadn't done it earlier. But then again, maybe they already had, who was to know... Maybe there was already somebody in the crew, who was writing daily reports to authorities on what we were doing.

Anyway, whoever he was, Chumakov certainly was qualified for the job and got hired just before we flew to England. Meticulous, slow, and methodical, he turned out to be an excellent accountant. He kept our books in perfect order, and fought like a lion over every penny spent. Sometimes it was annoying, but in the end he saved us a lot of money. The only problem was he chronically distrusted foreigners and was thus very difficult to get along with. He didn't like Skip, and Skip generously paid him back in kind.

Valery Chumakov often could be found deep in the night sitting in our office, his thick, old-fashioned, rimless glasses pushed down his nose, sorting through endless bills and invoices and punching numbers on his calculator.

"Mmm... mm... this invoice? Vladislav, take a look at this..." In his usual mumbling voice, Chumakov would ask, handing me a piece of paper torn out of the notebook on which Jim had written his expense report, "Does this look like official paper? Do these guys really think that I can later present such a scrap to the auditors back in the Soviet Union and explain why I paid the money... Mmm... these Westerners ... they don't have a clue as to how to run a business properly."

There certainly were plenty of hasty purchases poorly documented, and this frustrated Valery a lot. "Now, look at this... Mmm... the invoice from Musto for the foul-weather gear for the entire crew. Didn't you tell me that we had proposals from different manufacturers to supply us free gear as a sponsorship?"

This one was a reasonable question, and I myself was surprised that Skip had paid for the weather gear. It's true that the Musto was great stuff, probably the best in the business at that time, but it's also true that often manufacturers were happy to provide complimentary gear in exchange for visibility in projects like ours. It's difficult to get cash sponsorship, but there were plenty of in-kind proposals, you just had to choose the best of them. Anyway, the foul-weather jackets were completely covered with Pepsi logos, it was essentially a Pepsi uniform, and if anybody was to pay for it, they certainly should have.

"You know, Vladislav, what I am thinking... " Chumakov usually spoke in a quiet, slow manner, as if he was unsure of what he wanted to say next, "Skip's just using us to build up his credit. He'll pay those guys now from our pocket, and then, when he needs them again, they'll give him everything for free."

I hated to think that Skip might do such things but I also didn't like Skip's reaction when confronted by Chumakov's reasonable questions. He usually just dismissed them as annoying and unjust without giving any explanations. I paid close attention to the quotes and estimates we were receiving and was confident that in most cases we were getting the best possible deal. But then there were some strange cases like a hefty bill for crew polo shirts, which Skip had ordered, some 400 of them. A huge quantity for just 20 crew. Come on, Skip, there was simply no need to spend three thousand precious pounds for all those polo shirts.

Each of those instances, no matter how minor, only served to make more fragile the delicate balance of trust between the East and West, which in the middle of 1989 had their unofficial, very human summit in the small village of Hamble.

Anyway, I was glad that we had Chumakov standing haughty guard over FAZISI's finances so I could concentrate on the boat's construction and preparation.

• • •

Among all the jobs to be performed on FAZISI, the worst was sanding and fairing the hull—all 1,400 square feet of it. What had been done in Poti under supervision of Anatoly Verba needed to be redone. But after attempting for two days to grind off some of the stuff that had been applied there, we realized that this was an impossible task. The soft, rubbery compound specially formulated by the Soviet State Chemical Research Institute proved to be a real bitch to take off. It gummed up the tools the same way chewing gum sticks to the soles of your shoes and refuses to come off. On the third day I decided that we would be better off ceasing this futile endeavor and made peace with the fact that the entire hull needed to be covered with another layer of fairing compound. This would probably add another 1,200 to 1,500 pounds to the boat, which was already overweight. Shit, that's a lot of extra weight! Well… to hell with it, for now. We needed to finish the construction as soon as possible, and then I would deal with the problem later when we measure the boat—I hoped I'd find a solution then.

To perform the job on time and properly, Skip suggested hiring the best team in the business. That was Ian Armstrong, the guy who finished many of Europe's finest sailing vessels, from America's Cup racers to luxury Mega yachts. As it turned out, he was not only a very gifted specialist but also a great guy, cheerful and tireless with an endless supply of energy he was ready to share with anyone. What an indispensable person for the job we were facing!

Simply put: it was a living hell. Imagine yourself working at the limit of your physical abilities, sometimes upside down with the hull hanging over your head, breathing poisonous dust that clogged your eyes, throat, and ears, all this for 12 hours a day. Four squads, four to five people in each, worked simultaneously on each side of the boat. They moved slowly along the hull, sanding it with flexible, 18-inch-long plastic pipe covered with sandpaper to ensure a perfectly smooth shape without any hollows or bumps.

All of this was reminiscent of the slave labor of old-time Russian boatsmen of the last century who, crawling along the shore with the ropes tied around their torsos, pulled heavy cargo barges up the Volga River. We even sang their songs such as "Hey, Uhnem" (The song of Volga Boatmen) while working. Like the sea chanteys of Western seamen, those songs had great rhythm, which helped us to move in unison. No matter how busy I was with other tasks, I felt obliged to put in at least two or three hours a day of sanding, working with the crew. Actually, I noticed that the simple routine of physical work helped to clear my mind and prepare it to meet other challenges.

With every new layer of fairing compound, the surface of FAZISI's hull was getting smoother and shinier, resembling the glazed sides of our future rivals, already proudly docked at the nearby marina. All the other Whitbread syndicates had their boats in the water now and were undergoing sea trials. Minor boat projects still continued, but in a much more leisurely pace than our frantic one. Of course, not everything went smoothly for them either. It almost never does in such a demanding environment as the Whitbread, and some boats had problems of their own making. On ROTHMANS they had to change their keel quickly; NCB IRELAND needed last-minute surgery to make changes to the shape of the bow, while some other boats had problems with measuring and getting a racing certificate. But, of course, none of them faced the sort of time shortage that we did.

The cream of the crop of the world sailing community was now packed into the small village of Hamble. Soon we became casually acquainted with the sailors, whose pictures we had formerly only seen in sailing magazines. After long days of labor, we were literally rubbing elbows with them in the crowded pubs. As Gennadi Korolkov, nicknamed "Crocodile," put it:

"Yesterday, when I was buying a beer, just guess who was behind me? Peter Blake with his guys from STEINLAGER! Then we sat at the same table and talked. How could I have ever imagined that I'd be drinking a beer with them? And you know what? Those guys are just like us."

• • •

Hard work, interrupted occasionally by short breaks, quickly consumed our first weeks in England, and suddenly the 2nd of August, the launch day, was right before us. The yacht, now a snow-white beauty with a bright, ruby-red stripe that widened toward the transom, and a giant Pepsi logo along its sides, was rolled out of the shop. The launch was organized in the "Russian style," at least as Hill and Knowlton, the public relations agency that handled the Pepsi account, pictured a Russian style event. There was a tent with champagne, vodka, and caviar; a band dressed in Russian folk costumes that played Russian melodies on balalaikas. Surprisingly, with the memories of the homeland suddenly surging forward, it was touching. But all the same, the circus was not really Russian, and strongly redolent of fakery. There had even been talk of bringing a trained bear to the ceremony, but luckily none was to be found in the area.

Amid the gently weeping balalaika, the huge Travelift hoisted the boat, carried her to the dock and slowly and steadily lowered her till the keel touched the water for the first time. Yes, I'm not mistaken; the keel actually touched the water for the first time, although FAZISI's christening ceremonies had long ago ceased to be a novelty. This was the fourth and final one. The boat's transom was covered with the Soviet and American flags. Alexey Grischenko and Skip slowly raised them, revealing the Pepsi logo to the cheering spectators.

Our boat was officially christened FAZISI-PEPSI. The words in the press release distributed by Hill and Knowlton sounded like Pepsi's commitment to continuation of the sponsorship. " 'The opportunity to sponsor FAZISI was one Pepsi couldn't pass up,' said Roger A. Enrico, president of Pepsi-Cola International. 'Our company has a long and productive history of doing business in the Soviet Union and we are very pleased to back the first Soviet entry in the Whitbread Round the World Race.' "

11

FAZISI-PEPSI MINUS PEPSI

We were motoring out of the Hamble River and onto The Solent amid a huge flotilla of sailing and power vessels of all imaginable sizes and types. Hundreds and hundreds more were already cruising up and down the strait, staying along the side close to Cowes. FAZISI's first sail fell on the day of the start of the Fastnet Race, and The Solent was literally packed with racers and spectator vessels. The Fastnet, a 300-mile-long ocean sprint to the lighthouse bearing the same name near the Irish coast and back to The Solent, was a part of the biennial Admiral's Cup Series, the unofficial offshore yachting world championship. Traditionally, it is also a final training session for the Whitbread fleet before they plunge into the real race. It is a chance for the future competitors to get their first "taste of blood." Most of them were already there, sailing back and forth impatiently along the starting line in anticipation of the preparatory gun.

FAZISI, of course, wouldn't do the Fastnet. We had just gone out for her first sea trial. Certainly, I would have preferred to do it somewhere else, in a quiet spot far from sailing crowds to keep the inevitable initial mistakes private. As the Russian saying goes "The first pancake never turns out right," and it could be embarrassing to "burn" it in front of hundreds of the world's best sailors. In fact, we'd already had our first problem yesterday when we tried to raise the mainsail only to find that the boltrope on the luff was too skinny for the mast groove — an embarrassment for the North Sails guys. Working nonstop through the night, Kuli and Valery Safiullin had fixed the problem and now everything seemed to be ready.

Of course, there was risk involved in maneuvering a huge untried boat amid the dense crowd, as it would be a real challenge to slow her down below 10 knots in the fresh breeze of the day. And yet, the opportunity to use such an event for its exposure potential with all the media present was not to be missed. Besides, the endless stream of miraculous victories—some small, some big—that had already brought us so far, made me feel almost invincible. Obstacles and challenges were abundant, but there always was a solution. While being totally exhausted, I found myself in a sort of euphoric state of mind. I just knew that the first sail would go okay; I simply couldn't imagine that at some point my luck might run out. Well, one thing we should never forget when the winning streaks last too long: defeat is right around the corner.

Skip turned down the throttle, reducing the engine's RPM to idle, and as the boat slowed, pointed her bow into the wind. Following his command, four guys, facing each other in pairs, started grinding like crazy, and the smart mechanism hidden in the pedestals and below the deck, working through various gears, shafts, and switches, funneled their energy to the main halyard winch. The huge mainsail started to slowly, inch by inch, slide up the mast, as Juki tailed the halyard.

In about 10 minutes the main was all the way up, slapping in the wind and unfolding all of its 1,500 square feet of golden Kevlar, shining in the sun so brightly, it hurt the eyes. Next the genoa went up. Being much smaller and lighter, it was hoisted in a breath. With the engine off now and FAZISI still coasting slowly forward, Skip turned the wheel, bearing off, and her sails filled with wind for the first time.

It was a magical moment. The boat, conceived in my brain three years ago — just a crazy, impossible idea then — caught the breeze and was now piercing through the water, moving faster and faster toward a fleet of boats in the distance. In cautious anticipation, they all seemed to be awaiting her, intrigued to see two flags, the American Stars and Stripes and the Soviet Hammer and Sickle, waving off FAZISI's transom.

Despite my fears, the first sailing trial turned out flawless. Cheered by enthusiastic cries, horns and sirens from the spectator fleet, and reserved waves from the competitors' boats, FAZISI sailed in the vicinity of the starting line, where the racing fleet waited for the gun to signal the start. We stood clear of the line not to interfere with them. Then, after the gun fired, we trimmed the sails and followed the Whitbread racers to the west end of The Solent. On the first port tack toward the mainland, we sailed clear behind them. Then we tacked back, pointing to the Isle of Wight, and everyone onboard held his breath, waiting for the approaching moment of truth. As FAZISI was closing in on most of the fleet, which was still on the opposite tack, it became more and more apparent that we had overtaken a few Maxis. I figured those weren't the Whitbread favorites, but who cares! We have already beaten them anyway! As we cut across the bows of GATORADE and MARTELA OF, our crew was ready to explode in cheers. Instead, true to protocol, we passed them in silence and just waved briefly, then looked away. But, hey, inside we were all screaming with joy.

After five miles and passing two more boats, we still had the favorites STAINLAGER, MERIT and FISHER & PAYKEL well ahead of us, and the distance between us was not shortening. But it didn't seem to be increasing either. If we were able to do that well on our very first sail, imagine what's going to happen after we tune the boat and the crew gets some experience? — Dreams, dreams.

It was time to turn back. We hoisted our largest three-quarter-ounce spinnaker with the huge Pepsi logo on it and sailed through the Admiral's Cup fleet, spectators and media boats, as we started a month-long promotional marathon.

• • •

The PR company Hill & Knowlton, which managed Pepsi's International account in Great Britain, developed an exhausting sponsorship schedule for FAZISI that took most of our sailing time right up to the Whitbread start. The person in charge was Jock Wishart. A sailor himself, he never missed a VIP sail, enjoying the mixture of business and pleasure FAZISI provided. In addition to all the sponsorship obligations, we tried to use every day at sea as a chance to test the boat and learn the basics of her sailing. It wasn't easy because FAZISI was always overcrowded. At times we sailed with more than 40 people aboard. No wonder it created a pretty chaotic atmosphere, and sure enough, we had more than one pancake that didn't turn out.

The immediate challenge was the boat's sheer size. FAZISI was a huge powerful machine, twice as large as the boats any of us had ever sailed. Believe me, it made a world of difference. Skip brought along instructors, mostly his friends, who had sailed big boats before and were supposed to teach us. They were of course helpful, but, for the most part, they would just take over the boat and do most of the jobs themselves in the rush of the moment. The crew was not happy with such a setup and regarded the instructors as "foreigners", or unwanted outsiders.

The day after the Fastnet start, Wishart brought aboard a group of VIP guests, and we went out again. This time I insisted that Skip set aside some time to train the crew in performing basic sailing maneuvers. As we were preparing for the tack, I watched Jock trying to explain to Vladimir Musatov how to operate the mammoth primary winch, keeping his English as simple and as understandable as possible.

"Always – keep – three - wraps – on – the - drum." He showed Sergey a hand with three outstretched fingers. To make it even clearer, he put three wraps of the inch-thick line around the winch. "Load - is - tremendous. You - need - friction," he said as he put his hands on the top of the line trying to slide them around in an attempt to illustrate the friction. "Do - you - understand?"

"Sure," nodded Musatov and as Jock turned away, he took one wrap off the winch and with a wink said in Russian to Igor Mironenko: "These guys think we're stupid. Did you see that? He just showed me how to operate the winch, as if I'd never sailed before."

"Ready about," shouted Skip, and as a dissonant chorus replied, "ready," "yes," "*dah*" not in unison from all positions of the boat, he turned the wheel hard to the right. FAZISI's bow crossed the wind and the genoa swept to the starboard side. While the grinders started working, Vladimir Musatov at the winch trimmed the new sheet. The wind, caught the huge sail and pulled the sheet with such brute force that Vladimir, holding onto the sheet, flew a couple feet forward. Somehow he was able to hang on to it as it spun like a demon around the drum in a haze of smoke. Luckily, his hand didn't get caught in the wrap on the winch that would instantly break his fingers. Igor Mironenko saw the problem and quickly jumped in to help. Together they managed to hold the sheet as the necessary third wrap was placed on the winch, and finally trimmed the genoa properly.

Wishart was standing next to Skip, watching in disbelief.

"Are you sure you want to go to sea with these guys?"

"I hope they learn soon," replied Skip, without much confidence in his voice.

• • •

The pinnacle of the Pepsi PR campaign was sailing to London where the Tower Bridge was opened for us and FAZISI, under her big Pepsi spinnaker, sailed through. The maneuver was risky, the space very tight, but it all went smoothly. We anchored for the night on the Thames, right in the heart of the city. Klaus Wawer, who flew from Germany especially for this event, was ecstatic with the amount of exposure we got on British TV. Later that night over dinner he gave me an optimistic report on the status of our Pepsi sponsorship.

"Everything is going well so far. It's a hard job, believe me, to get somebody to commit millions of dollars. And it is slow. Corporate bureaucrats are not fast decision-makers. But be patient, we're getting there."

I already knew that they were slow. Bureaucracy doesn't belong only to the Soviet Union. Together with Skip we had already gone to several meetings with Pepsi and Hill & Knowlton personnel. We usually discussed details of upcoming promotional events, but inevitably there remained the big issue: what was going to happen after the start? I tried to be careful not to step on ASM's toes, yet I couldn't restrain myself from asking the direct question, "When will the final decision regarding the sponsorship for the entire race be made?"

I didn't get a straight answer, but all indications were clear that it would depend on how much publicity we would be able to generate for Pepsi, how good a promotional tool FAZISI proved to be.

And, boy, did they get publicity! In those six pre-start weeks FAZISI became a true media champion. No one, not even Britain's own high-profile entry ROTHMANS backed by the giant cigarette manufacturer and led by Olympic star and national celebrity Lawrie Smith, was able to overshadow FAZISI. At first, the tone of the media was a curious mixture of cautious friendliness and skepticism. But after FAZISI's launch it began to change gradually, as we proved that we could do the things everyone thought impossible.

Still FAZISI was an underdog. A dog of an underdog, indeed. Yes, she was graceful and looked fast and surprisingly advanced. Who would have expected this of a design from Russia, known for its ugly square cars, uninspired fashion and barely functional appliances? But then again, who knows, they had achieved Sputnik after all, and their military planes and warships did look pretty impressive and sophisticated.

Her crew proved to be dedicated, working practically around the clock to complete the construction, but they had absolutely no ocean experience, and the Whitbread, after all, was the most grueling sailing race in the world. The London bookies still had FAZISI at hundred-to-one odds that the boat would be able to complete the first leg to Punta del Este, let alone the whole race through the treacherous Southern Ocean.

But despite the skepticism, one thing was absolutely clear: no matter what, the media attention would be focused on FAZISI, constantly following her progress. Her sponsors would be the lucky ones getting the most exposure. FAZISI was not just a revolutionary racer from the Soviet Union. She was also the most fascinating story.

The sail to London and back was the first real sea trial for our yacht, and she passed it with flying colors. Everything worked well; there were no problems whatsoever — which was fairly rare for a brand-new boat. FAZISI's performance, which had already showed some promise during the Fastnet start, really sparkled when she hit 16-1/2 knots in a moderate breeze.

The future looked bright.

We sailed back into The Solent late at night. The wind had dropped to the lightest whisper, and the boat was gliding slowly over the glassy water. The huge golden disc of the moon was rising behind the transom, its broken reflection bouncing in FAZISI's wake. The whole crew gathered in the cockpit, speaking Russian excitedly, joking, and laughing, but in low voices, almost in whispers, as if they were afraid to break the spell of the enchanting moment.

Skip was sitting alone on the afterdeck, looking remote and lost.

"So far so good, Vladislav," he smiled when I joined him, but it was a sad smile. We sat silently for a while before he said, with his eyes glued to the jolly group of Russian sailors, "You know, I've decided to invite Jim Saunders to sail with me on the first leg. You were right. It would be tough. I'd feel as if I were locked up on the boat, alone with you guys for a month at a time without being able to speak a word of Russian. It could become very lonely."

We had had this discussion before, and I had suggested that Skip invite another English-speaking sailor aboard, at least for the beginning. He was reluctant at first, as he wanted to be the only American among the Russians. Another Westerner would ruin the uniqueness of his position. I didn't persist. After all, it was his decision. Besides, tensions among the crew as to who would be on the boat for the race, had grown substantially. All together, 20 guys had come with me on the Ruslan, but only 16 would actually race FAZISI on the first leg. They had already made peace with the fact that Skip was going, but, for obvious reasons, they would be opposed to another foreigner, who would take a position from one of them.

From early on — and we had discussed it many times — the crew had agreed that during the construction we needed extra guys, who would become back up crewmembers for necessary replacements along the way. After all, none of us had sailed on a boat like FAZISI before and, inevitably, some would end up performing better than others. It would be beneficial for the whole enterprise to continue the selection process during the race. This way we'd end up with the best possible crew and the potential to achieve better results.

But it is one thing to agree theoretically on the benefits for the team. Yet it is a totally different issue to accept the fact that you might be the person designated to stay on shore for the sake of the common good. I was already under a lot of pressure, and introducing any new crewmember, especially a foreigner, at this stage would only heat up the situation one step further. Still, I was glad that Skip had made up his mind. The only problem was that Jim's wife Liz was pregnant, expecting a baby any day. I wasn't sure if he'd go with us under such circumstances — well, maybe he would, sailors are a crazy bunch — but what about Liz?

"I'll talk to both of them tomorrow," said Skip reading my thoughts, "and I have a couple of other guys in mind if Jim chooses not to go."

• • •

In all the rush there had been no time thus far to measure FAZISI to obtain an official racing certificate. Technically, without the certificate, she was not a racing boat yet and couldn't enter the race.

Measurement of a sailboat is a complex and precise procedure aimed at establishing its performance potential. The boats in the Whitbread at that time were all different in design, and the measurement was a means of determining the proper and fair handicap for each boat. It was a process of obtaining all the necessary data on the boat's dimensions and shape. This information then went into the handicap program on the computer from which emerged the boat's handicap rating, a single number that represented the boat's performance capability.

The upcoming measurement worried me a lot. I knew that FAZISI was constructed with great accuracy as far as her lines. But I also knew that she was overbuilt and definitely weighed more than she was supposed to. It all started in Poti when, no matter how hard I tried to control the weight, it wasn't always possible to keep it to specifications, and even the bare hull had come out heavier than it was supposed to be. Then, in the rush of the last few days, we installed a lot of equipment and hardware without properly controlling its weight. By Ian Armstrong's estimate, the extra fairing compound we had put on FAZISI was at least 1,500 pounds, a huge chunk of fat that was not accounted for in the boat's design. But then we just simply couldn't avoid it. Every time I had to deal with the immediate problem on hand and put aside weight concerns. Now the time had come to take care of this problem. Of course, it wasn't totally out of hand. I kept as accurate weight records as I could and knew that a weight problem could be solved one way or another. However it was, in the end it would only be a question of time and money. But whichever, we were in short supply of both.

I knew that FAZISI was more than just a little bit overweight, and that the problem was very serious. To find out how serious, I needed to learn the boat's actual displacement. It was necessary to measure the height of FAZISI's freeboard and compare it to the design numbers. That would show me how much deeper the boat floated in the water and how much heavier she was built compared to the design numbers.

One evening, after the sailing with Pepsi's VIPs was over, I took a rubber dinghy and together with Alexey Grischenko went to measure FAZISI's freeboard, a task virtually impossible to perform at Hamble Yacht Services. With a strong tidal current running and the boat bouncing and heeling in the waves, it took us a while to get the measurements. I ran the numbers using my pocket calculator and got a rough picture. It was bad.

"Okay, let's do it again."

Alexey did a couple more circles, rowing around the boat while I took the measurements and put them down in the notebook. This time the numbers came out a bit different, but I knew they were still inaccurate. As the sun went down and the current diminished slightly, we performed more measurements. The numbers were still jumping up and down, but even the crude probe confirmed my grim suspicions: FAZISI was almost two tons heavier than she was designed to be.

Two tons, I thought, sitting dumbstruck as the dinghy floated aimlessly along FAZISI's shining side. Shit! Two tons… That's a lot of extra weight. What would this affect? Inclining test, of course. Now, as the total weight had grown significantly, the boat's ballast keel represented a much smaller percentage of boat's displacement. Plainly put: FAZISI was built less stable than she was intended to be and wouldn't pass the stability inclining test, a very important part of the whole measurement procedure. I continued my calculations, trying to find out how this would affect the boat's rating and what might be done to correct the problem. A few minutes later I discovered the scary truth. A quick fix wouldn't work, FAZISI needed radical surgery. She needed a heavier keel.

To make sure, we scheduled an official inclining test, took FAZISI to a quiet marina in Southampton where a certified measurer performed the test. It was definitely more accurate than ours, but brought the same result. The keel replacement was inevitable.

After learning the grim news, it was Skip who looked the most terrified. It was like a replay of his worst nightmares. DRUM, the boat he had skippered in the previous race, lost her keel and capsized just one month before the start of the race. And now again, a problem with the keel. Only this time there were but 10 days til the start.

The three of us, including Valery Chumakov, were sitting in our office silently looking at each other.

"Do something, Vladislav. There should be one or another way out. Do some calculations. Maybe we just need to shift the internal balance somehow or trim the boat differently, and that would be enough to get the proper rating?" said Skip.

I growled, "Nothing is going to work short of changing the keel. Just face it and get over it." I was too depressed to go into any deeper explanation.

Valery Chumakov reached into the bottom drawer of his desk and pulled out an opened bottle of Georgian brandy. He poured generously into three plastic cups with Pepsi logos. We had an endless supply of those (the cups, I mean) together with three-liter bottles of the famed drink, which filled two huge refrigerators in the corner of the office.

"Let's toast to our failure." Chumakov looked at Skip and smiled wearily. "It looks like this is your fate, Skip, to deal with keel problems. Soon people will start saying 'Where Skip is, there is always a keel problem.'"

When he saw that Skip was about to hit him, he smiled more apologetically:

"Okay, okay, I'm just joking. But isn't this coincidence funny?" I was surprised that Chumakov, who normally didn't talk much, had become almost jolly in this situation. I eventually learned that he always betrayed a great deal of strength when times got tough -- probably just another indication of his alleged KGB training.

Meanwhile, he continued in a sarcastic tone, "Of course, I'll lose my job, but that's okay. I have a beautiful *dacha* not far from Moscow... and I always wanted to be a gardener... Mmm... by the way, you all are welcome, any time... Vladislav would probably be sent to Siberia, and it looks like only Skip would lose nothing. Hey Skip, why is it that you Westerners are always better off, no matter what?... Tell you what, life isn't fair."

He poured another double brandy into our cups. I felt the burning liquid going down my throat, spreading comforting warmth. The first shock was over, and I started analyzing the situation more calmly, if not soberly.

I asked Skip if there were any manufacturers around who could cast a new lead keel on such short notice. A few quick calls, including one to Hans Waimer from Speedwave, which had built our original keel, quickly revealed that this would be impossible. At least 15 days would be our best bet.

"Well, if nothing else works, this would still be a chance. We'd miss the start of the first leg, but the race is nine months long. There would be plenty of opportunities to catch up with the rest of the fleet," — like a drowning man, I was grasping for even the smallest straw of hope.

"Oh, stop it, Vladislav, you just don't want to admit your defeat," Chumakov dismissed my proposal with a scornful gesture. "We did everything possible, but now it is all over."

A few minutes passed in absolute silence until Skip suddenly jumped up from his chair and ran to the door.

"Hasn't ROTHMANS just gone through a keel change? I think I've seen their old one still lying behind the storage container."

He was back in 10 minutes.

"I spoke to Lawrie Smith and he agreed to sell it to us for the price of the lead scrap." Skip certainly was the master of solving the keel problems. "It weighs 8.7 tons. Would this be enough to properly balance the boat?"

"I'm sure it's enough, but I can't perform all the necessary calculations without a computer. It would take me weeks if I used my pathetic pocket calculator. We need to hire a design firm to do this if we want to finish in time."

"I know Tony Castro pretty well," Skip said. "He lives right here in the village. Sure he could do it, but it would cost us an arm and a leg."

Skip was right. Tony Castro, a successful local designer, did a great job. In three days he came up with complete stability calculations, but his charge for the job must have made those three days the most profitable of his entire business career.

• • •

I knew and anticipated trouble, still the scale of it when it struck was devastating. After all, the boat, her design and the concept, the chance to see her sailing the Whitbread and performing well, were my primary motivations for starting the whole venture. I was confident that her design was the most innovative and probably the fastest in the entire Whitbread fleet. But now she would never have a chance to demonstrate her potential.

And disaster wasn't over yet. As it often happens, one problem started a chain reaction. The keel weighed much more now, thus putting more strain on the hull. The surrounding structure needed to be reinforced, which meant dealing with the welders again. I told Skip that this time we needed the outside guys, not the notorious gang that had caused so much delay before. Surprisingly, everything went smoothly without any complaints from the subcontractors or from the yard, and without the need of Nodari's motivation either.

Reinforcing ribs were to be welded on the top of the fuel tanks, and this made Alexey Grischenko extremely nervous.

"We shouldn't do this, Vlad. Even if we completely drain the tanks, there still will be some leftover fumes entrapped. As soon as those guys light the torch, the whole boat will blow into pieces.

"But why? This is diesel, not gasoline. I don't think its fumes can cause an explosion." But I was not really that positive and asked the welders.

"No worries, mate, nothin' happens," was their cheerful reply.

"Look, Alexey, these guys are not afraid to weld, and they would be the first to be concerned if there were any danger. They're experienced, they told me they have done similar jobs."

"I don't know, but this whole thing… if it's not one problem, it's another … I don't believe anymore that we'll ever be able to make it."

"Oh, come on, you're just too tired… we'll finish this, and then there'll be the start in just a few days, and then we'll be in the ocean… This is probably the last obstacle separating us from sailing," I hoped my voice sounded firm and confident. But honestly, I wasn't sure any more that there would ever be a time when all our troubles were left behind.

The following morning Alexey didn't show up for work, and the next couple of days he spent in his room, behind locked doors, refusing to communicate with anyone. Finally he came out, still looking weary and tired, "I hope I haven't let you down too much. I just needed time off to pull myself together again. I feel better now."

• • •

Our ordeal with the keel was not over yet, and before we even had a chance to breathe a sigh of relief, another, even more deadly blow struck. With just a few days now left before the start, Pepsi International informed us that they had chosen not to execute the option to expand the sponsorship for the entire race.

Actually, the first signs of trouble had become apparent a couple of weeks earlier. First, the checks, Valery Chumakov had been writing off the Pepsi money wired from the ASM account in Germany, bounced. In a panic, we called ASM and at first they reassured us that there had been some problems with the wire transfer, but now everything was sorted out. Then Michael Winterfeld changed the story and told me that they "decided to keep some money in an escrow account in case Pepsi didn't continue the sponsorship and ASM faced any unexpected bills." That didn't sound right. But worse still, during the next few days we were unable to reach ASM at all. They simply wouldn't call us back to answer our urgent messages. All this fell right in the middle of our keel epic, greatly multiplying my worries. Finally Winterfeld called and in response to my frantic questions, explained that there were concerns regarding the continuation of the Pepsi sponsorship, but they, ASM, were vigorously working with company officials and he was sure they'd come up with a solution.

"Look, we need some clarity here," Skip got involved in the conversation. "I think I'll better call Tony McGrath myself and ask him what's going on. I tried to talk with the Pepsi people here in England but was unable to get any straight answers."

"No, no, no", interrupted Michael, "I'm categorically against you talking with them directly. They are already totally confused, not knowing exactly whom they are dealing with, and that doesn't help the situation at all. First there was Dennis, then you got involved... then I was barely able to convince Vladislav not to talk to them directly. Do you know that the guys from Fazis Company in Moscow called me and suggested that they fly to New York to negotiate with Pepsi? That would be a total disaster. This whole thing is already a mess. Let's not make it any more confusing or desperate. Let me handle all communication and don't worry, all is not lost yet."

I didn't understand what he was talking about. Just a few days ago they assured me that everything was okay, and now it was a total mess? And it was not lost YET?

And then the fax came from America — a copy of an article from one of the major newspapers. I've never learned which one, because after looking at it only briefly, Skip furiously tore it into pieces and threw it in the wastebasket.

"What now?" By his behavior I realized that something serious had happened.

"Very bad news, Vladislav," I already knew Skip's tendency of never circling around the problem but going straight to the point, a great habit actually. "Apparently there was an interview, a pretty mean one, where Pepsi was accused of supporting the Soviets, while none of the American teams was able to find sponsorship to enter the Whitbread. It seems it got Pepsi scared, and they're going to end up their sponsorship."

In disbelief, I looked at Skip. I had never seen him so frustrated.

"I need to talk to Tony McGrath," he said as he reached for the phone. Tony McGrath was the executive responsible for Pepsi International marketing.

"Are you sure this is the right thing to do? Michael Winterfel doesn't want us to talk to Pepsi Headquarters direct..." I started.

"Look, we need to find out right now what's going on. From Pepsi. Enough of those mediators."

I was struggling to comprehend the news. I simply couldn't believe it. Sure, the whole Pepsi deal had become kind of shaky recently, and I suspected that there were some problems. But I could never imagine that they would end their sponsorship with such a bogus explanation. Who could really believe that Pepsi was afraid of a negative reaction in America for being associated with "the Soviets?" Pepsi, one of the very first American companies to come to the Soviet market more than 15 years before, a sponsor of the 1986 Moscow Goodwill Games, and the first foreign company to buy commercial time on Soviet TV? The same Pepsi that was selling Soviet "Stoli" all over America was now afraid of sponsoring the Soviet sailors? If it was okay for them to deal with the Communist Government bureaucrats for over 15 years, who would believe that they were fearful of supporting one of the first private initiatives in the Soviet Union? And that's now, when our country was no longer the Evil Empire...

Come on, it didn't make sense. At that moment I was almost sure that this was some sort of mistake. Deep in my thoughts, I didn't pay much attention to Skip's conversation with the Pepsi headquarters until I heard his voice raising, "Decision has been made already? Damn it!" Now he was screaming into the phone, "If you're afraid to support Russians, support me for God's sake! I'm an American after all! Don't you remember, this is a joint venture and this boat now carries your name as well!"

He slammed the receiver down and ran out of the office pushing the door with such a fury that the whole trailer shook. My heart plunged down a bottomless abyss. It took me some time before I returned to normal thinking.

And my first thought was, it's all over. The end.

Konets.

• • •

I was totally crushed.

From then on only momentum kept me moving. It was as if we had been used and then thrown away. Maybe this is how a raped victim feels like. Whose fault was it? Ours, ASM's, Pepsi's? I didn't want to blame anybody. I had simply learned that the world, even the Western world, is not perfect, is not just. That's all. And my shattered dreams were the price I paid for this knowledge.

We passed the inclining test and got a rating certificate. Now FAZISI was officially in the race, but how far would she sail without the money? We could probably reach Punta del Este but that would be it. Fazis SP was not doing well and couldn't put any more money into the project. Actually they had already spent much more than they could reasonably afford. Tikhov came to England himself, looking calm and composed, but I sensed that he was completely devastated by the situation. I was pretty sure that at this point he regretted the day he decided to get involved in the whole affair. For me there was some small comfort in the fact that FAZISI at least made it to the start, and my crazy dream sort of came true. But for him, from the business point of view, it was a complete disaster.

Needless to say, we all were under infinitely more pressure than anyone could have ever imagined. It was pressure that only a citizen of the former Soviet Union could understand. To be blunt, we were really scared. Back at the beginning we tried to be independent from the State in our venture but always felt as if we were under the watchful eye. As subjects of the last great empire, we knew all too well that if we succeeded, the officials would be jumping all over for joy, proclaiming another glorious victory for the State, but if we failed, they would crucify us. And we had come pretty damn close to that.

After talking it over with Victor, we decided that I wouldn't sail on FAZISI. Instead I would try to do whatever possible again to raise money in a last desperate attempt to save the project. Under other circumstances, it would have been an extremely disappointing decision to make. But now my limits of disappointment were exhausted; I was totally empty emotionally. Only a few days ago I was struggling to make the tough decision of who would go on FAZISI and who wouldn't. Now I had decided not to sail myself.

But what could I do? We had already exhausted all our options to find sponsors. We had worked really hard and failed. Jock Wichart of Hill & Knowlton was still trying to keep our hopes from dying completely and to convince us that the deal with Pepsi was not over yet, not entirely. "Don't give up. You need to start by any means, to fulfill completely your Pepsi contract. I'll continue working on those guys."

Sure, we'll start. And go as far as we could. But who needs this anymore? By now this was just too much for me. The whole Whitbread venture had turned so sour. It had become nothing more than endless torture. The very moment I'd overcome one obstacle, I would be immediately knocked off my feet by another. As soon as I'd try to rise again, another, even more terrible blow would crush me down. This was a clear case of the punishment not fitting the crime. After all, it was just a dream I was trying to fulfill. What was so wrong with that?

All my emotions were gone—and my will too. Only momentum was still dragging me forward. But for how much longer?

On the morning of September 2, I was steering FAZISI as we motored to the start of the 1989-90 Whitbread Round the World Race. In striking contrast to my mood, the day was absolutely gorgeous. Jam-packed with spectator boats, big cruise ships chartered for the day by wealthy sponsors, and press boats, The Solent was glimmering under the bright azure sky. Pristine white clouds flew past swiftly, pushed by a fresh breeze. At any given moment you could spot at least a dozen helicopters hovering above.

No matter what our situation was, the start of the Whitbread turned out to be a great celebration, and we were a part of it. Despite all the obstacles we had made it. My dream had come true, hadn't it? *Dah?*

Only then did I spot an unfamiliar face among the crew, a blond one, with a boyish look.

"Brian Hancock," Skip introduced him and we shook hands. "He is going instead of Jim. We've sailed together for years. Brian was with me on ALASKA EAGLE and DRUM. Great sailor."

"Nice meetn' you, man." Brian was speaking with an unfamiliar accent. "I'm from South Africa, but live on Cape Cod now. Skip called me yesterday morning so I didn't even have time to pack my personal gear." His smile was open and sympathetic. "I think my wife still doesn't believe I'm off sailing again." A few minutes passed in silence as I maneuvered FAZISI closer to the starting line through the thickening crowd of boats. Then Brian continued, "Skip told me you won't sail FAZISI on the first leg. Sorry, man... but don't worry, we'll take good care of her."

And then I saw Tony Castro approaching us on his tender, as we had earlier arranged. For the last time, I wished the guys a safe sail and jumped off onto Tony's boat.

At noon the gun from Her Royal Majesty's ship AMBUSCADE announced that the fifth Whitbread Round the World Race had begun, the race that would become the greatest ocean race of the century. FAZISI got an excellent start, getting the preferred windward position and crossed the line second only to STEINLAGER. Thousands of spectator boats immediately took off following the racers and with their wakes colliding and crashing into each other, turned The Solent into a raging sea. Our tiny tender was bouncing up and down like a cork, hitting a wall of white water that would catapult it high into the air, only to fall down the six-foot troughs, as water cascaded over our heads. We followed the Whitbread fleet all the way to the Needles, where the wind changed a bit, and FAZISI was again flying her Pepsi spinnaker. We had fulfilled our sponsorship obligations completely, but did it matter?

Filled with equal amounts of excitement and exhaustion, I couldn't take my eyes off FAZISI as she sailed farther and farther away and disappeared into the pale, hazy mist. Yes, there was still some left-over excitement in me, but as soon as that was gone, and FAZISI was swallowed up beyond the horizon, I laid dead sick for the next couple of days. The sounds of "Deep Purple" coming from the tape player only added to my mood. The weeping guitar solo of my favorite "Child in Time" fitted perfectly.

"...If you'd not been hit, oh, by flying lead... you'd better close your eyes, bow your head, waiting for the ricochet..."

Barely back on my feet, I was dragged by Gerd Butdzek to more meetings in search of sponsorship. Again, they yielded nothing. I didn't care. I had totally lost the ability to be disappointed.

● ● ●

A few days later I flew back to Moscow. I didn't want to, really. I didn't feel that anything was connecting me anymore to my old motherland. FAZISI's escape on that Ruslan flight had become my personal escape as well. I didn't want to go back to the USSR, but it didn't seem as if the West was welcoming me either.

Even in my senseless state of mind, returning to Russian reality was shocking. As we drove from Sheremetyevo Airport toward Moscow center, I looked around to see dilapidated buildings in desperate need of upkeep and empty dark streets that appeared almost uninhabited — the picture, drastically different from the perfectly manicured British landscape. We followed Gorky Street down to Pushkin Square, where the driver said:

"There is a big protest rally going on near the *Mossovet* (City Hall) and the road's closed." He turned left and took a detour through the maze of narrow back streets. We could see a huge mass of people in the distance and hear the roar of thousands shouting and on top of it, a speech of the leader, indecipherable and echoing off the dark buildings. Many people were waving torches, and the whole eerie thing gave those Moscow streets the appearance of a war zone. I couldn't recognize what they were shouting and didn't know who the people were — new democrats, old communists, nationalists, fascists, whatever.

After the peaceful and orderly West, I was amazed to see the scale of political changes that were sweeping over Russia. New parties, groups, and movements were popping up every day in scary quantities. In addition to the whole spectrum of real political parties from ultra right to ultra left with everything imaginable in between, there was also a party of beer lovers, of "blue gays," of women, of agrarians, of Donsky Kazaks and so on and so on. It was entertaining to see the curious forms that the recently unleashed social energy of the Soviet people were taking. It was a circus, yes, but a scary one as the country was quickly sinking into anarchy. There was lots of noise, slogans, and promises, but everyone was pulling in opposite directions with any kind of progress clearly absent.

Gorbachev tried to steer a steady course somehow and to calm down the excitement with the promise of gradual reforms. Leading economists predicted significant improvements in the quality of life in five to ten years. "What? Ten years? Communists used to say they would build social paradise in 20 years… now these new guys are telling us to wait another 10 years? Fuck them! We want it all and we want it NOW!"

It was not only the brave and the ruthless who now took guns and went into the streets to shake down the newborn businessmen for a share of their profits. Everyone from ordinary working people to the highbrow intelligentsia, who always liked to think of themselves as independent-minded, flooded the streets in endless meetings and demonstrations. This was not a real revolution. Just a few years ago all these people wouldn't have even dared to raise their voices to request anything at all. In silent obedience, they had followed the communist leaders for almost 70 years to the promised new Utopia. Now Gorbachev's reforms allowed revolt — so they revolted. Yesterday's communism supporters had turned overnight into democrats and with the same enthusiasm were overthrowing and crushing their former idols. It was a disgusting sight to watch. If tomorrow another tyrant were to rise, they would follow him with the same ease. Russia again was full speed ahead on the road to nowhere.

Obviously, democracy is not something that can be born overnight. A craving for freedom should burn deep in your heart, and no politician can implant it there. The most terrible thing about a totalitarian system is that it corrupts generations of people, making them so obedient even in their riots.

At about the same time Lech Walenza, the Polish dissident and leader, made the following remark in addressing the scope of problems his country was facing in its transition from a totalitarian system to a democracy, "It is very easy to turn the aquarium into fish soup. It is much more difficult to reverse the process." Well, Mr. Walenza, if you're right in your grim comparison, it seems like the chances of reversing the process are pretty futile. Soup is soup. End of story. I just honestly wished that it was not really all that bad, that there was a hope for my Russia...

If you haven't noticed yet, I was in a very grave mood upon my arrival in Moscow. Understandable, considering the circumstances. Returning to Mother Russia was the final drop that overfilled my cup and turned the whole situation into too much for me to bear. I plunged into a deep depression. It wasn't just a mental state. I felt physically sick and eventually went to see a doctor. He was extremely puzzled, telling me my symptoms were those of a man who had suffered a heart attack, yet there was nothing physically wrong with me.

I don't know what brought me back, probably the simple routine of everyday work. I realized that I was on my way to recovery when I began to develop a weak interest in following FAZISI's progress in the race. I started polling faxes from the Whitbread headquarters twice a day, marking FAZISI's position on a big map. My boat had sailed away and I had been left behind, but I didn't lose touch with her. The present was grim, the future — uncertain, but FAZISI bravely continued sailing through the ocean.

She had become my only hope.

12

THE BOAT. PART II

To appreciate the extent of the disaster of having to change FAZISI's keel, it's necessary to make a short detour into the nature of the measuring rules that governed the 1989-90 Whitbread. Of the 24 boats that entered the race, only 11 were Maxis like FAZISI. The rest of the fleet belonged to smaller handicap classes. The smallest was the French boat LA POSTE, only 54 feet long, as compared to the average length of 80 feet for the Maxis. It is quite obvious that a larger vessel, carrying more sail area, is more powerful and potentially faster than a smaller one. To make the race fair and open to a wide variety of sailing designs, the racing results were not based on the actual sailing time of the boat but on its so-called corrected time, calculated in accordance with each boat's handicap. Here's how it worked.

First, the boats were designed to the special IOR (International Offshore Rule) formula. This was a very complex formula; the book describing it consisted of more than 200 pages. While it was possible to make the computations using a simple calculator, it was a long and tedious process that usually took days. But this was the way our calculations were done. Western designers used computers, of course. If only we'd had them...

In a nutshell, to provide a fair rating for both faster and slower boats, the formula punished long hulls, light displacement, and large sail area, and credited broad beam, bulk, and other sorry features that prevent a boat from sailing fast. It might seem that the IOR promoted slower boats but, in fact, it just provided an exciting and even playing field with plenty of room for designers to employ a range of combinations of factors that affect performance.

Then, during the construction, the utmost attention had to be paid to the accuracy of the process to ensure that the actual boat was as close to the design as possible. In practice, this is almost an impossible task, and there are ways to deal with deviations later. In FAZISI's case, however, the weight was regrettably far off the usual deviations and acceptable tolerances.

Once construction was completed, an official certified measurer measured the boat. The process was long, tedious, and precise. The data received was entered into a computer, where the calculation, according to the IOR formula, was made. Out came a single number called the boat's rating. For some strange reason — maybe just to add to the confusion — the rating was measured in feet, though the final rating has nothing to do with the boat's length. For example, all Maxis used to have the same fixed rating of 70 feet, though their lengths varied from 72 to 85 feet.

Sound complicated? Well, it is. The IOR had been a cumbersome rule, but in the end it did provide a fairly even playing field for a large variety of yacht types. (Recently it has been replaced by so called IMS formula, which is even more cumbersome and confusing).

Anyway, complicated as it was, the IOR did promote diversity, and, as result, among the entries to Whitbreads have been craft small and large, light and heavy, sloop- and ketch-rigged. This was a reflection of each designer's own approach to the IOR system in an attempt to come up with the magic balance for the best, winning combination. It's because the rule really worked that Maxis, despite the fact that they were theoretically the fastest boats, had not always been the overall corrected winners, as listed here:

1973-74	SAYULA II (Mexico)	65 feet long
1977-78	FLYER (Holland)	65 feet
1981-82	FLYER (Holland)	76 feet (Maxi)
1985-86	L'ESPRIT D'EQUIPE (France)	58 feet

Now let's go back to FAZISI's problem. When she came out heavier than designed, her ballast keel became a smaller percentage of her displacement, meaning that the boat became slightly less stable. From a sailing standpoint of performance and safety, this wasn't much and nothing serious to worry about. But in the context of the boat's rating, it was actually a very big concern. The measuring procedure included an inclining test performed on the water to read the boat's stability. It was a lengthy and awkward procedure with the boat's spinnaker pole weighted at the ends and set out perpendicular to the hull. Heeling angles were measured; methacentrical radii and righting moments were calculated. If, as a result, a boat was found less or more stable than the rule required, it was penalized. And so our FAZISI was.

The problem was that the IOR rating tops out at 70 feet. That's the rating of a Maxi, and that's what FAZISI was designed to. If, with additional penalty, the rating comes out higher, then it's tough luck; your boat simply can't race.

Now, there was one peculiar thing that needs some additional explanation. Normally if a boat is heavier, its rating should drop, as it is obviously slower. This was not so in FAZISI's case. Theoretically, the larger keel installed later should have been compensated by a lower rating. But FAZISI's design was too sophisticated and complex to play by the usual rules. To ensure the best balance (and it was in fact excellent), we moved the keel well aft, much closer to the stern than had ever been done before. As a result, the new, much heavier keel caused the boat to sit differently on the water and to take trim at the stern. This was an absolute no-no under the IOR. Her new trim with the stern sitting lower in water increased the measured length (waterline), and pushed up her rating. This is why our last-minute keel change represented much more of a problem than anyone had probably imagined.

With the help of Tony Castro and his powerful computers, at the time the best around, the problem was solved in a couple of days. But the resulting boat came out a far cry from the extreme sailing machine it was intended to be. The comparison chart demonstrates how different the modified boat had become from the original design, and shows the negative handicap FAZISI was carrying as a result. (See the chart on page 150).

The last two lines of the table are the most important. The sail-area-to-displacement ratio (SA/Disp.) shows how powerful the boat is relative to her weight, an indicator of the light-wind performance. As designed, FAZISI was at the top of the fleet, on par with STEINLAGER. The modifications diminished her light-wind potential by more than 10 percent. The displacement-to-length ratio (Disp./Length) reflects the ability of a sailboat to get on a plane, start surfing, and exceed its maximum theoretical speed. The smaller the ratio, the faster the boat can go. While, according to the design, she was supposed to be the fastest boat in the Whitbread fleet, FAZISI never got a chance to prove it. Yet even after all the changes, she remained a fairly swift boat, which she would demonstrate soon.

I hope now that all this technical stuff is somewhat clear. If not, the only thing I can recommend is to re-read this short chapter, or, perhaps, just disregard the design complexities all together and follow me further through FAZISI's voyage. For the human story of the voyage was far more incredible than FAZISI's technical aspects or even the sailing itself.

And now we are at the threshold of the most dramatic point of it all, the FAZISI's triumph and tragedy.

PERFORMANCE COMPARISON CHART

	FAZISI as designed	FAZISI as built	STEINLAGER2	UBF	CHARLES JOURDAN
Length Overall (ft.)	82.8	82.8	83.7	82.7	72.2
Beam (ft.)	19.2	19.2	18.9	19.0	17.4
Displacement (lbs.)	38,200	49,000	77,000	67,000	36,900
Sail Area (sq. ft.)	2,800	2,700	4,300	3,76	2,670
SA/Disp.	38	32	38	36	32
Disp./Length	57	73	114	106	43

Note: All above numbers are approximate and provided only for comparison.

13

ONE MAN'S DECISION

The beginning of the race had been hard on FAZISI and her crew. Leaving me behind in Tony Castro's tender, bouncing about the turbulent Solent, they bravely plunged into the ocean. The learning process, started in the Hamble and interrupted so many times by sponsorship activities and last-minute FAZISI modifications, had continued. Only it was entirely different now. The boat sailed the high seas, where every mistake could cost dearly, and Skip didn't have on board the group of instructors that he had relied upon before. Together with Brian Hancock, he was among a bunch of strangers, who spoke a few distinctive tongues, none of them English, and had grown up in a society so different, they might as well have fallen from the moon. Here's how Brian recalls the beginning of FAZISI's voyage.

I had arrived at Ocean Village in Southampton the day before start, jet-lagged and tired. The previous 24 hours had been a mad scramble to get ready for the race. Skip called on Thursday morning and asked me to join the crew for the first leg to Uruguay.

"It should be fun," he said, "the guys are great, and the boat seems fast. You need to be here by tomorrow night," and so it was Friday afternoon when I dragged my bags out of the taxi and over to the breakwall where a crowd had gathered. I wondered what they were watching. As I elbowed my way to the front, I could see a sleek, low-slung yacht short-tacking up Southampton waters. The Soviet flag snapped briskly in the wind, as the crew maneuvered the yacht with practiced ease. My ride had arrived and all seemed well, but my sailing and communicating skills would soon be tested.

I scrambled on board while Skip did a quick introduction, and then he departed for more pressing issues. I was left to my own re-

sources. I nodded at the crew who had no idea who I was or why I was there, and made my way down below. The crisp red and white paint job of the exterior was in marked contrast to the dull gray of the rough interior. The low-slung freeboard that gave the yacht its unique watch-out-here-I-come look did nothing for the interior, and there was only a small crawl space between the back end and the forward section.

I found my bunk jammed high in the aft end, nestled among the salamis. The cook was busy stowing the food and had a variety of sausages strung from the overhead. Later in the trip when the tropical sun beat down on the afterdeck, the salamis would drip oil all over the sails, but for now they added a certain charm. I stowed my gear, wondered for a moment if I had lost my mind, and then headed for the hospitality tent.

Race day dawned bright, but my mood was dark, the effect of too much beer, too little sleep, and the news Skip had given me as we tossed the dock lines ashore.

"We've hardly sailed this boat," he said, "the crew have no clue what they are doing, they don't speak English, we've run out of money, and you're on the opposite watch." Skip delivered the news in the same cavalier manner to which I had become accustomed, but this time there were 6,000 miles of open ocean ahead of us and my heart sunk. It sunk a notch further when I noticed one of the crew spinning the winch to see which way it turned before he wound the line around it. They had no clue. No idea what they were getting themselves into, and no sense of the difficulties that lay ahead. I envied them.

As the start gun fired, I was filled with a sense of elation and dread. It was an uneasy combination, but the dread was soon washed away by the excitement of the crowds and the unbridled enthusiasm of the crew. They were just happy to be out from under the boat and anywhere but the Soviet Union. The recent odds handed down by the London bookies did nothing to deter their enthusiasm. They had been betting 100:1 that Fazisi would not make the start, let alone the finish, and we had just proved them wrong. If victory comes in small packages, we had just opened our first, and there would be many more to come. There would also be days of frustration and problems ahead.

My immediate task was to reprogram my mental Rolodex. Names are hard to remember and uncommon names delivered in a strange tongue are near impossible. Igor and Viktor were easy but Nodari and Gennadi were not. "Hey You!" didn't cut it because of the language barrier, and so I ended up remembering those with nicknames first and gradually figured out the rest with time. Elephant and Crocodile were *extroverts and became my immediate conduit to the rest of the crew. They understood more English than they let on and had a good grip on sign language and universal gestures. Some of the others were harder to figure out, and I had the nagging feeling that they were still wondering why I was on board.*

Next came the problem of sailing the boat, but to my surprise and delight, she seemed to sail herself just fine. She slipped through the water with hardly a trace; a few bubbles in the wake were the only sign that we had passed by. Luckily, we had good weather for the first few days, and we romped into the Bay of Biscay under full spinnaker and mainsail. We were in sight of some of the other yachts. I found time to figure out the deck lines and halyards, and learn some of the Russian names. I had one of the crew translate "I need food," and "I need sleep," and I used the two phrases as often as I could. It seemed to amuse the guys and got me what I wanted.

Despite the language barrier and the difficulty we had learning to sail the boat, we all — the crew, Skip and I — had settled into a routine and life on board fell into the usual pattern. We sailed, slept, ate our meals, and carried out maintenance on a rotating schedule, all the while trying to hold our own with the fleet. The weather had been good and as long as the mild conditions prevailed, we probably would be fine. I was worried that the good times would end and we would be tested. I didn't have long to wait.

During the night of September 13, less than two weeks into the race, we had our first near call. Under ordinary circumstances, it would barely have been noted in the logbook, but these were not ordinary circumstances, and the weaknesses among the crew, myself included, would soon be laid bare. We were approaching the northern group of islands in the Cape Verde chain, spinnaker up, and the boat surfing easily. Skip was below resting and had left instructions with Nodari, the stand-in navigator, to wake him when we got close to the islands. I had expected the wind to increase, as it funneled through the gap between the islands, but the increase came quicker and with more strength than I had anticipated, and to add to our troubles, it swung aft.

The night was clear with a sliver of moon, and ahead of us we could see the dark outline of land. Nodari was bobbing up and down the aft hatch, checking the chart and scratching calculations on a pad. He looked worried. I knew that he would not have anticipated the change in wind condition, and the scared look on his face confirmed my suspicions. I had checked the chart and knew that even though it was a narrow passage between the islands, there was enough water to transit through safely. I aimed for the middle of the gap.

But as the wind kept swinging aft, I was forced to sail more and more by the lee, risking an uncontrolled gybe at any moment. It definitely was time to call for a gybe before it was too late, but I did not trust the crew to pull it off without incident in such a strong wind and in the darkness. I should have called for it earlier but had been lulled into a false sense of security from a week of easy sailing. With the wind still increasing, we planed on the almost smooth water through the narrowing gap. Black rocky masses on each side seemed to be pulling closer and closer, and soon they were towering over us, covering the moon and the stars, and the next moment we were flying with an increasing speed in complete darkness.

The hum of the hull woke Skip, who looked over at Nodari sitting at the nav-station and immediately knew there was a problem. "I saw the bewildered look on his face and knew we were in the shit," Skip later told me. "The radar was a mass of interference. I shot on deck and all I could see was the dark outline of land hardly a hundred feet off our beam."

Skip added to an already precarious situation by overreacting. I understood his concern. He was the skipper after all, responsible for everything, but we were just fine, and his sudden outburst only wound the tension one notch tighter. It was too late to do anything anyway, other than to hold our course, and hold our breath, and in a few minutes we were out the other side and back in control.

The Cape Verde Incident, as it came to be known, pointed to weaknesses in us all. Skip and I had become too used to sailing with professionals and expected a different reaction from the crew. They, on the other hand, had not offered an opinion before the incident, but offered many afterwards. They argued among themselves ranting back and forth. Nodari was clearly the scapegoat, and he had paid a price for it. I felt bad for him. Maxi boats move quickly and a navigator's reaction should be the same, but Nodari did not have enough experience and was too proud to ask for help. It would take time and a lot more close calls before our crew work was on par with the rest of the fleet. I only hoped they would survive this time and the conflict among themselves.

• • •

Clearly, the beginning of the race was not easy on FAZISI, and after the first two weeks of struggle, she lagged hopelessly behind most of the fleet. Then, approaching the equator, something changed in my boat's behavior. One day the report showed her in 15th position and then the next day she was in 12th. A few good decisions, like picking up thunderstorm squalls in the doldrums, moved her right behind the leaders, sharing fifth to sixth place with THE CARD. While the same distance from the finish line, they were quite far apart from each other off the coast of Brazil, but on converging courses.

The next few days saw fresh breezes with waves built up to 20 to 30 feet and excellent sailing conditions. Right in her element, FAZISI was surfing at speeds exceeding 20 knots through a vast expanse of deserted ocean. But it only seemed empty. Slightly ahead to port far on the horizon appeared a small triangle, then vanished again as waves rose in front of the view. A few seconds later it popped up again. The radio below came alive, and through the cracks and static was Roger Nilson's voice: "This is THE CARD, Whitbread Maxi, sailing from Southampton to Punta del Este. Do you read me? Over."

"Roger, copy you," Brian replied in his thick South African accent.

"Do you see me?"

"Can see you bloody well, you're moving, man. Over."

"Who are you and where are you heading?"

"I am a 50-foot cruising sloop returning to Cape Town," Brian winked slyly at the guys listening to the conversation without the slightest idea of what was going on. "Had a bloody good time in Brazil."

By the end of the day, both boats were still able to see each other, but now FAZISI had moved slightly ahead of THE CARD. During the next radio conversation Roger Nilson's voice sounded really annoyed, "Where do you say you are heading, guys?"

"Cape Town, mate, I told you."

"And how big is your boat?" Now Roger got completely frustrated.

"50-foot cruising sloop." It took Brian a lot of effort not to laugh out loud.

A few minutes later, they could see THE CARD's mainsail go on the other side as the boat gybed and soon disappeared in the other direction. The first thing Brian did after finishing in Punta del Este was head aboard THE CARD for a little ribbing of Roger Nilson.

"Hi, mate, I am a small 50-foot cruising sloop from South Africa..." That time he didn't hold back his laughter. Later he told me he had played this joke twice before in the previous Whitbreads and it had always gone smoothly.

• • •

Just before the finish, THE CARD managed to slip ahead, pushing FAZISI to sixth place, but even this was a great victory and enough reason for euphoria among the Russian crew.

A week later, I flew to Uruguay with Chumakov. We arrived in Punta at midnight, and I went straight to the dock. There she was, my boat, proudly docked next to the leg's winner STEINLAGER. She had crossed the ocean and now was resting peacefully, getting ready to continue her journey. It may sound like a time of triumph, but I felt happy only for a brief moment. The reality was grim and I couldn't see any ray of hope for the future. We were completely broke. Fazis SP didn't have any money to spend on the project, and our slim chances that Pepsi might change its mind and renew the sponsorship after our first leg's success had not materialized, despite all of Jock Wishart's enthusiasm.

I left the empty dock and headed back to the Palace Hotel where we were all staying. Despite the late hour, its bar was packed, and I was glad to see most of the FAZISI guys again and celebrate the first leg's finish. Around 3 a.m. Skip and Brian wandered in with a noisy mob from ROTHMANS.

"Oh, Vladislav, here you are! Welcome to Punta!"

"Thanks. And congratulations on the great job you've done! How was it? How's the boat?" I asked, and with drinks in hand, the three of us headed for a quiet corner.

Skip started, "So far so good. The boat is great, had no problem whatsoever. Very easy to sail. Bloody wet while sailing upwind, but downwind she's the sweetest thing I've ever sailed. What a shame you weren't with us to enjoy it… the helm's fantastic… you control her with just a touch of the fingertips. I remember on DRUM we had to have two guys on the helm, and even then, at just 20 knots, forget it – nobody could control her."

"Great, let's drink to FAZISI." And so we did. I can't tell you how happy I was listening to Skip describing it all. But then he continued, "As for the crew performance… we have a big problem here. Your guys completely lack motivation and the communication is terrible."

"Well, we'd expected the language barrier, hadn't we?"

"It's not only language; I'm not talking just about them and myself. It seems they have a real problem communicating among themselves. First of all, they don't have any desire to make their own decisions. Then, when I tell them what to do, Eugene translates it to Alexey, and they have a meeting, sometimes short, sometimes not so short. Alexey explains to them what I told them to do, and they discuss it for a while. Sometimes they start arguing but do nothing. Even when they do something, it's so slow, with lots of mistakes. It's scary. It's not the way to operate a racing yacht. Don't misunderstand me, on a personal level I like them a lot, at least most of them… but as a team…"

Despite the festive atmosphere surrounding us, Skip now looked really troubled. After we ordered another round, he continued. "Maybe I'm not getting it right, but it seems as if there's always some sort of conflict going on. If it's not the Ukrainians against the Georgians, then it's the guys from Odessa against the guys from Kiev."

"Welcome to the Soviet Union, my friend. I suspect you are used to a different attitude. But that's how we live there. I understand that it must be difficult for you guys…"

"It's more than difficult," interrupted Brian, "it's dangerous. The first leg was an easy one, and yet we have already had some scary situations. It will be the Southern Ocean from now on. If FAZISI has a crew like this, I don't think she'll ever make it to Fremantle."

Oh no, not another grim prophesy. Hadn't I had enough of them? Guess not.

As I didn't respond, Skip continued, "Brian has to return home, and I certainly can't do it alone. I need at least three good professional guys who know how to sail… Hopefully, that'll do it, and then maybe your guys would improve as well. But they learn so slowly… "

Well, that meant three crewmembers should be sent home — another problem I would need to face. But then again, who knows, maybe Skip just exaggerated the situation. Despite his reputation as an emergency manager who shines in tough situations, I knew he could over-dramatize things.

In the meantime Skip continued, "I'd like to invite Jim, he probably could leave Liz now; baby's doing great. And I've already spoken to two other guys. Bilou is French, a great sailor, one of those crazy French cohorts who sails around the world alone. Another is Dale Tremain from New Zealand. Has plenty of offshore experience as well."

"Okay, okay. Don't rush it. We'll come back to this later after I talk to Alexey. You know we can't sail with 18 people on board. That means we have to make room for the new guys," I wondered, how I was going to tell the crew.

"Any suggestions on who might stay ashore?" I asked Skip.

"Well, we can start with the cook," he said.

This came as a great surprise to me. Alexey Drosdovski, our

cook, was actually the crew doctor as well and had been invited to join FAZISI at the very last moment at Skip's categorical request. Skip had simply refused to go on the boat if there were no doctor on board. Amazed at how easily he'd changed his mind, I listened as Skip continued, "There wasn't much for him to do as a medicine man and he's not good in the galley. It seems as if the other guys don't care for him as well."

"I don't know, Skip," Brian chimed in, "Doc's got his problems, sure, but you know as well as I do that cooks the world over get a bad rap. This guy has been kicked around and used as a political football. I'm not sure we understand some of the nuances that go on among the guys."

Brian's point was well taken. It was too easy to blame the cook. Was he just a symbol of a larger problem, I wondered? Was there a much larger danger looming, or was it Skip just exaggerating? Hard to tell—and I still hadn't heard Alexey Grischenko's opinion yet. I wanted to talk to Brian more as well, but it was too late. I was too tired and jet-lagged after my long journey, and he unfortunately was leaving on an early flight later that morning.

How bad could it be? They had managed to come in sixth after all, hadn't they?

• • •

I could see right away that the first leg had put a lot of strain on Alexey. He seemed happy with the results and had enjoyed sailing on the ocean. We chatted about his experiences for a while, and with a spark in his eyes, he told me about FAZISI's performance, about the moments of sheer joy while surfing among the mountainous waves. She was his boat as much as mine, the fruit of his labors, which he, unlike me, had been lucky enough to sail on the high seas. I was almost envious.

But then the sparkle faded away when he said, "It was great, but also tough. After this experience, I honestly don't think that either FAZISI or the crew is ready for the Southern Ocean. I made a long list of what needs to be done to prepare the boat, but it seems like no one wants to do anything anymore. Discipline is totally out of hand and I am tired of pushing them. And I know they are tired, too. I don't believe we will be able to make the boat ready for the second leg…"

Not wanting him to concentrate on this negative generalization, I suggested we go through his list of things to do instead. The biggest job was to insulate the deck and topsides with one-inch-thick foam, sheets of which were packed in one of the two containers we had shipped from England. Outside temperatures in the Southern Ocean could often drop well below freezing, making life unbearable inside an aluminum boat without insulation. The job would require at least a full week, but that's okay, we had time. There were still three weeks before the start of the second leg. Among other necessary jobs on Alexey's list were: to build proper food storage, a dry locker, and arrange a basic bench for sail repairs under way. And then, of course, routine maintenance of the boat, checking and re-tuning the rigging; dismantling, cleaning off the salt and lubricating the winches; and checking every seam of the sails and making repairs as necessary.

It was enough to keep everyone busy for the whole stopover, but no matter how you looked at it, it could all be easily completed without putting a strain on the crew, while still having enough time for rest. The situation was drastically different from the pre-start rush in England, and I couldn't see why Alexey was worrying so much. It seemed like both co-captains were unhappy, albeit their concerns were different. I wasn't sure whether Skip's reasons were justified, but it was apparent that Alexey wasn't assessing the situation adequately. More than anyone else, he seemed in need of rest to restore his usual positive attitude.

His other concern was the future of the whole project in general. His view was that it really didn't make much sense to do anything, to work hard and prepare the boat to continue, when we had no money to go any further. I kept my fingers crossed that we wouldn't have much of a bill from the Uruguay stopover. If we were careful, we would be able to cover most of the routine expenses with the leftover money we still had. But that would be it.

Of course, the money concerns were very serious indeed, but to give up now, after FAZISI's first triumph? I had already made peace with the fact that we'd probably never get our big break, that the project would remain agonizing. Yet, with hard work, a little luck and God's providence, we just might be able to continue. We had gone so far, hadn't we? Somehow we would find a way to keep moving, and step after small and arduous step, we would inch forward. There's always hope. Only if we give up, then that would be the end of it.

We just needed to concentrate and pull it. Besides, there was no road back to Soviet Union, other than after successful completion of the race.

• • •

Fundraising was again the main task at hand.

"Forget about it," Skip told me. "Uruguay is such a remote country, no one cares about the Whitbread here. Besides, there isn't a lot of money here to start with. Don't even waste your time. Let's just hope that Jock Wishart is able to do something. If not, we're history."

I wasn't so sure. First of all, I didn't believe that Jock's talks with Pepsi had gone anywhere. That whole chapter was history, granted. Then, another of Jock's darlings, some huge anonymous Soviet company — he refused to provide us with the name — was supposedly ready to jump in with major sponsorship. As we hadn't left any stone unturned in Russia, that sure sounded like more bullshit. Russia's economy was rapidly deteriorating. There simply was no company that would be able to spend hard currency, much less the huge sum Jock was talking about. I knew this was a dead end. We had no other choice but to rely on ourselves.

A couple of days later, Chumakov and I drove to Montevideo, visited the Soviet Embassy and the Chamber of Commerce, and got a list of local companies doing business with the Soviet Union. Methodically, we called each and eventually came upon Amenco, Otegui, and Comurex, three local companies selling wool and leather goods to a subsidiary of a Russian *Vneshtorg* monopoly called *Novoexport*. The companies wanted to expand and considered supporting FAZISI as a way to improve their stature in the eyes of the Soviet authorities. Of course, we couldn't guarantee them successful lobbying before the authorities, but luckily it had turned out that Alexander Kedishvili happened to know people at *Novoexport* who were dealing with the Uruguayan companies. He quickly arranged a meeting in Moscow to discuss a deal that would benefit everybody. It wasn't our break yet, but at least it was something, the first ray of hope.

• • •

I don't think the guys in the crew were fully aware of our desperate situation, and I didn't want to depress them with details. Even if I tried, they wouldn't care. The triumphant finish in Punta had instantly changed their status from underdogs, who attracted only curiosity, and had instantly propelled them into celebrity stardom. They had overcome insurmountable odds and now claimed respect. After accomplishing what everyone thought impossible, who knows what these guys

Everybody hangs on as FAZISI is broadsided by another big wave.

FAZISI slides effortlessly through the waves on a broad reach.

Top: Beautiful sailing day in the Atlantic Ocean.
Middle: Monstrous iceberg hides behind the foggy mist. Photo: Juki Tsomaya.
Bottom: Before the start of fourth leg in Auckland, NZ.

Top: Training session in Auckland harbor.
Middle: Sunset paints capricious patchwork of light and shadows on FAZISI sails.
Bottom: Kuli seems oblivious to the attention of huge crowds in Auckland, NZ.

Top: FAZISI construction at Poti Shipbuilding Yard.
Photo: Fazis SP.
Left: Valery Chumakov (on the left) is checking Edgar's work servicing the rig.
Right: Juki repairs cracks on the rudder. Later, during the third leg, the whole blade practically got off the carbon fiber stock and was replaced in Auckland, NZ.

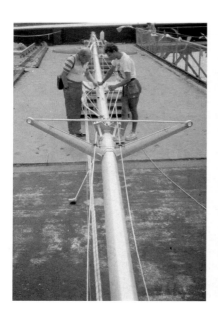

FAZISI in the row of Whitbread yachts during the Fremantle stopover is being readying for the next meeting with the ocean.

Bow section of the boat forward of the mast was totally empty and separated by a watertight bulkhead. Clearly visible is a sophisticated structural framework that supported the thin aluminum shell.

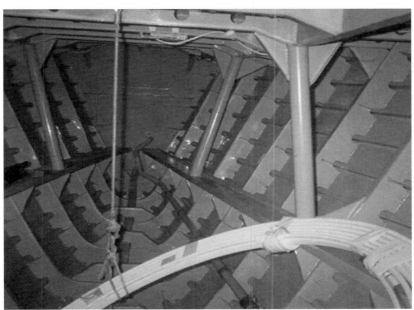

Tatiana and I are standing in front of our improvised office in Palace Hotel, Punta del Este during her short holidays in Uruguay.

Trying to figure out how to patch a huge gap in the sailcloth, the crew swarms around the mainsail torn into pieces in the ocean after rounding Cape Horn.

Skip at the navigation station. In front of him is chart table; to the left -- a shelf with radio stations, Decca/ Loran and GPS.

Battling THE CARD during the stormy start of the third leg in
Fremantle.
Relaxing after watch. I am sitting (on the right) together with
Edgar Terekhin and Dave Mathews.

Water rushes over the deck with power of fire hydrant.

Airborn ballet during a spinnaker change.

Victor Pogrebnov (on the left) and Juki Tsomaya look happy at the sight of the Isle of Wight.

might be capable of. Working practically nonstop, they had completed FAZISI in time, gotten her to the starting line, and then performed a miracle, beating most of the fleet on a completely untried boat.

But now unexpected glory was too much for the crew to handle, and overwhelmed with the euphoria of their first success, they completely lost a sense of discipline and self-control. We all know what sailors are like when coming to port after a lengthy sea voyage. Try to imagine what it was like for these guys, who in effect had disembarked off the ironship of the Soviet system, where they had spent their whole lives.

All they wanted now was to celebrate, resisting any attempts to steer them toward a life of hard work and responsibility. Not again! The tensions were building gradually until one of our usual short morning meetings, when we discussed the projects for the day, turned into a spontaneous protest.

It started with angry remarks, some crewmembers had thrown at Grischenko and me. Then Anatoly Verba stepped forward and proclaimed, "We have a very serious matter to discuss. The whole crew disagrees with the way the project is being managed. We've prepared a list of grievances and request that it be faxed to Fazis SP office in Moscow."

He handed me a long memorandum. It was clear now that the protest was not spontaneous at all and had been carefully prepared and orchestrated in advance.

Under other circumstances, most of their requests might have been reasonable, like a pay increase, or bringing their wives to every stopover. If only there was enough money. They also requested reduced working hours and more free time — again, guys, don't you want this boat to be ready for the next leg? Don't you want to go sailing anymore?

It seemed as if they were forgetting that the whole project was ours — theirs as well — initiative. Fazis SP had no obligation to make it easier or more comfortable for them. Tikhov had backed us with a lot of money and did as much as he could. Actually, he had gone much further than was reasonable or prudent. He was risking a lot; no one realized just how much — at least his position, his future, and maybe much more, all just to make the project a success. And now these guys demanded still more. These pure, altruistic sailors, who just a year ago didn't even want to talk about pay, who were ready to do anything for the chance to sail around the world, now wanted more money — and less work — and they wanted to be taken care of. The mentality of the

Soviet system of dependency had been too deeply implanted in them.

"Okay, are these all your requests?"

"No," said Anatoly, trying not to meet my eyes, and continued, "we also do not like your having so much power in the project. We are in the free world. It's a democracy here. Now we don't need bosses anymore. We know better ourselves what to do."

"Are you finished now? "

"Not so fast," he answered, getting into the leader's role and becoming more and more confident, "we want Chumakov out of the project. We don't need commissars anymore. And we don't need any foreigners either. We could sail this boat much better ourselves without someone directing our every move."

Anatoly was definitely feeling as if he was already FAZISI's captain and was full of himself. The mood of the crew had clearly shifted to his side. Obviously, all the guys from Odessa supported him, but now Eugene Platon, who belonged to the Kiev contingent, sensing the shift of power, abandoned his partisan interests and jumped to the opposition's camp. It seemed only Igor Mironenko remained loyal to Alexey Grischenko. It was not a mutiny yet, but getting close to one.

Alexey was even more distressed now. He felt as if he had lost control of the crew completely, and that was not far from reality. He had already made the decision to skip the next leg of the race, go home for a couple of months, and join the crew later in Australia. He needed the rest badly. It was obvious that he was totally exhausted and couldn't continue at this point. But he also understood that if he left now, the crew might not accept him as captain later. Besides, he was probably reluctant to go back home to the humiliation of being a loser, as his fellow Russians would view it, as the captain who was not strong enough to go all the way. I realized that he was under a lot of pressure, but at no point did I imagine what really was going on in his mind. He couldn't make his decision for a while, and when he finally did, it was the worst one.

On October 9, 1989, Alexey committed suicide, leaving a short note that explained nothing.

The night before he had been unusually cheerful and told me that he was really looking forward to going home and couldn't wait to see his family again. He had already bought some souvenirs and presents for his newborn daughter and wondered whether they would be right. It was his first baby and he had no experience at being a parent. With Valery Chumakov's help, Alexey had scheduled the date of his departure and inquired about the formalities he might face at the airport.

The next morning he showed up for our usual brief meeting, but I didn't see him on the boat at all during the day. I became slightly alarmed when he didn't appear for dinner, which we always had at El Metehon Restaurant with the whole crew. Igor Mironenko, Alexey's closest friend, had not seen him all day as well, but reminded me of the time in England, during the keel change, when Alexey locked himself away, disappearing for a few days. Together we went to his hotel room and knocked on the door, but there was no answer.

"He probably went for a walk along the shore. He likes to walk alone late at night. Recently he has preferred to be alone," Miron said, then wished me a good night and headed for his room. Considering Alexey's current state, I was alarmed but still didn't worry too much. He was, after all, a grown up man and had a right to his privacy. He would probably show up tomorrow with the same explanation as in England, "I needed time to gather myself. I'm okay now."

But he didn't.

By the next morning I became seriously worried that he might have had an accident. What if he had been hit by a car or wandered into a bad part of town and gotten into trouble? Maybe he was in the hospital somewhere, lying unconscious or, not knowing a word of Spanish, was unable to explain who he was. Skip and I walked down to the Whitbread office and talked to Race Chairman Admiral Williams. A great person and a real old-fashioned gentleman, he had run the race for many years and contributed a lot to its success. For all of us Whitbread sailors, he became almost a parental figure, and we knew that in case of trouble, he would always be ready to provide advice and support.

Admiral Williams was serious and attentive listening to our story, but then tried to reassure us that probably nothing bad had happened, "You know, sailors are sailors. It's nothing extraordinary for a sailor to disappear for a day or two. Especially after what you guys have been through, one would probably need a break."

Nevertheless, he promised to inform the Uruguayan police.

The next morning while I was working in the office, Admiral Williams walked in with Skip.

"Vladislav, I am afraid there is very bad news. Alexey Grischenko committed suicide." The word was new to me and I didn't understand its meaning.

"What happened? What's he saying?" I said looking at Skip.

"Alexey hanged himself." Skip made a gesture around his neck to make sure I understand. "His body was found in the forest. Now the police need someone who knew him to identify it. Would you go?"

I sat frozen, refusing to accept what I'd heard.

Admiral Williams took a step forward and put his hand on my shoulder, "I am very sorry ..."

He hanged himself? How could it be? How could someone make such a terrible, such an ultimate decision, no matter what the circumstances were? He seemed to be okay the last night I had seen him and was really looking forward to going home. What made him change his mind?

Later, I heard nasty rumors circulating among the crew that Alexey had in fact come to our rigging container the morning he disappeared. He was weary and exhausted, as if he'd spent a sleepless night. Apparently someone told him, "You look like shit. Dead people look better. If life's so miserable, why don't you take a rope, there's plenty of them here, and go hang yourself?" Probably it was meant to be some sort of stupid black humor, but in Alexey's state this phrase could be enough to break the fragile balance of his mind. He did, in fact, use a rope from our container.

But no, I just rejected the thought that there might be such an asshole in the crew who could have pushed him. They were not angels, no, I knew it all too well, but not cruel people either. Besides this was just a rumor, just a whisper in the corner, which no one had the courage to say out loud.

The news of Alexey's death spread immediately through the entire Whitbread camp. Every team sent their representatives to a vigil that night, held according to the Orthodox tradition. A long line of unusually silent and solemn sailors wound across the courtyard, each entered the small, empty, and dim candle-lit room, passed Alexey's portrait decorated with flowers on the opposite wall, drank a glass of red wine, and read the eulogy written in English by Eugene.

The next few days were a total blur. I was acting like a zombie, doing my routine job, but with only one thought pounding in my brain the whole time, "If only I hadn't started this whole thing, nothing would have happened. Why did I go and invite Alexey? Why did I decide to do this damn project in the first place?" The thought overwhelmed everything, and there was no answer, nor escape. Alexey's death took me to the bottom of the barrel. Skip told me later that I had gone to the morgue to identify his body. I didn't even remember.

Three days later, unable to cope with the grief, I went to a local store, bought a bottle of vodka, and drank almost all of it that night. It helped to reduce the pain for a few hours, but in the morning it was back again, along with a terrible hangover. Surprisingly, the only man who supported me and helped me get though this ordeal was Valery Chumakov. Who would have expected that this emotionless and sometimes boring man — not any of my romantic fellow sailors — would become the only person I could count on in crisis?

• • •

There was a night when walking along the empty rocky shore, I stumbled onto a small chapel nestled far out on the edge of the tide line. It was like a tiny shrine, maybe six feet tall with a statue of the Virgin Mary inside. I fell on my knees and prayed.

I do believe in God, though my faith back in Russia was rather naïve and more emotional than spiritual. I didn't go to church often, as it was a place of older people, and they wouldn't have appreciated a representative of the younger generation wandering in. Orthodox religion is extremely strict, and there is a whole code on how to dress and act inside the church. I was simply unfamiliar with it. Besides, the service was performed in old Slavic, which I didn't understand for the most part. I had a Bible that had been passed on to me from my grandfather. I liked to read it, but it was written in the same old language too, which was really difficult to read. And honestly, I wasn't persistent enough.

I very seldom talked about my faith. I didn't feel like a missionary in my soul, and anyway, I knew too little for that. Besides, I must admit, I had a fear — not of persecution, because the era of being jailed for your beliefs was long gone — but a fear of being ridiculed. On those rare occasions when I shared my beliefs, people would just laugh, "You're a smart guy, Vladislav, how could you believe in all that stuff in our scientific age? Hopefully you don't believe that the Earth is flat?" Blindsided by ideology, they arrogantly considered themselves too educated or too intelligent to be believers. Sadly, 70 years of communist brainwashing had worked.

Growing up in the 1930s under the watchful eye of the Communist Party, my parents were not religious people. But my grandparents, like most of their generation, were. They were born at the end of the nineteenth century and brought up before the Bolsheviks took power in 1917. Close to the end of his life, my grandfather was a very sick man, practically immobilized. He couldn't attend services at the church, so instead read the Bible most of the time, so much that he got to the point of being able to recite long passages by heart, page after page, without ever glancing at the text. His favorite was the Book of Revelation. Hour after hour, he would tell me about the end of the world when the righteous would walk out of their graves and rejoice in the eternal kingdom.

To a small child, it was extremely scary but also irresistibly fascinating. I was a curious kid and early on had started questioning what life is, whether it has any purpose, and what kind of miracle had brought us into the world. The evolution theory, which we were taught at school from the early grades, was not a good enough answer for me. How could such a glorious universe emerge from chaos? "Following the laws of nature," answered the teacher. Well, if there are such laws, then someone should have established them? Certainly they couldn't have emerged from chaos. And human beings couldn't have created them. Those laws are too powerful and universal for mere mortals. Then there had to be someone with awesome supernatural powers? God?

No matter how hard my teachers tried to hammer the doctrines of materialism into my head, there was enough evidence all around me to see the superiority of the spirit. Besides all the reasons, I was also blessed with faith.

At first, my faith was childish and naïve. I remember praying to God and asking him to improve my grades on exams. And He did! Since then I often felt the presence of God in my life, though sometimes — many times — I got confused and failed to follow the right path.

My Whitbread endeavor certainly had its purpose. I didn't know what it was exactly, but there was God's plan that had led me through the obstacles that I would never have been able to overcome on my own. From the beginning, I knew that this would be a difficult road, a real test. But why, oh Lord, did this test have to be so terrible, so ultimate?

While I prayed, I sensed peace entering my soul for the first time in many days. Walking back to the hotel, I felt different — much stronger. I still didn't have any clear answers, and the future remained uncertain, but I felt as if I had received encouragement to overcome this tragedy and go on.

• • •

A few days later we received a sponsorship offer from Otegui, Comurex, and Amenco, enough money to cover the stopover in Punta and a promise for more when we returned to Punta on our way back.

Alexey's death had sobered the crew. What Russians are capable to do best is to unite in face of tragedy. The rebelous attitude had evaporated without a trace, and the crew had again become a disciplined team working hard on the boat, determined to continue the race. A new seven-page memorandum, drafted by the crew and signed by each of them provided enough reasons to show Fazis SP and the Soviet authorities that despite the tragedy, the crew "is psychologically and functionally ready to continue the race, the boat complies with technical requirements, and is completely prepared for the race." It also stated that "it is worthwhile to include into the crew several experienced professional sailors, led by Skip Novak." Evidently, no one was against foreigners anymore.

Unfortunately, now the continuation of the race no longer depended on the crew attitude, nor on the additional financial backing we had received. The tragic incident had become big news worldwide – and in the Soviet press as well — probably getting us more publicity than we had ever received during all the preceding time. And it was the worst kind of publicity. The tone of some of the articles was really mean-spirited. *Komsomolskaya Pravda*, one of the major Soviet newspapers, published a feature story headlined, "Would the boat hold, would the people hold?" The author went on, "... I intentionally never use the word Soviet characterizing this boat. FAZISI was not registered in any of the Soviet registries." (That was a lie. In strict compliance with the regulations of the USSR, the boat, in fact, was registered on the roster of the port of Poti). "No Soviet port allowed the vessel into the sea... in a word, we are talking about private initiative. Moreover, from the very beginning, the design raised a lot of doubts among the specialists."

Then three interviews followed: with the Russian Olympic star Vladislav Akimenko, who initially had been on FAZISI's crew list and had spent some time in Poti during the construction, but later drifted away; with Boris Nemirov, the first Soviet sailor to circumnavigate the globe just a year earlier; and with an official from the Sport Committee, who claimed that FAZISI's design had never been approved by the Russian Sailing Federation. Not true. I had presented full set of documentation that was officially approved by the Technical Committee, although bureaucrats from the Sport Committee fiercely fought against it. Moreover, the American Bureau of Shipping, an organization that certainly carries much greater respect than the Soviet *Goscomsport*, approved the design as well. It was one of the safety requirements of the Whitbread that every participating boat must have its design approved by ABS, and we had passed the test with flying colors.

Probably well aware that their arguments were "sucked from the finger," as Russians say, everyone quoted in *Komsomolskaya Pravda* nevertheless condemned our project in one way or another. Boris Nemirov said, "For me it was obvious that disaster was inevitable. Of course, no one expected it to happen this way. I'd rather be inclined to expect someone would be washed overboard."

Sailors from Alexey's Kiev Yacht Club prepared an open letter, which was published in a few newspapers. It read, "...we have to express our doubts on the reliability of the existing version about the suicide of A. Grischenko. We believe that his death couldn't have happened without direct or indirect outside assistance ... we request the initiation of a criminal inquest into the death of A. Grischenko, and conduction of a thorough investigation of the causes and the circumstances surrounding his death."

There also were requests to prohibit FAZISI from continuing to fly the Soviet flag. Not that the privilege to carry it mattered that much to me any longer, still it was painful to realize that my own country was not supporting me – and our entire crew — in such a tragic time, but was rather looking for ways to punish.

All this media outcry scared Fazis to the point where it was on the verge of pulling the plug and abandoning the whole project altogether. Victor Tikhov requested that I fly back to Moscow and report to him, in person, on what had happened.

PART III

BACK TO LIFE

14

TROUBLED WATERS

Waiting for the Aeroflot flight at the Buenos Aires International airport, I tried to rationally assess my options. There certainly was a risk in returning to Moscow. The suicide of the Soviet skipper had become international news and a worldwide embarrassment of perestroika, and, overwhelmed with grief, I was also sick with worry and fear. The phrase from the Cold War novels, "He was recalled to Moscow to report" now bore new and personally frightening meaning to me. In those novels, after he went back, you never heard of the guy again. Now it was me who was recalled to fly back to Moscow to report.

According to unwritten protocol, when something really bad happened in the Soviet Union, it was never considered an accident, an act beyond human control, but rather someone's fault or even a deliberate ill-intentioned deed. The Bolshevik's paranoia, developed after the 1917 revolution, saw enemies and conspirators everywhere, and resulted in the terrible Soviet tradition of finding a scapegoat to punish for any incident, without much consideration of whether the person was guilty or not. The tone in the Russian newspapers after Alexey's death was ominous, and I was really afraid to stick my head back into the lion's cage. I certainly didn't want to become the scapegoat.

Here in Buenos Aires was the headquarters of world-famous naval architect German Frers, who had two boats of his design in the Whitbread, MARTELA from Finland and BRITISH SATQUOTE DEFENDER. I was fairly sure he was aware of FAZISI, and I probably wouldn't need any introduction. For a while, I was seriously considering walking away from the airport, taking a taxi, and showing up in his office to apply for a job and political asylum. Surely, this would put an end to the whole Whitbread affair, and instead of plunging into the treacherous Southern Ocean, FAZISI would be returned to the Soviet

Union. Who knows, maybe that wouldn't be such a bad idea. It would cut short her agony.

I toyed with the thought for a while. It was so tempting—and yet I wasn't ready to give up. Besides, if I chose to stay in Argentina, I would probably never see my family again. I was still considering the options when the boarding for my flight was announced. I picked up my bag and slowly walked onto the plane. Half an hour later, I was high in the sky heading back to Russia.

Only three weeks before, flying to Punta to meet a triumphant (but totally broke) FAZISI, I was sure that we were in the deepest trouble yet, with the project reaching its inevitable dead end. The only comforting thought then had been that it couldn't get any worse. But it had. A lot. Yet some strange and wonderful thing had also happened to me back in Punta, on that rocky shore where I had encountered the little shrine. Now, despite Alexey's death, I was returning home more at peace than when I left for Punta.

Tikhov's stern order for me to return to Moscow notwithstanding, I was almost sure that he wouldn't back off now. I knew him too well for that. The man was a fighter, and he would stand up and continue struggling as long as there was even the slimmest chance. Of course, both of us would face really tough times defending our decision to continue FAZISI's voyage, but I felt that he would be on my side. I just sincerely hoped that things had now changed enough in Russia so that the decision was within Tikhov's power. Only a couple years ago, one phone call from the Party Committee would have been enough to bring the entire project to a dead halt and put our lives in misery. Who knows, maybe it still held the same power.

With nothing yet settled in Russia and the future more uncertain than ever, I couldn't help looking beyond the inevitable ordeal awaiting me at home, beyond even the next stopover in Fremantle, which I knew would be a tough one to get through financially. I was looking toward New Zealand.

First, it was Skip who told me time after time, "If only we can make it to New Zealand... you'll love the country. Nearly every family there owns a boat and has something to do with sailing. The country is more than a thousand miles long from north to south, but at no place are you more than 30 miles from the ocean.

"Auckland is practically surrounded by water. It's so beautiful, you must see it to believe it. They don't call it a sailing paradise for nothing.

"In the previous Whitbreads, there always were at least one or two boats from New Zealand, totally supported by people, without any corporate backing. Imagine how high the enthusiasm toward sailing is there. And they love to support underdogs.

"This time both New Zealand boats are totally sponsored by big guns, and there's no 'people's boat' in the race. Imagine the possibilities..."

Still in Punta, I had talked a few times to Peter Blake and Grant Dalton, skippers of the two New Zealand entries, and they enthusiastically shared with me their invaluable local NZ media, marketing, and PR contacts. Grant Dalton was even able to get his sponsor, the manufacturer of home appliances named Fisher and Paykel — and closely affiliated with Panasonic — interested. Their last word before I left Punta was, "We are considering specific things we could do for FAZISI."

Next, the Tremain family got involved.

Dale Tremain, the New Zealander invited by Skip to join the FAZISI crew for the second leg, was the younger brother of Carol Tremain, who ran the North Sails portable service loft. With a small team and a full workshop in a container, she followed the Whitbread fleet, providing repair and maintenance services at all stopovers. As almost all of FAZISI's sail inventory had come from North Sails, Carol was already very much involved with our project. Now, with Dale Tremain joining the crew, the time came for their older brother to get involved as well. Clive Tremain was a freelance boatbuilder and small-scale entrepreneur in Auckland. While I was still in Uruguay, he got in touch and suggested organizing a grass-roots fundraising effort.

"By the time FAZISI reached New Zealand, at least $100,000 NZ would be waiting for her," said Clive, sounding really enthusiastic and confident, "It might be even more, if we start right away and allow ourselves more time. FAZISI and her crew have already made quite a stir here and people are amazed at what you've accomplished so far. I am sure they will do what they can to help you."

Clive went on in his Kiwi accent, "I'll establish a FAZISI fund, where they can send their contributions. Tis' a small country, but everyone loves sailing and many'd be eager to participate. The centerpiece of my effort will be a merchandising program with different types of FAZISI T-shirts, hats, pins, you name it. I already have some great design ideas. How 'bout 'The Russians Are Coming!' slogan printed up front? Believe me, this T-shirt will be a smashing success! So hang in there, guys, just keep moving. Remember, we're expecting you here."

If only we could make it to New Zealand, I prayed high in the sky en route to Moscow. It would be the halfway point...

But as the plane continued its flight, with the USSR getting closer and closer, my unfounded optimism began to diminish, giving way to grim anticipation of what was awaiting me ahead.

• • •

The reception at home was bad, but not actually as bad an inquisition as I had expected. Of course, the officials from the Sport Committee and the people who had been rejected from the team earlier on enjoyed their revenge now. I went through lengthy meetings, plenty of accusations and rude questions, yet I was surprised to find that many people understood what I had been through and even tried to console me. Even so, the calamitous times following my return from Punta remain to this day painful — even after so many years. It still hurts to think about it.

The worst was the trip to Kiev to meet Alexey's friends and family, and to deliver his belongings and his last note to his wife and mother. It was a heart-breaking ordeal, and I probably would not have been able to get through it without the support of FAZISI crewmember Nodari Teneishvili, who volunteered to go to Kiev with me. Over and over we were asked the same questions. Over and over we repeated the little that we knew about Alexey's ultimate decision. First it was his wife, then the next day his mother and sister, who still refused to accept the tragic reality, and finally his friends in the Kiev Yacht Club.

And not only friends. I knew, Alexey had also had a lot of hostile rivals at the club as well, those who did not like his straightforward and frank attitude. A great boat builder, he had been elected the technical supervisor for the yacht club's fleet. He took that responsibility very seriously, making sure that all the boats, especially those homebuilt (which were plentiful in the Kiev Yacht Club), were technically sound and safe. Extremely demanding on himself, he expected others to maintain the same high standards. Those standards were probably too high for some and occasionally led to disagreements, leaving many alienated and discontented. But it seemed that at least in his death they had finally made peace with Alexey.

According to the old tradition, the yacht club arranged a lengthy vigil in Grischenko's honor. There was an empty chair for him at the head of the table with a full glass of vodka and a piece of rye bread on a simple white plate in front of it. People came and went, silently drinking to Alexey's memory and asking us the same questions over and over, again and again, as we continued to repeat the tragic story — that tormenting evening seemed to last forever.

It was clear that those who had gathered for this farewell ritual knew very little about our project, except for the scarce information, which had been released by officials. They had no clue as to why such a strong and cheerful guy as Alexey would commit suicide. And who could blame them? It was too difficult even for the crew to grasp the pressures he had felt... I would like to believe that with our help, in the end his close friends were able to recognize the scale of Alexey's accomplishments and, to some extent, understand the enormous odds he was fighting against. I hope, they began to register at least a glimpse of the tormenting doubts that tore him and ultimately pushed him to his grave decision.

Many, however, were simply unable to understand all this, inclined instead to stick to a theory that circulated around Kiev Yacht Club for quite a while and even penetrated into the Soviet press. They were convinced that there was a sort of international conspiracy going on intended to prevent Soviet sailors from entering the most prestigious ocean race, to stop FAZISI at any cost. They suspected that Alexey had fallen victim to it.

It was well beyond midnight and too many people had come and gone. The same torturous questions had been asked too many times. Everyone had too much vodka, and when it ended, I was absolutely exhausted by the vigil, which at times had seemed more like the prosecutor's interrogation. Nodari and I felt cornered by the endless inquiries that had been hurled at us. We knew full well that, no matter how many times they asked, no one would ever find out what was going on in his mind that fateful day, what made him to do what he did.

While they were contemplating the theory of a capitalist conspiracy against the first-ever Soviet yacht, a question infinitely more important to me surfaced again in my mind — the same one that haunted me during the sleepless nights in Punta del Este, "Why did I start all this three years ago? Is it worth such a terrible price?"

And again, the vision of the tiny shrine on the ocean-buffeted rocks whispered an almost elusive answer, "Everyone chooses his own path... let it go. Losses are inevitable, but one must continue on... go on. Why are you so much in doubt? Why do you have so little faith?..."

• • •

As I had anticipated, Victor Tikhov stood firm on my side, committed to continue FAZISI's endeavor.

"If we stop now, after Alexey's death, all this tragedy and suffering was for nothing," he told me. "You've been able to get sponsorship in Uruguay, which everyone thought impossible. Now New Zealand looks promising. True, this whole thing has turned totally opposite of what we had anticipated. But we simply cannot give up now. Let's keep working, hoping for the future. We must complete this journey."

Again, I found myself not only deep into day-to-day Whitbread project management, but also into the Fazis SP business as well, helping Tikhov to capitalize on whatever positive impact our project might still have. Flipping through the pages of my old appointment book of that time, I can find notes of conversations with boat builders, sailmakers, and yacht brokers from all over the world, as I tried to establish a solid boating business for Fazis SP. It seemed so logical: we had good designs, access to the best materials (now more easily available from the downsized military industry), inexpensive labor, and even some experience and international contacts. Together with our new friends from Otegui, we also tried selling Poti-built hydrofoil ferries to Uruguay to establish an express service between Montevideo and Buenos Aires, with possible extended service to Punta del Este.

In the end, none of it materialized. I think Fazis SP was just trying to do too many things simultaneously, sinking in the everyday struggle without a clear vision of the future. The net that had been thrown was much too wide—from selling pigskin to building Mega yachts with everything else in between. What a combination indeed—but I can't judge Tikhov. After all, he was only trying to survive in those crazy times, doing whatever possible pretty much the same way I did with my Whitbread project, one day at a time.

After all the events in Punta, my first priority was to develop a long-overdue, formal structure for the FAZISI project. It would be almost like a strict corporate plan. Who's who, who's in charge of what, etc. Hoping it would clarify their positions, rights and obligations, I also drafted a pro-forma contract for the crewmembers. I had learned the hard way that romantic attitude of the project's idealist beginning had completely evaporated. For better or worse, it had grown into a strictly business affair, and subsequently, it had to be run as a business. Of course, I didn't hold any illusions that these structural improvements would eliminate all future problems, but at least it would provide some common ground for solving them.

Again, I pulled out my old list of potential sponsor contacts and went through the most promising ones. Alexander Kedishvili added a few new names from the rapidly changing Moscow business arena. We actually made some progress in our negotiations with the Dresdner Bank, but soon it became clear to me that it was all too late now. After Pepsi had grabbed the publicity cream off the top, it was totally naïve to expect major corporate sponsorship anymore. All we could hope for was local support at each stopover.

In the meantime, Jock Wishart kept me entertained with his faxes about yet another potential sponsorship deal, which this time would finally rain upon us with so longed-for money. Sure, Jock.

All in all, it was a very busy month in Moscow.

• • •

This time I was much more interested in FAZISI's progress than during the first leg, and talked frequently to Skip through the SSB marine radio via a ship-to-shore station in England. The reception was great. It was, in fact, unbelievable, considering that we were on the opposite sides of the globe. The news from FAZISI — well, it was mostly bad.

Of course, she made the start of the second leg, the longest leg not only of this race, but also of any Whitbread thus far. The route, more than 7,000 miles long, would take the fleet from Punta del Este to Fremantle, Australia, through the most treacherous waters of the Southern Ocean, leaving the southernmost tip of Africa to port. But first, before the boats reached the Roaring Forties with their steady westerlies, they would need to pass through the area of light variable winds that surrounds every major landmass, South America included. This was the area where FAZISI suffered the most. After the mutilation she had been through during the keel change in Hamble, she was no light-wind champion. Much heavier than intended, she really hated light, unsettled weather, and during the first few days after the start of leg two, FAZISI quickly dropped down to the middle of the fleet in ranking.

Then the storms finally came, one following another, and FAZISI came alive in her element. But bad weather soon started taking its toll. One day, after a spectacular crashing broach performed by Elephant, FAZISI recovered sans spinnaker, with a broken spinnaker pole (luckily there was another one on board), and the headfoil shattered into pieces. The next day Skip grimly informed me that two more spinnakers had been ripped apart. Result: FAZISI's downwind inventory had been reduced to half, and together with the inability to make fast headsail changes due to the loss of the double-luff headfoil, she was greatly disadvantaged. And, of course, also gone was my hope for a small repair bill in Fremantle.

It was only the beginning. With just ten days since the start of the second leg and so much breakage already, I knew that more bad news was bound to come as FAZISI plunged deeper and deeper into the Southern Ocean. Sure enough, the next crisis was not far off.

"Vladislav, we have another big fuck-up here," the message came straightforward and to the point, in Skip's usual manner, "the spare mainsail had been washed away from the afterdeck. Sorry, man. It's been tied there all right, but then a big one came from the quarter, hit us real hard, and the next thing we knew there was no main on deck."

Bye, bye $35,000. Don't you guys have any idea of how to secure the sails properly? And how am I supposed to take this news to Victor Tikhov? Shit, hadn't we had enough? "Why the hell was it tied on the afterdeck and not down below where it was supposed to be?" No comment. Now I feared talking to Skip and would start shaking nervously even long before I called him on the marine telephone.

"Vladislav, we had an accident... Eugene fell overboard but was immediately recovered, no harm's done... he's fine and the good thing is that now everybody's much more careful on the deck."

What next?

All this emotional roller coaster probably would have been much easier to bear had I been on the boat. The worst thing about the whole situation was that I had absolutely no control over it. Anticipating doomsday at any moment, I was gradually becoming a nervous wreck, "You always knew it wasn't going to be easy," I tried to remind myself, "This is the Whitbread, after all, the most grueling race of them all ... What else did you expect?"

At last FAZISI was in her element and soon, as on the first leg, she started to show what she was capable of. No more bad news came during my next radio rendezvous with Skip.

"We are having our best day ever! One hundred ninety-five miles in 12 hours, noon to midnight. We're into a 400-mile day!" His voice was ecstatic, and though half a world apart, I could feel the rush they were having.

Skip continued, "Now, as I'm talking to you, we're making 22 knots, wait a moment, it's 23.5 now and rising! It's 25 knots! Yes! Yes! ... I wish you were here, you would love it."

I wished it too. But I was stuck in the Fazis SP office and, as it was, all this excitement resembled nothing more than telephone sex.

Skip continued, "The night is beautiful, with bright skies and a half moon. The wind has subsided to about 40 knots, but the waves remain the biggest I've ever seen..."

They didn't make that 400-mile day but came very close. When the smoke cleared, FAZISI had covered 386 nautical miles in a 24-hour period, noon to noon. That's an average of 16.08 knots hour after hour, day and night! Not bad at all for a newcomer. As her designer, I was possibly just as ecstatic polling the faxes with my boat's positions and following her progress as were those guys in the ocean riding the biggest waves of their lives.

It turned out that FAZISI's 386-mile day became the second largest run for a 24-hour period of the entire Whitbread fleet during the race. Only FORTUNA did slightly better, topping it with a 394-mile day.

• • •

Now I was polling faxes from the race office at least twice a day, analyzing the performance of FAZISI and her rivals. On November 16 they arrived in the vicinity of Kerguelen Island, a barren mass of inhospitable rock, constantly pounded by monstrous breakers, and the only major land between Africa and Australia, some 2,300 miles from Fremantle. From her zigzag course, I could tell that at first Skip couldn't make up his mind whether to leave Kerguelen to port or to starboard. But as it became evident that another deep low system slightly to the south of the Great Circle was catching up with the fleet, he decided to play it safe and turned north of Kerguelen. The choice was made and as always consequences followed.

FISHER & PAYKEL and FORTUNA, who were in the lead now, had chosen the northern route as well, while STEINLAGER, MERIT, and MARTELA led the southern group. At this point, FAZISI moved forward into sixth position again. It seemed that once more she was emerging victorious from troubled waters. Would she be able to hold on and repeat the result of the first leg?

The very next day brought the answer.

Skip's voice was as frustrated as I've ever heard — more bad news, I knew it, and my heart sank.

"We've broken the boom ... It happened before dawn this morning, and by now we have pretty much squared things away. We already have a jury-rig in place, sort of Chinese-junk style, with improvised sheets leading down from every reef line. And you know, it works surprisingly well ... "

I didn't even try to imagine what a hell of a job they had performed in a full 50-knot gale, with a broken boom violently swinging around their heads. But I had known long ago that my guys really did shine when times got tough. Just like Mother Russia, which apparently could always find the strength to pull out from any hopeless situation. Who knows, maybe there is a bright future for her after all? If only she could figure out what to do after the tough times are over.

Skip continued, "In this wind we are doing probably as good as with our normal rig. Let's just hope that the wind doesn't die on us."

Three days later on November 19 they were still holding on. With about 1,300 miles to go, FAZISI clung to sixth position, now sharing it with THE CARD — again! FISHER & PAYKEL, 160 miles ahead, was still in the lead, followed closely by FORTUNA, STEINLAGER, and MERIT. Slightly behind FAZISI were GATORADE and MARTELA, and 180 miles to the southwest was a group of outsiders, including NCB IRELAND and SATQUOTE DEFENDER.

Unfortunately, in deciding to sail north of Kerguelen, FAZISI was pushed farther north than any other boat in the fleet. Her jury-rig, very difficult to control in the storm, only added to the problem. And now a huge area of high pressure with its inevitable light winds, slowly descended on the fleet from the equator, catching FAZISI first.

Just another stroke of bad luck. She was caught in the wrong place at the wrong time, a heavy-air boat sitting hopelessly at the edge of a high-pressure zone, while the others still enjoyed a decent breeze, sailing away little by little. If only Skip had stayed south longer, letting FAZISI have the wind she so enjoyed. But hey, he did exactly what I had asked him to do before leaving Punta. Actually I hadn't merely asked him; I had ordered him to play it safe during the second leg. And it was probably the right thing to do. Even north of Kerguelen, conditions were bad enough to break the boom. Who knows what might have happened had they ventured deeper south?

On November 22, still 630 miles from Fremantle, she fell 230 miles behind the leaders, while the boats behind shortened their gap to only 90 miles and just kept rolling on.

During the next radio conversation Skip was not a bit disappointed, but rather took it philosophically, "We're doing just fine considering the circumstances. As usual in light wind, the Russian contingent is spending most of the time sunbathing and reading old newspapers. I wonder, how the hell they keep them dry on this submarine… Dale is sailing the boat pretty much alone. Jim occasionally helps him, but who knows if that's worth it anymore. Seventh place, ninth, what's the big difference? ...Me? I am trying to finish Tolstoy's "War and Peace" before we reach Australia. Then there certainly won't be enough time ... it's a thick book, you know, so I'd better go back to my reading. See you soon in Fremantle."

Crippled FAZISI with her under-motivated crew kept moving slowly toward Australia for another five days. On November 27 they crossed the finish line and sailed into Fremantle harbor. They finished tenth and they managed to survive. Good enough for now.

15

THE ROUTE

The first Whitbread Round the World Race in 1973-74 followed the traditional eastbound route around the world established long ago by the clipperships seeking to get maximum use of the following winds. The very direction of the route was determined by the prevailing westerly winds in the Southern Hemisphere where most of the route lies. There were three stopovers: Cape Town, South Africa; Sydney, Australia; and Rio De Janeiro, Brazil. Over the years it went through changes and grew longer with more legs and stopovers. Some ports of call were eliminated and new ones established. In protest to the apartheid policy of the white-dominated regime, the Cape Town stopover was cancelled for the 1989-90 Whitbread. (It was reinstated for subsequent races after the first democratic elections were held in South Africa), and for the first time, the North American stopover in Fort Lauderdale was included. This brought the race to the United States and increased its worldwide exposure.

As a result, the route of the fifth Whitbread Round the World Race in 1989-90 was shaped like this:

Leg 1. Southampton, England, to Punta del Este, Uruguay, 5,950 nautical miles

Leg 2. Punta Del Este, Uruguay, to Fremantle, Australia, 7,260 miles

Leg 3. Fremantle to Auckland, New Zealand,   3,272 miles

Leg 4. Auckland to Punta del Este,   6,215 miles

Leg 5. Punta del Este to Fort Lauderdale,   5,475 miles

Leg 6. Fort Lauderdale to Southampton,   3,818 miles

The starting gun was fired on September 2, 1989, and the boats arrived back in the UK during the last week of May 1990. About half of the nine-month race was actually sailing, with the balance of time divided between five stopovers, each about three weeks long. The total race distance was 31,990 nautical miles. Of course, that was only the measurement of the shortest distance between the stopovers. In reality, the racers followed the wind, tacked, drifted, and in the end, sailed a much longer course.

Because of the curvature of the earth, the shortest distance between two points doesn't appear as a straight line on a map, but rather curves to the north in the Northern Hemisphere and to the south in the Southern, following the so-called Great Circle Route. That's why after leaving Punta del Este on leg two, the boats dove deeply south to latitude 50 degrees—some of them went even more south, closer to Antarctica—before sailing back north again to Fremantle. To understand the nature of this phenomenon, imagine yourself looking down at Earth from a satellite hovering directly above the South Pole. You can easily see that the shortest way from South America to Australia cuts through Antarctica, very close to the Pole itself. Now it's clear why those crazy Whitbread captains try to venture as far south as they dare, enduring the cold, the snowstorms, and the danger of collision with icebergs. They are simply trying to take a shortcut.

But it's not all that simple when Mother Nature comes into play. The empty, desolate body of water that surrounds Antarctica is called the Southern Ocean, though it couldn't be further from what people usually associate with the word "south." It's so cold there, even in summer, that were it fresh water, the ocean would be frozen. A human can only survive a few minutes in water of such temperature. Magnificent towering mountains of icebergs, broken from Antarctica's permanent ice shield, float in packs pushed by the wind and currents.

The Southern Ocean stretches up north to latitude 40 degrees where it meets much warmer waters and the hot, dry lands of Australia, South America, and Africa. These opposites never meet peacefully. When warm and cold waters and air masses collide there is always a continual struggle. And that's what happens on the entire 15,000-mile-long perimeter of the Southern Ocean. A gradient of pressure between cold and warm air generates strong winds, often reaching hurricane force. As the wind keeps strengthening, the air mass starts rotating (clockwise in Southern Hemisphere), creating a mighty cyclone, a huge vortex that can extend to 1,000 miles in diameter, or even more. The wind blows from the west in its northern quarter, but it could come from the east with all its fury in more southern latitudes. That's why there is always a limit to how far south the boats might descend without being hit by the heading storm.

Pushed by the so-called Coriolis force, the cyclones in turn move eastward themselves. This force, the result of the Earth's endless spinning around its own axis, affects everything, from the way water drains in the bathtub to artillery shells, directing the flow of mighty rivers, controlling the weather.

Nowhere on the planet does the orgy of natural forces take such a violent form as on the treacherous waters of the Southern Ocean. For the wind and waves to build, they need to have a significant open span (called fetch) with no obstacles. That's why a gale might blow on the open summit, while only a light leaf-rustling breeze exists deep in a protected valley. That's why waves on broad lakes can grow much higher than on small ponds.

Now imagine this: the open span of the Southern Ocean is endless.

The same cyclone could circle the Earth several times, compounding its strength; the same rogue wave could go around the globe again and again interfering with other ones, rising up to 50 feet, to 80 feet, to 100 feet. Who knows, maybe they could grow even higher, but the people who have met such enormous killer waves in the Southern Ocean never came back to tell the tale.

The place has no mercy on humans. Old salts who sailed these waters during the last century on square-riggers used to say: "Below 40 degrees south there are no God's laws. Below 50 degrees there is no God."

The inevitable question needs to be answered: why do people sail in those terrible waters? Why do they risk their lives in such a forbidden place? In the past the answer was simple: because of necessity. There was no other way to maintain commerce between Europe, America, and India, and between China and other Pacific countries than to sail around the great capes of the Southern Ocean: Cape Horn, Cape of Good Hope and Cape Leeuwin.

But that has long since changed. In recent times with the construction of the Suez and Panama Canals, all commercial traffic uses other, less-dangerous routes, and the Southern Ocean has become an even more uninhabited and desolate place. Now only a few hundred of the world's most brave stalwarts dare to challenge these waters from time to time during the Whitbread or the Around Alone, or some other crazy sailboat race.

Why? Because nowhere else on the planet does the joy of sailing come even close to the thrill of riding the monstrous waves of the Southern Ocean! Almost everyone who has been there returns again.

The remoteness of the place breeds a very special camaraderie among offshore sailors, for everyone knows that in case of disaster only a fellow competitor can come to your rescue.

• • •

The Atlantic Ocean legs of the Whitbread route are perhaps not as dangerous, but they offer challenges of their own. They can be more damaging to the yacht's race results, even if they don't pose a real physical threat.

The biggest question mark, of course, is presented by the doldrums, or as it is scientifically known, the Intertropical Convergence Zone (ITCZ). The blend of unsettled winds and prolonged dead calms spanning around the equator separates the northeasterly trade winds of Northern Hemisphere from the southeasterly trades that blow below the equator. Depending on local conditions, this area could greatly vary in its width and is not always calm, as the common perception has it. Fed by the energy of the hot tropical waters, short and violent thunderstorms are brewed there. Stirred by changing winds from all directions, confused waves and eddying currents add another element to the ITCZ enigma. It is only a matter of luck and to some degree your ability to use even the slightest changes in the weather that enables you to slide through the doldrums instead of being held captive for long windless days. And this could mean the difference between winning and losing the entire race.

Don't forget also that the area around the Equator is a breeding ground for hurricanes and tropical storms during the hurricane season. Its peak falls on September, exactly the time when the Whitbread fleet crosses this area during the first leg.

The next most important factor in the Atlantic is the Gulf Stream, a powerful current flowing along the general northeastern curve of the North American continent from the Gulf of Mexico toward Europe. At places the Gulf Stream reaches speeds of four knots, which could become your bonus if you knew how to ride this powerful river within the ocean.

Next come the hazards of the Newfoundland Banks, where the cold Labrador current meets the warm Gulf Stream waters, creating — if on a smaller scale — a macrocosm of the Southern Ocean, with dense fog, gale-force winds, and icebergs. To make matters even more interesting and to add to the challenge, there are also the Horse Latitudes and the Azores High with their light, unpredictable winds.

Modern racing yachts are well equipped to meet all these challenges by forecasting the weather with a good degree of accuracy. Each has a set of nautical almanacs containing a wealth of recorded information and the ability to receive weather faxes of up-to-date weather maps. Many boats even have weather computers with powerful software, enabling them not only to predict the wind changes, but also to calculate how such changes would affect the yacht's performance and recommend the optimal course in any given conditions.

We on FAZISI had a weather fax but no computer, and consequently our forecasts included too much guesswork.

16

FREMANTLE –
UNKNOWN WHITBREAD

In fifteen minutes after taking off from Delhi International airport I saw through the airplane's window to my left a pristine white strip of what I first thought was a row of huge clouds along the entire northeastern horizon. As the plane slowly closed on it, I realized they weren't clouds at all. They were majestic snow-capped peaks beyond our altitude —a wall indeed—stretching as far as the eye could see, piercing the dark blue sky.

It was the Himalayas, the mysterious land of supernatural beauty and spiritual splendor. Home of the world's three great religions, the place where generation after generation of wisdom seekers has gone in search of answers to the ultimate question of life, the Himalayas slowly unfurled before my eyes, floating westward past the left wing of the plane. An endless chain of ragged summits, some disappearing only to give way to others of even more grandeur. Some resembled paintings by one of my favorite artists, Nicholas Roerich. I used to spend hours enchanted and unable to leave, gazing at his work in Moscow's Museum of Oriental Art.

As I studied the Himalayan majesty from my plane-eye view, something changed in me. The grief and worries since Alexey's death two months ago no longer seemed so overwhelming. All of a sudden I felt stronger and regarded the project differently—a mission to be brought to fruition – and this mysterious change in my mindset was brought about by a brief touch with the Himalayan universal magnitude.

I was on a flight from Moscow to Perth, Western Australia, to meet the heavily battered FAZISI and to try to pull her further along the round-the-world journey. I had to make a stop in Singapore, where my free flight on Aeroflot ended, and I stepped into a Singapore Airline first-class cabin. Lucky me, it was the only seat available. For the first time in my life I traveled like a real big brass, surrounded by attentive flight attendants, as beautiful as they appear on TV commercials, and sipping champagne long before the plane even started taxiing down the runway. In a few hours — going through the scariest thunderstorm I'd ever experienced — I was finally exiting into the 110-degree, dry heat of the Australian desert.

The customs officer looked pretty typical in his formal jacket and tie. It was only after he stamped my passport that, while passing through, I caught a glimpse of his legs. He was wearing shorts, and it struck me as a funny combination with the straight-laced-military-jacket look. In Russia nobody wore shorts even on vacations, let alone while on official duty. The airport was small and there weren't many people who came to meet arriving passengers. It was easy to spot among them a figure resembling a yachtsman in a classic polo shirt and docksiders. Sure enough, it was Scott McAllister, a local America's Cup hero, who would become FAZISI's shore manager for the Fremantle stopover.

During the legendary 1983 America's Cup match when the Aussies beat Dennis Conner and took home the Cup for the first time ever, Scotty has been a member of that glorious team. In one of the elimination races AUSTRALIA II's spinnaker halyard snapped and Scotty was sent up to repair it. The swells around Brenton Reef shoals off Newport could be quite violent, and on this day, with the swells heaving, the 12-Meter's 80-foot mast was swinging in 40-degree arcs. Scott somehow lost his grip and for several minutes was tossed around like a rag doll, with each swell being whipped against the mast until the crew finally got him down. He was severely injured and ended up in the hospital. Though disappointed in missing the Cup racing, he went on to become one of Australia's best-known sailors and a local hero as well.

I remembered watching the entire horrific episode back home on video, seeing his unconscious body swinging around and hitting the aluminum mast with such force, it was gruesome to watch. But here he was now, alive and well, smiling in front of me. And as I shook his hand, I felt again how small the sailing world was. Only a few hours ago I'd been in snowy Moscow, then had gotten a brief --oh, too brief -- insight into the scope of the Universe while flying over the Himalayas, and now here I was in the middle of the Australian desert's furnace, barely managing to breathe.

• • •

With a population of only one million, Western Australia is separated from the country's East Coast by 3,000 miles of desert and is about as remote as it can be. If you took the outbound highway from Perth, eventually you'd come to the sign "Highway Ends." It didn't mean the road merely downgraded to a secondary road. Within one mile the asphalt would literally end, dissolving into the sun-baked reddish dirt of Western Australia with its rolling hills spreading ahead into infinity. Yet, only two years prior to my arrival there, in 1986-87, this lone metropolitan outpost had become the world's sailing capital, the arena for the fiercely fought America's Cup battle.

Now, however, the excitement was gone, along with the Cup.

My first impression upon arriving in Perth was not encouraging. No way could we get any sponsorship here. An exhausting brainstorming session with Scott and his father on the porch of their house overlooking the beautiful Swan River was time well spent but didn't move us forward much. Watching the famous black swans gliding majestically on the water painted the ruby red of the sunset, we managed to come up with a few ideas. But even with a liberal support of premium Foster Lager our imaginations brought meager results.

The plain truth was that the Whitbread was virtually unknown in Perth. This was the first time it was coming to Western Australia, and unfortunately the race organizers hadn't put enough effort into promoting the stopover. On top of that, Western Australians are an independent lot, happily living their own totally isolated life, and often not taking world views and perspectives into account. Mind you, theirs is a great life with the beautiful Indian Ocean as their front yard and a climate that you come to appreciate the more time you spend there. The Australian bush has its unique exotic beauty, as deserts go. Throw in a classic lamb-on-a-spit barbecue under the southern stars, and in addition to all this — the cultural life of the vibrant one-million-populated metropolis.

They had all they wanted. "The Whitbread?"

"Which Whitbread?"

A complication was the fact that the stopover was actually not even in Perth, which is about 15 miles up the river, but in the port of Fremantle. The Whitbread fleet used the first-class yachting facility that had been constructed for the 1987 America's Cup. But, unfortunately, while the set-up was good, the place just wasn't attracting the crowds.

It wasn't entirely hopeless, however. The day after my arrival,

Scott took me to the local Rotary Club as his guest, and its members eventually led me to some valuable business contacts. This was my first introduction to the Rotary, an organization simply unheard of in Russia. I was amazed to discover how businessmen and women of different walks of life were able to combine pleasurable time with business and charitable activities. Perhaps it was due to the isolation of Western Australia, but the club was very well organized and strongly associated with the entire network of Rotary Clubs in the area. The Apple Cross of Perth was the main club that took care of FAZISI, but these Rotarians also got their affiliates involved as well. In addition to cash contributions, the Apple Cross members provided food for the crew and picked up the tab for some of the boat's maintenance.

It wasn't much, but with the remains of the sponsorship money from Uruguay, we figured that by watching our expenses closely, there just might be enough to keep our heads above water through this stopover. Fortunately, FAZISI's repair bill didn't appear as massive as I had feared, despite the beating she'd taken. First, we needed to repair the boom. While there is no such thing as warranties in this major-league game, Sparcraft, the boom maker, took some responsibility and gave us a decent discount. The sails needed a lot of work, but most of it could be done by Kuli, who had just arrived from Russia to join the crew on the third leg and Valery Safiullin. They were immediately put on sail detail. Our largest loss was the spare main washed overboard into the Southern Ocean. Well, this wasn't the first time an expensive sail had been washed off a Whitbread racer, and at this point we just had to eat the loss.

I never anticipated that the Rotary's generous offer of meals for the crew would present any problem. But, in fact, it made some of the guys furious, "We are not beggars, we are looking for sponsorship, not donations. We are ashamed to hear everybody gossiping around of how poor we are, unable even to buy ourselves a pint of beer. That's bullshit, man!"

Russian pride is a very powerful emotion, sometimes much stronger than hunger. Besides, it was the project that was broke, not the crewmembers. They were being paid $25 per day, not much by Western standards, but still almost equal to the monthly salary at that time in Russia. Even if Fazis SP wanted to pay more, and had the money, in accordance with Soviet regulations, it couldn't do it. Fazis was not a completely independent enterprise yet and, of course, it worked within the strict state regulations, especially when hard currency was involved.

Valery Chumakov justly suspected that given the amount of visibility our project enjoyed — or suffered — the probability of an audit was very high. There would be no free interpretation or, God forbid, stretching of regulations even one iota. To be safe — and not end up in Siberia upon returning home — he played it strictly by the rules. It didn't matter if the crew liked it or not, the rule was: all Soviet citizens working abroad were entitled to only the salary they were receiving back home plus $20 to $25 per diem, depending on the country they were in. And for our crew it was just pocket money, as their lodging and food expenses were completely taken care of.

Of course, aware that their modest pocket money represented a fortune back home, some of the crew saved all of it, choosing not to spend it for anything, even for a pint of beer or a pack of cigarettes. At the end of the race such thrift resulted in a good chunk of money, at least a few thousand dollars US.

Was it sufficient payment for a whole year of danger and suffering — a year that happened to also be the greatest adventure of one's life?

Sure, it wasn't much. But let's not lose perspective. At that time, with the average Russian salary of less than the equivalent of $30US, the amount earned by each FAZISI crewmember was equal to 10 to 15 years of hard labor in Russia. The labor, certainly not as dangerous as that of the Whitbread, but not as thrilling either. In addition, they were paid in stable, Western-world currency and not ever-rate-changing rubles.

So all the talk that the Russian crew was poorly paid was true and untrue, depending on how you looked at it.

• • •

FAZISI was lifted out of water, taking her place in a row of beautiful sailing machines, all recovering from the tough second leg. Only then did we discover the cracks on the rudder blade close to the stock. The rudder was a high-tech masterpiece of carbon fiber and epoxy, built by the highly regarded German company Speedwave. It was supposed to be an engineering marvel. Yet now Juki, in a cloud of deleterious carbon-fiber dust, was busy grinding and sanding down the cracks. Hoping that it would hold at least till New Zealand, we put a double laminate over it. It was really a Band-Aid repair. When we had more money, we'd do a proper job.

Luckily, this job rounded up our work list. Despite all the beating FAZISI had taken, her hull was in excellent shape. Amazingly, all the breakage occurred only with Western-constructed gear and equipment, while the Russian-made parts seemed to hold together fine. Maybe we, Russians, are capable, after all, of building great boats — particularly when working for ourselves, not for Big Brother.

I was proud of FAZISI's toughness. All of the Whitbread fleet suffered some damage on the brutal leg, and some teams had substantial repairs to make. In all, there were five broken booms and practically every boat had broken at least one spinnaker pole. No one even bothered counting the number of broken halyards and the sails torn apart. Some composite-laminate boats showed signs of delamination. These boats, built of thin layers of carbon fiber or kevlar with a layer of lightweight foam and then sandwiched with resin, had begun to come apart after the month of non-stop pounding.

As I passed MARTELA, I noticed a bunch of guys swarming around her keel again. They had already performed a major overhaul in Montevideo after hitting an underwater oil pipe on approach to the finish line in Punta. The pipe survived, the keel didn't, almost being ripped right off the hull. That was punishment for sailing into a restricted area in the heat of competition. It seemed that the problem had persisted even after that repair.

It was just the normal Whitbread routine: the fleet licking its wounds after a tough Southern Ocean leg.

Despite these common problems we shared with our fellow competitors, I still looked at the other teams almost with envy. The fact that they had much more experience and far larger budgets was only a part of it. For most of the sailors, racing the Whitbread was a game, a way to take life to it fullest. That was exactly what sport was meant to be. But for us it was both more and something else. It was the chance in of a lifetime to us. No, actually it WAS our life.

We had struggled more than any one else just to be in this race. We had little sailing experience, much less in ocean racing. We'd had no exposure to the West, no previous experience of living here and doing business here. We had never known this freedom, nor glimpsed at so much opportunity, all laden with dignity. We were strangers in this world where the other sailors, born and bred in it, had lived with these wonderful things all their lives and had taken them for granted. Indeed, we were just uninvited strangers.

Deep in unhappy thoughts, I walked my usual way back from the marina to the hotel. As a rule, I skipped the ride on the crew bus, opting instead to take the three-mile walk, which always energized me and helped to clear my mind after the day's work. It was also about the only time to look around and get acquainted with Fremantle. That day a small pet store on the main street attracted my attention and I walked in. There were rows of brightly-lit fish tanks lined up along the walls. Each tank had a different species of fish. Standing there and looking around, I suddenly felt as if a cold hand had squeezed my heart. I wasn't sure whether it was real physical pain or just a shot of loneliness suddenly stabbing me. The aquariums around me, full of colorful fish, looked exactly like the one in my son's room back in Moscow. By some strange association this pet store sharply reminded me of how far I was from home. I didn't even know when I would see my family again. Why had I left? What have I forgotten in this foreign land?

I don't know how long I stood there, but a woman behind the counter looked at me strangely as she asked politely, "Are you all right?"

"I am fine, thank you." I rushed out trying to look away so that she wouldn't see the tears brimming in my eyes.

Why had those stupid fish made me so emotional?

• • •

Among the problems that filled my days, I noticed that Skip had started to lose interest in our project. His lack of enthusiasm had become pretty evident by the frustrating end of the second leg, but that was understandable. There was more to it now. I was worried that at any moment he might abandon ship altogether. He made vague remarks to me a few times that went something like, "I've already done three Whitbreads, more than most sailors have ever dreamed of … If only this project had any chance of doing well, then it would make some sense for me to continue … The crew totally lacks motivation, and I just don't have the desire to push them any more."

I was afraid that the next time he would add, "Okay that's enough for me. I'm packing my duffel."

That would be a terrible problem to deal with. I knew for sure that at this point we certainly couldn't do it without Skip. No one was qualified to take the captain role.

In addition to Skip's attitude, there also was the issue of his pay. Initially, it had been agreed that he would be paid $10,000US for each leg sailed on FAZISI. This was a rather modest sum for a professional sailor of Skip's ability and experience, especially compared to what the other captains were supposedly getting. While no one knew for sure, there were rumors that rock stars like Lawrie Smith were being paid six-figure salaries to do the race. But regardless of how relatively puny

Skip's check appeared in comparison, for us it represented a lot of money and was a tremendous burden on our pitiful budget. When we first agreed to the amount back in Moscow, it was assumed that big sponsorship money would be coming in, which of course never happened. The deal, however, had been struck. Now, when I pleaded with Skip to consider our plight, I didn't get far. I asked him to consider his job as, in part, an act of Goodwill and wave the next paycheck as a gesture of sharing our common hardship. But Skip stood firm.

"If you want me on FAZISI, it'll cost you 10 grand for the next leg. If you don't even have that much, I don't see a reason to continue."

"Come on, Skip, this leg is only half the length of the previous one," with a smile I tried to soften his position and gain some bargaining ground. "And conditions will be much easier. I must agree that the Southern Ocean leg was definitely worth $10,000, but a pleasant ride to New Zealand…? "

It didn't work. Ten grand or bye bye.

It seemed as if we had no choice. Skip received his check, signed by a discontented Valery Chumakov, and would remain with us at least until Auckland. But what if we just couldn't come up with ten big ones next time around? After discussing the situation with Valery, it was clear that in order to be ready for the possibility of Skip's departure, we needed an alternative skipper. The only one whom I still could consider from my original list was Valery Alexeev. He was initially involved in FAZISI's construction in Poti but, citing personal reasons, later left the effort. Somehow I suspected that he just didn't believe that the project would really happen. But who cares what his reasons were. He was a good, experienced skipper and that's what mattered. I knew that he was eager to return to FAZISI. And so we arranged for him to join us in Auckland.

Victor Pogrebnov of the same yacht club in Sochi and one of the best Black Sea sailors, and the Soviet Olympic star Sergey Borodinov would come with him. Sergey had also been involved in the project at the start but then had opted instead for the perks of being a member of the Soviet national sailing team. Now he'd rethought his decision and had been persistently calling the Fazis office asking to be included again. We could certainly find a place for a sailor of his caliber. After the second leg I was confident of FAZISI's potential. With this reinforced crew, we might be able to push the boat harder and see what she was really capable of. In the meantime, the important task was to keep Skip on board, not losing him before we reached New Zealand.

An unexpected break, that helped to fire up Skip's enthusiasm, came with the arrival of Paul Smitt, a handsome, cheerful New Zealander. He flew to Fremantle to visit his Whitbread pals made from the Auckland stopover of the last race. Surprised to find Skip leading the Soviet boat, he became fascinated with the whole set up. He proved his interest by getting on the phone to his friend Barry Everard, an Auckland entrepreneur and the owner of the radio station 89FM. As it turned out, Barry had already heard of the FAZISI campaign and was curious to learn more.

One thing led to another, and two days later I found myself flying to New Zealand to meet our future sponsors.

• • •

Approaching Auckland International Airport, I could instantly see what Skip meant when he called this land a sailing paradise. From far above, it appeared like less land than water, which was dotted with countless specks of boats of all sizes and shapes, pulling their white wakes across beautifully carved bays and amid emerald-green islands. As the plane descended lower and lower over the water, I wondered when I would finally see a strip of land large enough for a runway. It didn't appear until landing, and I breathed a huge sigh of relief upon feeling a nice touchdown instead of one giant splash.

Our grass-roots campaign organizer Clive Tremaine and his girl-friend Margie Gray met me at the airport, and drove to downtown Auckland for the meeting at the radio station. Paul Smitt, Barry Everard, and his assistants were already waiting for us. Skip, who left Fremantle a day earlier, stopping in Brisbane to visit his girlfriend Julia, was there as well.

I could instantly detect a sort of rivalry between the two groups of New Zealand supporters. In his early 50s and looking the part of a poster playboy, Barry certainly made it clear that his effort would be a higher class affair than Clive's down-to-earth grass-roots program. Maybe it had something to do with the fact that Clive came from the common folk, while Barry and especially Paul Smitt, who supposedly drove the only Ferrari on the North Island, certainly crowned the social pyramid. But then again, maybe I was wrong. Maybe it was just a personal thing. After all, New Zealand society, despite all its diversity, seemed a pretty equal one compared to what I'd seen in Great Britain and Uruguay with their closely guarded walls between the social classes.

"The biggest advantage we have as a radio station is unlimited ability to generate publicity for you," Barry told us. "Ours is a small country with not too many FM stations. In fact, there are only two in the Auckland area. So with us, you're instantly getting access to at least half of the local population."

With a proud smile, he continued, "Every major business has an advertising account with us. We could offer them free airtime in exchange for contributions to FAZISI. There are plenty of other opportunities that we've been discussing with Paul. The groundwork has already been laid, and a few meetings have already been arranged for you today. Let's not waste our time."

Barry was a real businessman and we didn't waste any time. In the next few hours the outline for the entire New Zealand program was drawn up. In even the worst-case scenario, the sponsorship deal with 89FM packaged with Clive Tremain's efforts looked good for at least $200,000. That's New Zealand dollars, of course, at the time worth 70 US cents. Nevertheless, this would be enough money to pull FAZISI through the middle-way point. Now things were certainly looking brighter. New Zealand was expecting us. Full speed ahead!

17

MIDDLE OF THE WAY

For the two weeks before the start of the third leg, the weather was absolutely beautiful — sunny days with a nice fresh breeze, not too strong, just enough to make the scorching Australian summer bearable, even comfortable. But last night a gale bringing cold rain moved in off the ocean, and by starting time it was already blowing Force 8.

As Skip was motoring to the starting line, I thought back on the Fremantle stopover. It turned out much better than I had feared it would at the beginning. We managed to perform all the necessary work on FAZISI and the crew was well fed and rested. Skip was still on board and would stay with us at least until Auckland. And best of all, we got sponsorship for the next stopover. I had met many great people, learned a trick or two on how to run a business, and was slowly putting the tragedy in Uruguay behind me.

The only disappointment was the fact that I was too busy to do any justice to this beautiful country. There was no time to go with the crew to the big lamb cookout party on a farm deep in the bush, or to join them on the trip to a local winery south of Perth. The wine was excellent, or so I was told. I had no time to enjoy the beautiful Australian beaches and took a swim in the Indian Ocean only once. I didn't even see any kangaroos, emus or koalas. Maybe next time — well, I had already seen them in the Moscow Zoo.

Skip killed the engine and under the number three jib and the reefed main, maneuvered FAZISI in vicinity of the starting line. Dale Tremain stood next to him, counting time, "One minute to the gun... Thirty seconds... Twenty..."

"Trim for speed!" shouted Skip. Sheets were quickly adjusted and our yacht darted toward the line.

"Ten seconds... Five, four, three, two, one. Go!"

The gun fired and my personal Whitbread started.

For the first time everything—even the project's financing—had been taken care of and finally I could treat myself to sailing one leg on FAZISI. Only 3,000 miles long, this would be a short one; nevertheless, it was considered one of the most difficult. After dipping down into the Southern Ocean around Australia, the fleet would cross the notorious Tasman Sea with its violent storms and steep seas. The infamous Sydney-to-Hobart Race, held in these waters, claims sailors' lives with frightening regularity.

For the crew it would be another tough leg in the ocean, but I was honestly looking forward to it—almost like a vacation. After working in the salt mines of managing arguably the most challenging campaign in the Whitbread, everything, even sailing the Whitbread itself, would feel like a vacation. And I certainly needed one.

I always liked the routine of long-distance racing. Nothing helps more to relax and forget problems than the precise schedule of watches and the routine of boat management that sets in on board after the first few hectic days. Day-to-day life narrows to the simple act of sailing, which is essentially nothing more than a way to survive on the ocean while moving in the direction you desire. The outside world becomes irrelevant, and every day survived without an accident brings you closer to the destination, and by itself, becomes a small one-time achievement.

Unlike dealing with the social, political or business complexities of life on land, at sea you deal with the elements, which are neither good nor bad, just natural. Only a tiny toy at their mercy, the boat can be easily crushed by wind and waves, with the danger increasing greatly if you fail to treat the nature with respect. But elements do not have evil intentions. They simply live by their own rules, oblivious to your existence. Respect those rules and you will not only get a chance to survive, you might enjoy the journey immensely.

The primitive, atavistic nature of the ocean has always been an irresistible lure for generations of sailors. Just like the highest mountain peaks, it will always remain pure and innocent, even if it occasionally kills brave souls who dare to challenge it.

• • •

My first watch was over, but I didn't want to go below yet to rest. I was too excited for that. I glanced at the brightly illuminated jumbo displays mounted at the mast base. The wind was 32 knots at 40 degrees apparent with boat speed dancing at around 14 knots. Not bad for such a close reach. In the thickening dusk, I could still make out the yellow hull and the two-mast rig of THE CARD. We had had a fierce duel with them for a couple of hours just after the start, but now they had chosen to go lower and slowly disappeared behind the curtain of rain. For Skip battling THE CARD was sort of a personal vendetta, after the project he had founded was taken over by his friend and project manager Roger Nilson. It had become Skip's obsession to chase and fight THE CARD.

I could feel the wind increasing in the last few minutes, the waves hitting harder and harder, and the boat heeling more. A quick look at the wind repeater confirmed that it was blowing around 38 now, a full gale. Skip poked his head through the aft hatch, stood for a few seconds looking around and said: "Okay, guys, it's time to change to the number four." We were sailing under the number three jib since the start and the smaller headsail would mean less heel and better boatspeed in the increased wind.

No one made a move. Instead, a heated debate in Russian erupted between those who supported Skip's decision and those who argued it was just bullshit. No one treated it as a command. It was merely something to talk about. The crew, having been raised on a system so imbued with pressure from on high, were Soviet to the core and had developed a totally relaxed attitude toward commands. It was like an immune reaction. Let the bosses push, even threaten, that's what they are for anyway. We'll wait and see. Maybe we'll do something eventually.

How could Skip, an American, even begin to understand it, I realized watching this display. He looked back at me betraying a strange mixture of disappointment and triumph on his face. "I told you. Nobody cares about sailing the damn boat. They should've changed the fucking sail long ago without my kicking their asses. But no, they just sit and argue," he hissed, brimming with fury and frustration.

Skip and I had talked about the problem many times: what to do about the crew's lack of initiative. But that was on shore and that was just his opinion. Now, however, by my own witness, I saw the confrontation: Skip versus the crew, the crew versus Skip. And I couldn't agree with him more, it was not a pretty sight. But I just kept silent. While I was the boss of the operation ashore, here on the boat, I tried to be just a crewmember, like any one of them. The last thing I wanted was to make matters more complicated with my intrusion. Finally, two guys stood up and went to the afterdeck to untie the sail. I joined to help them.

The number four jib is a small but heavy sail made of very strong fabric to withstand a gale even sailing upwind. It was a tough job for the three of us to lug it forward on the dancing deck. Besides, our safety harnesses were a nuisance. As a rule, every man on deck had to wear safety equipment that consisted of a strong web harness with a tether hooked to the boat, thus preventing being accidentally washed overboard. The tether's hook was designed to glide freely along the jacklines on either side, but it often got tangled around one thing or another. As I unhooked my harness, freed it, and hooked it again in front of me, ready to move, somebody else's line would get tangled up, and I would need to stop again. Dragging the 200-pound bag forward on the wildly gyrating deck was almost too much for the three of us to handle, as we struggled with our harnesses not in unison.

But to go forward without a harness seemed too dangerous to me. It was my first day on the boat, and I had yet to develop the feel of her motion, which was very violent indeed. FAZISI was at least twice as big as anything I'd ever sailed before and twice as fast. Her moves were sharp and quick. Sailing upwind, she would spring almost half of her length out of the water, hitting the crest of a wave, and then fall down into the trough with a crashing sound, bury her bow and send a wall of water rushing aft over the deck. If you were not careful all the time, it would wash you right off.

All in all, it took us more than 20 minutes to muscle the sail to the foredeck, hoist it, lower the old sail, pulling it underneath the new one and then onto the deck and fold it. It was all done as the deck leaped up and down under gushers of cold water. I felt totally exhausted after the ordeal and made my way down the aft companionway in search of a little food and some rest.

My bunk was on the bottom to starboard. It was conveniently located close to the hatch for plenty of fresh air, to the drier for easy dressing and undressing, and to the nav-station, so even when resting, I was close to the nerve center of the boat. Of course, there's a downside to everything. For ventilation, the aft hatch was left open all the time, and when an occasional boarding wave hit, my bunk would get flooded. Plus, being near the information center could be noisy. There always was some conversation or argument going on about routing or weather, or the radio was squawking, intruding into my shallow, alerted sleep. Even proximity to the drier could be a disadvantage, as the smell from it was awful at times. But when you're exhausted and have just a few short hours before the next watch, who cares.

The bunk next to me was Dale Tremain's and behind us were Skip's quarters with a luxurious single bunk and no one around. A canvas bulkhead, with convenient pockets for things like a flashlight, book or Walkman with your favorite tapes—a nice touch of privacy—separated the bunks. On the opposite side were three bunks for the watch captains and the navigator. The aluminum shell surrounding us and protecting us from the ocean's fury was but an eighth-inch thick, that's it—but mind you, it was Russia's best aerospace-grade aluminum, the best in the world, as far as we were concerned. There was practically no insulation so the constant hissing of water could easily produce an illusion of being in the middle of a waterfall—or inside a washing machine, if you're less romantic.

The nav-station, the command post of the boat, was located on the centerline directly ahead of the aft companionway for easy communication between navigator or captain below and helmsman above. You had only to step up the ladder a little bit, poke your head through the hatch (in those rare moments between waves, of course) and shout: "Okay, guys, ready to tack in two minutes" and dive right back into the coziness of the space below. Let the guys on the deck digest the command and argue a bit. Who knows, they might just be ready to tack in two minutes.

The big chart table was made of mahogany and added a nice warm touch of luxury to the submarine-like, stripped-out aluminum interior. Next to it were three radios: an Icom VHF for short-range communications, the huge Scanti long-range single-sideband radio (SSB)— a beautiful piece of electronics that worked marvels—and finally, a small emergency radio with its own independent battery supplies. The assortment of electronic equipment on FAZISI was fairly good and included radar, Decca/Loran, and GPS. The Global Positioning System, which had just become available from the military, was a brand new thing in the late-1980s. We never ceased to be amazed at how accurate it was; you could actually determine your position within just a few yards.

All this stuff represented a quantum leap for us Russians. The only navigation equipment we had on our boats back home was a compass and a transistor radio for taking bearings off the radio buoys. That's it. But then in Russia we didn't venture far offshore either. We were practically landlocked with almost all sailing taking place on the small lakes and rivers. A hundred miles out into the Baltic and Black Seas were our farthest destinations. But now we were on a real ocean and were properly equipped.

The performance instruments on FAZISI were by Ockam, considered at the time to be the best in the business. There were four displays at the chart table with up to 30 different displayable functions—probably much more information than we could ever use. Four other huge repeaters almost a foot long, called jumbos, were mounted at the mast base, where they were visible from any point on the boat. We also had a weather fax, an absolute necessity, but no meteorological computer. This, as it turned out, was a severe handicap. There was also a sextant stowed under the chart table, but I doubt if anyone of us would call himself adept at celestial navigation. The era was long gone when you had to wait patiently for a break in the clouds and then try to get a bearing on the sun or stars from a violently jumping deck.

I took off my foul weather gear and inched my way through the low and narrow passage between the engine and dryer into the main salon. It was much bigger than the aft cabin, and there was even standing headroom in places. This was the quarters for eight crewmembers with the galley in the middle.

Our new cook Rami Leibovich was sitting in his comfortable swivel chair, his face pale with beads of sweat covering his forehead. It was his first leg on FAZISI as well. He nodded toward a bunch of plates sliding around on the improvised table on top of the diesel generator and croaked, "That's your supper out there." Then he reached for a black garbage bag and threw up. Feeling a surge of nausea myself, I rushed up the companionway into the fresh air. Supper would have to wait until better times.

• • •

The next day began with trouble. Dale was the first one to spot the threatening mast bend. While trying not to make any unnecessary fuss, he calmly pointed it out to Skip and me. During the stopover in Fremantle, FAZISI's mast had been removed and every fitting checked and serviced. Once restepped, the rig was tuned. It was all done under the supervison of riggers from Sparcraft, the company that had built the aluminum mast. Despite all that care, only the second day out of Fremantle, it became obvious that something had gone terribly wrong. The second starboard diagonal had given way, and the mast had developed a visible transverse bend in the area of the second spreaders. This was bad. And it might get even worse.

A modern racing mast is supposed to be flexible but only in the longitudinal direction, from bow to stern. This way it allows adjustment of the shape of the mainsail, making it flatter or fuller, depending on the wind condition. From side to side it is supported by the spreaders and a system of stainless steel rods, called shrouds, vertical and diagonal, and should be absolutely straight, "in column," as sailors say. If not, the enormous compression loads could cause the mast to lose balance and fold. The shrouds are under such tension that it is practically impossible to re-tune them under load — you'd just shear the threads.

There were only two alternatives: return to Fremantle for repairs or keep going, hoping the rig would somehow hold together. We discussed both options with Skip, but basically it was my call. No longer was I a humble crewmember, it was a time to put my project leader hat back on — if only someone else would take it from me. First, I sent Edgar Terekhin, one of our own riggers, up the mast in the bosun's chair to check and secure the shroud fitting, if possible. He came down confident that it was not something that just happened, it simply was improperly tuned during the stopover. It was not a fitting failure, and it probably wouldn't get any worse, he thought.

It seemed to me that we could go on, keeping a close eye on the mast for any sign of further trouble. I knew it was slightly overbuilt and believed it would hold if things did not get any worse. Well, who knows, I could be wrong. But we were in the race, and the risk seemed reasonable to me. After all, I'd taken a lot of risk before and certainly was not going to turn back now.

I moved my eyes from the mast to the sky above and prayed silently: "Oh, Lord, don't let this happen, please. I believe you wouldn't let my sailing be over now, when it has only just started." It was a selfish prayer, but I felt as if it was heard, and that gave me more confidence. I am not always a good Christian, I must admit, but deep in my soul I know that God sometimes hears my prayers.

As the whole fleet moved toward Tasmania, a big area of high pressure with light, fluky winds was slowly catching up with us. First it overtook the stragglers, NSB IRELAND and the pair from Finland, BELMONT II and UNION BANK OF FINLAND. We still had a light, unsteady breeze but were making good progress, as we constantly trimmed and changed sails. The best thing about this fluky wind was that it allowed us to tack and momentarily relieve the tension on the loose shroud. Edgar went up again and after 20 minutes of hard labor on the swinging chair 60 feet above the deck, was able to tune it almost as good as it should be. We tacked back. The mast was still not absolutely straight but certainly looked much better.

If the wind continues to diminish, with luck we might simultaneously ease the shroud tension slightly on both sides of the mast and tune the rig properly. It would be an extremely risky thing to do in the ocean, and I wasn't sure if it was worth it. The mast now looked pretty good as it was.

The next day, roughly 200 miles southwest of Tasmania, the wind died completely, but the swells remained ten feet high. FAZISI became a helpless toy at their mercy, as they tossed her from side to side, shaking any leftovers of wind off the sails. Hour after hour passed by. The ocean just heaved heavily in the silence broken periodically by the slapping of the sails, loud as cannon fire. Powerless, the boat was rolling so violently that tuning the rig now was out of question. In all honesty, it was a relief as I was not at all looking forward to the procedure. It seemed way too risky, and we could easily end up with the mast overboard.

The calm weather was even more exhausting than the storm and especially frustrating, because we knew that the leaders still had good wind. The gap between us quickly increased to 240 miles. Only with the arrival of night did we finally feel a light breath of air again — then a bit more, and the boat started forward. My watch was over and with a sigh of relief, I went below and headed for my bunk. Before I was even snug in the comfort of my sleeping bag, Eugene Platon suddenly sounded at the top of his lungs, "Mast is going down!" Thinking this was some cruel joke, I stormed out through the aft hatch only to see the mast standing proudly just where it was supposed to be, sails now filled with the freshening breeze, and the boat moving lively. But then I heard agitated comments coming from below. Eugene, Skip, flashlights in hands, and half of the crew were gathered around the mast step deep in the boat's belly. Now what? I thought as I plowed through the crowd.

The flashlights were pointing to the two thick pins, which secured the mast from moving in the step. They were an inch and a quarter in diameter and incredibly one of them was broken. Shit! How could this happen? And how long will the other one last by itself? The load on the mast step was more than 20 tons, but it was all compression, not shear load, that had snapped the pin. Besides, for safety reasons, the pin was supposed to have three times the strength needed. Theoretically, this couldn't be happening, but there it was. Well, to hell with the explanation, we needed to secure the damn thing first. Taking whatever materials we had in our spares kit, Eugene together with our second technical whiz Igor Mironenko started shimming the mast, while Skip and I assessed our options.

This time I was not confident at all. Of course, we could change course for Hobart, Tasmania, and try to do repairs there. We would lose this leg of the race—not a big deal really. By this time we were among the outsiders anyway, and losing the leg was infinitely better than losing the rig. So, "ready about" and turn toward Tasmania? Well, the problem was that we left Fremantle with virtually no money and even a simple repair might be out of question. We might get stuck in Hobart forever. On the other hand, a sponsorship was awaiting us in New Zealand — assuming of course that we could make it there. Big assumption.

I knew that this time the risk was much higher, indeed a gamble. But as Americans say, "no guts, no glory," right, Skip? Still wrestling with prudence, I gradually grew willing to take the chance. Skip toyed a bit more with the idea of turning to Tasmania, but realized as well that this would mean pretty much the end of racing for FAZISI, probably forever. Sometimes when you're facing a tough decision, it's almost a blessing to have no choice. Together we checked Eugene and Igor's job.

"Looks pretty safe to me," I said, trying to keep my voice firm.

Skip was ready to throw away his doubts as well. "Okay, I am with you." And so we kept sailing.

• • •

Two days after the start in Fremantle, Christmas came — at least in the Western world. Actually, according to the Russian Orthodox calendar, Christmas is January 7, but we were in the West now and of course would honor both dates. Back in Russia, the Christmas celebration was just a quiet family holiday, its true meaning much obscured after 70 years of Bolshevik religion suppression. They worked really hard to make sure that faith would be totally replaced in Russian souls by the communist ideology. Saints were traded for the whole pantheon of proletarian martyrs crowned by Vladimir Lenin. The Mausoleum on Red Square with his glass tomb perpetually on display had been turned into the place of worship for millions of Russians.

There were other, more subtle differences. In Russia, Santa Claus wouldn't come to reward good children on Christmas. Instead, *Ded Moroz* – Grandfather Frost, would bring presents to kids on New Year's Eve. Well, one way or another, children had their fun anyway.

We too, with three holidays to celebrate during this short leg, had been looking forward to the festive times at sea, despite all the worries about our rig. Rami cooked a delicious Christmas dinner — no freeze-dried food this time, it was banned for the day. Instead we had turkey (what else?), fresh vegetables, salad, and fruit. For desert there was a huge pie delivered by our friends from the Rotary Club just before the start.

Skip was very excited, somehow getting the mistaken idea that his Russian shipmates were celebrating Christmas for the very first time. He even put together a press release about this and dictated it over the radio. I had no desire to correct him, as he had already explained to me many times before that media is not about information, but about sensation. "It's not news when dog bites man, when man bites dog that's news." And then, there were other trivialities, like, "it doesn't matter whether the publicity you are getting is positive or negative, it's the amount that matters." Well, I could be cynical too if I chose to. Still, I couldn't understand why he cooked up this phony anecdote with Russian flavor when there were so many real and remarkable things going on. But I let it go. Who needs a confrontation at Christmas time?

New Year's Eve is traditionally a much bigger celebration in Russia. That's when people decorate a tree, get together for big parties, open champagne at midnight with the clanging of the Kremlin clock bells. Eventually, champagne would give way to more substantial drinks, food would be extraordinary, one delicious course after another, and the party would last until dawn. Sometimes it would be followed by enthusiastic snowball fights outside with lots of squealing and laughter. It was so different here in the middle of the ocean, far from home. We would surely remember this exotic celebration for the rest of our lives, but it felt so lonely and sad without our friends and families. Of course, we had our champagne, only instead of President Gorbachev's face on a TV screen, it was Skip, live, who made the toast. And the music we listened to wasn't a cheerful Soviet march. It was — oh, yeah — "Gypsy Kings," what else. We first discovered their music in Punta del Este and it had since become our favorite.

Then, briefly, I played the Ded Moroz part, handing out greeting cards to everyone from their families. I had collected them well in advance and secretly kept just for this moment. There were also faxes from Fazis SP and the Soviet Sailing Federation, but they got a far less emotional reception. For a minute, silence fell on board, everyone deep in personal thoughts and memories. Finally, I made a last toast for the success of our journey and a better future for Russia, and our celebration was over.

• • •

In the midst of our ordeal with the wrongly tuned mast, we got news that UBF had been dismasted, which only added to our own concerns. At the moment we were very close to them, sailing in the same conditions. The wind was moderate, ranging between 12 to 15 knots true, but it was right on the nose, so the apparent wind felt like well over 20. The seas were not big but steep, causing frequent and severe pounding. In such conditions Maxi yachts sail at about 10 knots, which is enough to occasionally get half-airborne before crashing down into the trough. The mast starts acting like a gigantic pendulum, swinging back and forth and from side to side every few seconds. Repeated a hundred times day after day, constant loading and unloading causes metal fatigue over time and could eventually get to any part of the rigging. A small piece such as a broken clevis pin could cause the whole 100-foot mast to tumble down.

The steering technique became absolutely crucial in such conditions. Some helmsmen had a natural ability for it and just knew how to guide the boat through the waves with maximum speed and little pounding. Even below, I could instantly tell that FAZISI wasn't anymore caught at the bottom of each wave with hundreds of gallons of water washing over her bow, but was, instead, riding up and around it. That meant Kuli, or Edgar Terekhin, or Dale had taken the helm. Jim Saunders steered well for the most part, though he could occasionally lose concentration and throw FAZISI into a pretty violent crash. Igor Mironenko was perhaps the most reckless driver, constantly testing the very limits of the boat. He was capable of packing a couple of Gs into every movable object inside the cabin, sending it shooting up to the ceiling and making one's jaw clench with such a force, you'd need to check if your teeth were still in place after every wave's hit.

It won't take long in such conditions to lose the mast, especially after all the troubles we already had. I just kept praying that it would hold, taking Ludde Ingvall's frustration personally.

The Whitbread is an extremely competitive race. It is a never-ending battle along the entire route, with fierce, even finishes, when boats cross the line nearly side by side. (After almost a month of racing the 7,000-mile marathon through the Southern Ocean, only 26 seconds separated MERIT and ROTHMANS at the finish in Fremantle.) Yet it is a competition of unique camaraderie that only sailors who have been through the same storms can appreciate. This spirit is greatly reinforced by the clear understanding that in the remote areas around Antarctica only your fellow competitors can come to your rescue.

Now all the fleet was on standby in case UBF needed any assistance. A few hours later Ludde finally advised that they had managed to set up a jury-rig from parts of the mast and the boom. He was confident that they would make it to Auckland on their own. It was a great relief to us all.

I felt sorry for Ludde. He was the first Whitbread sailor I'd ever met when in the summer of '88 he sailed into Leningrad to promote his recently launched boat. Since then we had run into each other a few times on different occasions during the stopovers, and I had grown to respect and like him. Ludde started and ran a scrupulously organized, well-funded campaign backed by a major European bank. Indeed, it certainly looked as the "proper" one that most Whitbread sailors only dream about. With the boat on water more than a year prior to the start and everything optimized to the highest degree, checked, tested, and re-tested many times, Ludde had positioned his entry as a serious bid for the victory. And yet, here he was, in the middle of the Tasman Sea, with his mast broken, and his dreams for any good standing in the race shattered.

Talk about preparations and luck ...

The next distress call came from CHARLES JOURDAN. The boat had hit a whale at full speed and put a 2-by-6-foot hole in her carbon-fiber hull. The whale was apparently injured, as the water around the boat turned red with its blood. For the French crew the danger was that the boat could sink. After first radio communication when they reported the incident, they went silent, ignoring calls of concern from other boats.

In the void of silence, Skip suggested grimly, "They're probably dictating their last wills to relatives and friends in France ... Or they might very well already be drifting on the life raft with their boat resting peacefully on the bottom. With a hole that size, it would take but a few minutes."

Luckily, CHARLES JOURDAN was heeling to the deck at the moment of impact (the poor whale might have been just carelessly sleeping on the surface). As a result the damage occurred above the water-line. So as soon as they tacked to the other side, the hole was out of the water. The crew, relieved that the boat was out of immediate danger of sinking, quickly fashioned a temporary patch, using a floorboard and spare sails. If the weather won't deteriorate, they'd probably make it to New Zealand.

A few days later, the New Zealand newspapers carried a story about a dead whale washed up on a beach not far from CHARLES JOURDAN's encounter. It had deep wounds, and the natural assumption by many was that this must be the same whale that JOURDAN had hit. The story caused a lot of resonance. New Zealanders are environmentally attentive, so when CHARLES JOURDAN took her place at the dock in Auckland, the reception was noticeably cool. Oblivious to the public disapproval, skipper Alain Gabbay went ahead and actually consented to a photographer's request to pose with a sledgehammer hitting a huge inflatable whale stuffed into the hole on the side of the boat. The picture sparked an explosion of outrage and propelled the French boat to the status of public enemy number one.

But that would come later, after the finish.

• • •

Sailing for the first time on FAZISI, I witnessed all the problems within the crew firsthand and tried to figure out what should be done so FAZISI could get through the entire race. Watching Skip grow ever more dissatisfied, I was almost certain he wouldn't stay on for much longer. He was spending more and more time below, writing and dictating articles for the British newspaper The Daily Telegraph. True, it was more publicity for us, but it was the sort of publicity we certainly could do without. I read some of the articles. They were all clever and funny stuff, but at the expense of FAZISI's Russian contingent, and full of exaggerations on Skip's own importance in sailing the 'unprepared entry' with 'unmotivated crew'.

He painted himself as the only one on board trying to race the boat, while the others remained mired in squabbles among themselves. Well, unfortunately not all of that was false. To a point, a lot of what he wrote was true, but it was the arrogant way in which he expressed it that made me angry. It sounded as if he was the only good one on board, stuck on a boat with inferior crew. Now, that was just bullshit.

Yet I must admit, he was a true professional. On those rare occasions when he would come up on deck to "kick ass" the boat's performance did, in fact, instantly improve. He would yell and swear, jump from one spot to another, trim a sheet, ease another, and check things. And just in a few minutes FAZISI would be sailing a bit better — if only it didn't have to be done in such a hysterical manner.

He was complaining more and more about the crew attitude and wanted me to replace a few guys. Beyond his requests, I knew that Anatoly Verba and Eugene would have to go to ease tensions on board. Their ambitions were bigger than FAZISI. Anatoly, watch captain for the leg, had grown particularly annoying. For the longest time I tried not to step in, no matter how much I disapproved of the way in which he handled his watch. But finally, when I couldn't take it any more, I asked him if we could have a few words together.

"Anatoly, how come everyone steers during your watch, no

matter whether he's good at the helm or not? Don't you remember that we decided long time ago that each crew would be assigned a specific position and only good helmsmen would steer? This is especially important in the current situation. You're perfectly aware of the serious problem with our mast ... and with such a constant pounding, who knows how long it will hold."

"It was your opinion to allocate specific positions. I never agreed to that. As I see it, everyone pretty much performs at the same level. Besides, they all worked hard to build this boat, and now they all equally deserve to steer her. After all, steering is the most fun in sailing."

"Oh please, cut the crap. Fun is fine but we are here to race first of all. Some guys are better helmsmen, others can trim sails better or they are good in something else. We need to give them a chance to do what they do best. The boat's performance will benefit too." It all was so obvious, and we had discussed it so many times...

Totally frustrated, I continued, "I don't want to explain to you things that you already know yourself. Enough of these arguments. Just do what needs to be done."

Visually upset, Anatoly went below and spent an hour making a chart with everyone's name on it along with rows of watches. For the next two days he was deeply involved in measuring time and boat speed, and performing endless computations. Finally, it was over and he approached me with the chart all filled with numbers.

"I don't want to argue with you empty handed, so I've performed a scientific experiment. As a result, I have proved that the average boat speed doesn't change, no matter who's steering the boat. Take a good look."

I took the chart and looked at it, if only to be polite. It certainly didn't convince me.

"Anatoly, we're not talking about average speed here. What I am trying to do is sail the damn boat efficiently, with the best man on each position. If we'd be able to shave off just a few minutes here, a few there, at the end of the day we'd have sailed a couple dozen more miles. And who knows, maybe by the end of the leg, we could even catch up with the leaders. Don't you get it?"

I am sure he understood. After all, he held a master's degree, was teaching in the marine academy, and had sailed all his life. This whole thing was probably just a show to demonstrate that he was going to run his watch however he felt like it.

Fine. If you don't want to race, you'd better leave the boat. The only problem was that for some strange reason, which had never been explained to me, Tikhov wanted to keep Anatoly aboard and resisted all my attempts to get rid of him. For a while I let it pass and didn't confront Tikhov on it, but not anymore. With Anatoly's attitude, FAZISI would never stand a chance of doing well in the race.

Of course, I recognized that she probably wouldn't do really well any way, with or without Anatoly. There were just too many factors to the equation, but that wasn't the point. We had to at least try to do our best, try to race FAZISI as she was supposed to be raced, as others were racing their boats. Otherwise, what's the point of it all?

On the phone with Fazis, I was directing the crew replacements that would be made in Auckland. I tried to be discreet and didn't want to spread a fire of rumors and speculations aboard. It was tough in the close quarters of the boat. All of the politics and juggling with egos and interests was really getting to me, making me sick. How far things had deteriorated since our romantic beginning, when everyone was eager to contribute to the success of the project.

I had hardened a lot and grown bitter over the course of the last year. There had been so many disappointments. But I had also become much stronger. I had started this project and was responsible for it, and I knew now no one could manage it better than I. Sometimes I felt like a warrior, powerful and skillful, fighting for the success of my mission, but was neither happy nor proud of this. Sometimes I hated decisions I had to make torturing myself with doubts later. The only comforting thought was that, deep in my heart, I was honest and my intentions were good.

• • •

We rounded Cape Reinga on New Zealand's northern tip in the early morning hours and slightly ahead of GATORADE. We were now on a short straightaway for Auckland, 200 miles away. The sailing was beautiful with brisk breezes and an occasional powerful squall hitting during the day. As we sailed past the ragged, rocky islands piercing from the sea, the mainland coast unwinded to starboard in a string of gently rolling emerald hills. What an unbelievable shade of green! It belongs only to New Zealand.

Leaving Cape Brett and the Bay of Islands to starboard, we turned more south, now practically on a direct course to Auckland. The spinnaker went up and the speed followed to the upper double digits. With the wind increasing, Poor Knights Island to port flew by in an instant. Then a very powerful squall hit, bringing winds of well over 30 knots and shifting to the east, but it was well anticipated. Our radio had been left on 89FM, which was constantly bringing race updates. After hearing about the havoc wreaked by the same squall on the leaders just a short time before, we didn't waste a minute getting the spinnaker down.

The day was quickly coming to an end, together with the third leg of the Whitbread. Despite the late hour, the first spectator boats came far out into the Hauraki Gulf to cheer us. Each minute their numbers grew larger and larger. We crossed the finish line shortly after midnight, surrounded by hundreds of spectator boats with our deck brightly lit with their searchlights. Amid the powerful cacophony of the myriad horns and sirens, we motored slowly toward the Princess Wharf.

If the reception at sea seemed great, what awaited us at the dock was simply unimaginable. All three decks of the pier were filled with cheering crowds, which did not disperse till 4 a.m. A VIP party arranged by Radio 98FM, on FAZISI's deck, brought so many people, the boat sank almost two feet deeper into the water. Lucky us, it had been built strong enough to hold everyone. Yet during the first couple hours of the party, I had an uneasy feeling it might crumple at any moment under the load of more than 250 people. That's about 40,000 pounds!

Who knows, what's more dangerous for the boat: the fury of the ocean or the unlimited enthusiasm of FAZISI fans? Certainly, in designing the boat, we never took into consideration the strength factors for such an occasion. I tried to warn Barry Everard about the potential danger and regulate the unstoppable flow of the guests, but it was to no avail. In the midst of such a great celebration, who cares! Drinks were plentiful and one of the waterfront restaurants delivered endless trays of food all night long.

It was what you'd call a real reception, New Zealand style.

Sometime by the middle of the party I'd had enough drink to relax and to put aside my worries about FAZISI's deck. It was holding up just fine. Okay, no problem. From that point on, carried away by the surrounding atmosphere and sinking deeper and deeper into soothing half-consciousness, I remember only short snatches of the events. I could vaguely recall that at some point the radio station brought a person dressed up in a chicken costume to stroll on board. Or maybe, more appropriately to the location, it was a Kiwi bird. I don't know. Some crewmembers, who had grown wild after three weeks at the sea (combined with all the drinks they consumed during the last couple hours), persistently tried to determine its sex, groping and squeezing her (or him, let's just say IT).

The layer of feathers covering it was too thick to find out anything, and soon the guys lost interest. Moreover, there were plenty of real girls around—not disguised by the silly chicken outfits—young and beautiful. And quite drunk as well, at least to the point that they seemed ready and eager to discover how good the Russian sailors were after their long abstinence. The poor forgotten bird soon got completely drunk too, rather strange considering the nature of its costume with a long solid beak made of painted papier-mâché, which seemingly had no entry for drink. Later on two guys from the radio station staff tried to drag the chicken back to the dock down the FAZISI's sloped, 10-foot long transom (the boat was tied stern-to at the dock). Sure enough, all three of them slid right into the water, sending up another wave of cheers from the crowd.

As the party progressed, attempts to disembark FAZISI grew clumsier with swims becoming more and more frequent, until one lady hit an underwater piling after falling, and broke her leg. Strangely, the calamity caused by an ambulance arrival only added to the festive atmosphere.

The next day I saw an attractive lady approaching FAZISI on the crutches and my heart sank at the thought of the possible liability. But she just introduced herself with a happy smile and said:

"Welcome again. It was such a great fun yesterday... Oh, the leg... It's okay. Doctors told me it would heal, no problem... Well, you know what? I own the restaurant across the street. I'd like to extend an invitation to you and your entire crew to have their daily lunches there during the stopover. It's my treat."

Skip was right. New Zealand was a sailing paradise.

●●●

By the time of our arrival, the sponsorship program was already in full swing in two basic directions. Barry Everard and Paul Smitt arranged a raffle with tons of great prizes. The top one was a gorgeous BMW 3–Series, donated by a local dealer, Coutts BMW, in exchange for the free airtime. There was also a flight for two to Disney World in Orlando, Florida, presented by Continental Airlines, and a whole array of home appliances from Fisher & Paykel. With such great prizes, the raffle tickets were going like hot cakes. A bunch of college kids on their break were hired by Barry Everard to sell tickets on every Auckland corner at ten-percent commission.

The government permission to hold a raffle, which normally takes a few months to process, had been obtained in just one week. The

Prime Minister of New Zealand, Sir Geoffrey Palmer, gave a speech on the radio, personally imploring New Zealanders to take FAZISI into their hearts under the slogan "Let's put wind into their sails." Grant Dalton of FISHER & PAYKEL spoke as well. He was joined by New Zealand's rising sailing star Chris Dickson.

Barry Everard was occasionally involved in sponsorship activities, but he also had the radio station to run. Skip didn't have a desire to get tangled in the routine management himself, so the real soul of the FAZISI campaign became Paul Smitt. Every morning, with a light hangover still lingering from the previous night's fundraising party, he'd show up at the 89FM office and immediately fill up the space by talking, laughing, making phone calls, and throwing out more ideas for yet another fundraising event.

"Yes, hon, you' brilliant... I think this fashion show with al' the models will be the biggest fucking success... Is there really no bloody way they could be topless? What a pity, hah, hah," said Paul while taking notes in his notebook. His New Zealand accent sounded so strange. I was amazed to find how many different variations of English language existed. As soon as I got slightest grip on English English, formal and sophisticated, we had already arrived in Australia with its own Aussi English, strong and optimistic. And now it was yet another variant, New Zealand'. These foreigners were not making it easy for me.

Paul continued, "Oh, yes, that's fantastic. We'll put a couple of handsome Russian guys at the podium as well to accompany the models. I think Juki would look absolutely stunning in a black tuxedo... Oh, you've already heard about Juki, haven't you? Well, who hasn't ... Oh, yes, those Russians really know how to party... Yes... That's right ... Brilliant idea, sweetie, just keep working on it. That's my girl, I just love you! Have you already booked a convention hall?... Sure, I'll hold..."

He covered the microphone with his hand and with a funny grimace turned to me, "My head is literally crushing... How do you Russians survive all this vodka without any visible damage? Anyway, yesterday's party at Southern Spars... it was a riot, wasn't it? I'd guess there weren't less than a thousand people, what do you think? At ten bucks a head it's ten grand right there! Isn't it great? Our expenses had probably been $3,000, maybe a bit more... Three bands, food, and whatnot... That leaves us with seven big ones in just one night! That's the way to make money!"

At that moment a bunch of young men and women, raffle tickets sellers, entered the room carrying large cartons filled with money.

"Come on in, my friends! How was business yesterday? Looks like pretty damn good." Paul glanced into the cartons, took them from the kids and emptied all over the table. A stack of money at least two feet high looked impressive, and Paul's eyes sparkled when he continued, "Probably another four grand, Vlad, what do you think? Maybe five?" He jumped back to the phone, "I am here, darling, sitting in front of this huge pile of money. This is exciting, believe me... Well, getting back to the fashion show..."

The other, subtler, grass-root approach was taken by Clive Tremain, whose campaign of private contributions and merchandising program grew more and more successful each day. He was selling a variety of FAZISI T-shirts, hats, pins, and such in a store in the center of Princess Wharf and through mail order.

Too many sponsorship events were squeezed in between the maintenance of the boat. We all quickly got tired of this non-stop party routine, but the results were astonishing: FAZISI's fund grew larger and larger, along with our confidence.

• • •

FAZISI was hauled at McMullen & Wing boatyard where she received a complete check-up and a new deck paint job. She had never looked so beautiful.

With the boat out of water, we were terrified to look at her rudder. The infamous Speedwave masterpiece repaired in Fremantle had totally fallen apart. The blade was hanging to the stock only by the piece of laminate of Juki's repair. It was truly a miracle that we'd made it to Auckland. This time Cookson's Boatyard took care of the rudder, practically building a new carbon-fiber blade. We never had a problem since.

The new crewmembers arrived in the middle of the Auckland stopover. Together with Valery Alexeev, who would become the new Russian co-skipper, came Victor Pogrebnov from the same yacht club in Sochi on the Black Sea and the Soviet Olympic star Sergey Borodinov. The crew replacements sparked a brief rebellion (surprise, surprise), actively supported by Skip. That was weird, I thought. Hadn't he requested the replacements in the first place? Well, he had requested the replacements, true, but not the new Russian co-skipper. I suspected Skip was partly behind the plot, though mostly it was the fruit of Eugene's and Anatoly's labor. They had certainly felt that their days on FAZISI were numbered, and this stopover, entirely controlled by the radio station 89FM, would be their last chance to raise a final revolt against the "administration," myself and Chumakov included.

I was working on FAZISI with Valery Alexeev when Skip hurriedly arrived and announced in an utmost serious, almost somber, voice, "Vladislav, you need to come with me. The crew has called a meeting, and they sent me to take you to the radio station.

"What kind of meeting? Something happen?"

"I can't tell you anything. Just come with me."

"You are not arresting me, are you?" I couldn't resist a joke. "What is all this secrecy about?"

He didn't answer but I had already guessed it anyway. In some strange way Skip behaved exactly as he did during the crew unrest in Punta, before Alexey Grischenko's death. He had the same kind of dramatic excitement with his eyes sparkling and his gestures sharp and unnatural — he actually looked rather funny, and I smiled again. A stern glance was the only response as he kept driving, seemingly even more tense.

Skip once told me that, while attending the University of Chicago, he took an active part in the student unrest of the late '60s. That's where his obsession with fighting came from. Realizing that he had been a rebel at roughly the same time when I had grown totally fed up with the Soviet system, trying to resist it in my own way, I found it strange that that didn't draw us closer, rather the opposite. With all respect for Skip's right to protest the way he did then, I couldn't discard the fact that he was protesting the American political system. It may not have been a perfect system, certainly in need of improvement, but in my view the best one people had yet mastered, where free choices were guaranteed, and where even Skip's rebellion was okay.

At the same time I was rejecting the Soviet system, where it all was prohibited; the evil one, as Ronald Reagan had rightly put it. The difference seemed so obvious to me. We talked about this a few times, but as smart as he was, Skip never got it. My English was probably not good enough to explain.

Anyway, the differences of political opinion had put us on opposite sides of the barricades, luckily not for long. The mutiny was a short-lived one. Barry Everard stepped forward to calm down the yelling and shouting rioters as he made a brief speech on the essence of personal freedom and responsibility.

"Look, guys, we understand that you are unhappy that some of you have to be replaced by the new crewmembers and return home. But it's up to the Fazis company on how to handle this project. You may accept it or leave at any time. You are in a free world now, guys, the choice is yours. You could even start your own project if you wish. But for those of you who want to stay with FAZISI, we, as your sponsor, expect and require at least some discipline and organization. Only then can this stopover become the success we're all hoping and working hard for."

As he saw that the yelling and angry remarks had not subsided, Barry continued, "Let me assure you, nobody's going home now. You will all stay until the start and enjoy New Zealand. But we've agreed that Vlad and Skip will decide on who will have to fly home after the start, and I'm asking you to abide by their decision."

After it was all over, Eugene stopped me and in an apologetic voice explained that the improvised protest hadn't been his idea, that he had actually tried to prevent it. Then why all these apologies? Anyway, I really didn't care any longer. Over time, Eugene had proved to be exactly the man Grischenko had described to me before inviting him: a brilliant engineer, an average sailor, and first and foremost, an extremely ambitious person. Often unhappy and complaining about "the administration," quick to unleash his peculiar sense of humor, overly sarcastic, almost sardonic, he was a source of many conflicts. I had even heard rumors of fistfight he had had and, obviously, lost to Juki. I hadn't paid much attention. The conflicts weren't about the good guys and the bad guys. It was simply that Eugene and Anatoly were both ambitious men, and both wanted to be leaders in their own right, unhappy with their position within the project and unwilling to submit to the interests of the team.

They both talked a lot about their own future Whitbread campaigns, which would be much better than FAZISI's. Sure. That a way to go, guys! Now prove it!

Finally, Fazis SP, namely Tikhov, agreed with me that Eugene and Anatoly would sail their last leg to Punta, and then bye, bye. No matter what, I was determined to finally build the best FAZISI crew I possibly could.

• • •

As the start grew closer and the sponsorship program reached its peak, we started to realize that, regardless of how fast money came into the FAZISI fund, it disappeared even faster. All in all, about $150,000 NZ was raised during the New Zealand stopover. Not exactly as much as we all had expected in the beginning, yet still a great amount considering the shortness of time. This was the gross revenue, and a substantial amount of it went into expenses to organize the fundraising activities. A total of $60,000 NZ was paid to Skip and his team, including Monica Tingay and Jim Saunders and the and rest of the foreign contingent. This time there was no discussion; he just told Barry Everard how much he wanted and was paid exactly that. As not all the bills were paid yet, it was clear that again we would be leaving practically without any money.

The result of Clive Tremain's efforts went to pay for the crew accommodations but yielded nothing more. He claimed that he'd invested too much in the inventory.

"Shouldn't the inventory bring more money after it's all been sold?" I questioned, but didn't receive an answer from Clive. I didn't suspect any foul play on his part. He simply was not a good businessman, and his books were in disarray.

For us it was *deja-vu* — another lesson in comprehending the fine art of making money and losing money. This time there was nothing we could do about it. Neither Chumakov nor I had much control over the finances in New Zealand, which extremely frustrated Valery. But that was okay with me. Whatever, we'd made it past the midpoint.

Tikhov and Kedishvili, who both had come to Auckland, were visibly disappointed. Whatever their real feelings were, I didn't know, but somehow the openness and trust among us had vanished. Apparently in their eyes, I was too close to radio 89FM and to Barry and Paul, whom they didn't trust, and I came under suspicion as well. My relationship with Fazis SP executives had only grown more and more tenuous when Ray Glasgow arrived onto the scene.

A businesswoman from Perth, Western Australia, she was an active member of Rotary Club International and through that association, she'd first become involved with FAZISI during the Fremantle stopover. Ray followed our boat to Auckland, took a minor part in some fundraising activities, and came to the conclusion — and managed to convince Tikhov and Kedishvili as well — that we should've raised substantially more money, of course, if she had been in charge. I never understood where her persuasive powers came from, but as a result Tikhov signed a contract making Ray Glasgow an exclusive Fazis SP representative for the entire Whitbread campaign. Technically she became my boss. First, he put her in charge of investigating the results of the fundraising in Auckland. Then he had her fly to the United States to organize the sponsorship search there.

The decision to entrust FAZISI's future to a complete newcomer was strange, to say the least, but, again, I didn't object. Actually even if

I had objected, it wouldn't have mattered much, as no one was asking for my opinion any longer. But I can't even begin to pretend that their decision didn't piss me off completely.

In any case, Ray Glasgow seemed to be pretty energetic and also apparently smart. I couldn't care less at her being my boss. At least, it would be another brain and pair of hands that might come handy in Fort Lauderdale. So I decided to let it go; moreover, any fight would have only jeopardized my position further. But I certainly didn't want to leave everything up to Ray. Without even informing Tikhov and Kedishvili—we didn't have much communication lately anyway—I decided to fly to America myself, and to do whatever I could to prepare the groundwork for Ray's sponsorship search. Barry Everard helped with visa application, and few days later I was on my way to the country of my dreams.

PART IV

PROMISED LAND

18

WELCOME TO AMERICA

Followed by the usual farewell greetings of the flight attendants, I stepped out of the plane, walked through the folded jetway of the concourse extension and entered the Los Angeles International airport… I had finally arrived in America.

My friend Alik Aksharumov, who emigrated from a war-torn Armenia not long ago, was already awaiting me. When he left the Soviet Union, I didn't know if I'd ever see him again, but now here he was, smiling happily, elegant as usual, white suit perfectly outlining his new Californian suntan. We embraced. I was so glad the ticket that Barry Everard's secretary had booked for me included a stop in LA. She got a super deal, only NZ $1,200 for the entire trip from New Zealand to Moscow via a stop in America, but I had to take lots of connecting flights. I didn't mind it at all; it only added to the excitement. The actual route looked like this: Auckland – Honolulu – Los Angeles – Denver – Miami – New York – London – Moscow. What a journey! I was finishing up my round-the-world air loop started more than three months ago in Moscow with the flight to Australia.

While we waited for my luggage, Alik briefly told me about his life during the past year — tough, the prospects for the future – bright, and then he drove me to his apartment in south LA. It was already late at night and the streets were dark and empty. On our way we stopped for dinner in a small restaurant, where the food was delicious, and no one spoke a word of English, then continued our drive through a strange area that looked like a war zone. Alik lived in a dark, decayed three-story brownstone with barred windows and surrounded by a tall steel fence.

"Hope you are not living in a prison," I said, trying to hide growing uneasiness behind a joke.

"Well, it's not the best neighborhood, but I'll move from here as soon as I get a real job."

I needed to make a few overseas calls, but Alik didn't have a phone. So we drove to a street booth, stopping briefly at a small shopping plaza, where I changed $20 into quarters. I had already tried to make a call from the airport, and knew that as soon as I would pick up the receiver to make a call, a nice woman's voice would say: "Please insert $2.50 for the first two minutes ..."

We drove for a while until a working street phone was found.

"Oh, no, no, stay in the car," Alik said quickly when I tried to open the door. "Just roll down the window and reach for the receiver. I've parked close enough. It is too dangerous to step outside ... "

Wow, so far everything looked exactly like the Soviet propaganda told us America would look. Strange ...

• • •

Long before arriving here, I had had a very definite image of America, totally different from the reality to which I was exposed so far.

As long as I could remember, I had always been fascinated with America. Actually, not just fascinated. In my soul, I felt that I was an American. It all probably started at the age of three or four. My parents were building their own house then, and for the time being we were living in one tiny room. My father had a habit of listening to the news on the Voice of America radio station. This was a forbidden activity, so he did it late at night. He had a good receiver, and despite heavy signal blocking produced by the Russian military radio stations, the quality of reception was reasonably good. Voice of America became a part of my life.

Deep in the night, half asleep, I'd hear bits and pieces of transmissions cutting through the static. Catching glimpses of my father's dark silhouette , feebly lit by the mysterious green light of the receiver's tuning indicator, within an atmosphere of secrecy that surrounded his late-night activity, I grew more and more confident that he was not just an ordinary Russian dad, as all my friends had had. What if he was, in fact, a secret American agent, I thought, shivering from fear and excitement. His tales of wandering around Western Europe after escaping the German labor camp during WW II only added to the mystery. At some point, I had developed a strange fantasy that one day my father would tell us: "Okay, guys, it's all over now. My mission is accomplished, we can go home to America now." Well, sure enough, it never happened —and the childhood dreams eventually evaporated — but the seeds planted then fell into receptive soil and flourished.

That was in the middle of the Cold War, and America left not a single Russian untouched. It was a subject of hate or love. No matter how hard the Soviet propaganda tried to paint America black, for many Russians it remained a faraway dreamland. Many people still remembered the time when our countries had been allies in a fight against fascism, and were extremely grateful for the food and clothes they had received under the Lend Lease deal. I often heard older people speak fondly of America in sharp contrast to what was said by the official media.

But generally, information about America was scarce and fragmented. Then came Stanley Kramer's movie, "It's a Mad, Mad, Mad, Mad World." This hilariously funny story depicted a group of Americans from all walks of life who by accident had learned about a hidden treasure. Instantly abandoning everything they were doing, they rushed without even a second thought into hot pursuit of it, pushing aside and crushing all that happened to be in their way. Yes, those commissars in the *Ministry of Kultura*, who censored the movies shown, goofed and did allow this film to be shown in Russia, probably considering it an excellent example of how greedy Americans are. But many of my fellow Russians saw it differently. I'm quite sure that this film became the single most damaging factor leading to the collapse of the Soviet Empire. Before that no one in Russia had any idea of what American life looked like, but with this movie, millions got a first glimpse of America, and it was, oh, so alluring, so different from the drab Soviet reality. Just a schoolboy then, I remember going to the cinema with my friends to watch this movie over and over again, at least 10 times, maybe more. I could never get enough of the intoxicating sights of American cars, highways, and most of all, people who, well, did a lot of stupid things according to the script, yet were so spontaneous and free in their decisions and actions.

You may view it differently, but to me, three men destroyed communism: Stanley Kramer, Ronald Reagan and Michael Gorbachev.

Alleluia!

Later, rock-n-roll music had entered my life. Elvis, Jerry Lee Lewis, and then the Beatles, of course. Okay, okay, the Beatles didn't come from America, who cares, rock is American music anyway.

And later still, with lots of reading and thinking, came the realization of the stupidity of the Soviet system, which killed initiative of its citizen, bred dependency and obedience, and, by putting the whole nation on welfare, deprived it from many opportunities. With this realization came my desperate craving for freedom. In a sense, it led me into the quest around the globe, and finally to America — only it took so many long, hopeless years.

All those years, dreaming about America, I had no choice but to make peace with the Russian reality. Just face it: there was no escape. The borders were sealed tighter than bank vaults. I was not a Jew, so even the slightest hope for a refugee status was not for me. For quite a while during my adolescent years, I toyed with the idea of meeting a beautiful American girl who would fall in love with me, (after all, I was quite a handsome lad then and enjoyed women's attention) and would take me back to America. I was not sure whether this could be done legally within the framework of Russian matrimonial laws, but this was irrelevant to my dream.

During those gentle Moscow summer nights of my youth, I remember wandering through the shady alleys redolent with intoxicating scents of groves of lime-trees, dreaming how I would step onto the square in front of the Bolshoy Theater just as the big tourist bus arrived. Among the American tourists rushing out would be a dreamlike stranger who would slow down, look at me, and smile. Deep into my imagined world, I wasn't even aware of walking into the Bolshoy Theater Square, and was almost hit by a shiny tourist bus approaching the curb. It stopped, the door swung open, and a big group of American tourists rushed out, all of them ladies in their late '70s. They looked at me and smiled as I passed by.

Actually, I did get my chance once, but blew it. It was in the early 1970s, during one of the American exhibitions called something like "Research and Development in the USA," — don't remember exactly after all these years. Anyway, next to the booth where a nutty professor slightly resembling Albert Einstein, was entertaining the crowd with scientifically explained explosions, stood a gorgeous navy-blue AMC Javelin, a marvel of American technology. Overshadowing it was its guide, the beautiful American girl of my dreams with long black hair and an irresistible smile. There was always the largest crowd around her — or was it around the Javelin?

I was in a college then and would skip many lectures — probably enough to get thrown out of the Institute for chronic absence — just for the chance to return to the exhibition again and again to see that girl. Only once did I gather all my resolve -- and my knowledge of English — and spoke to her, asking something like, "What is horsepower of this car?" She gave me the answer, which I knew anyway, with that smile of my dreams—I probably just imagined all this. Soon the exhibition was over, and I was left to cope with my ordinary life again.

But then I met Tatiana and all dream girls evaporated in an instant — and the spring was around us, and we were young, and life was wonderful even in the Soviet Union. Soon we got married, our son was born, and everyday concerns became a priority. But the dream to see America, to breathe the air of freedom, just kept burning inside, no matter how deep it was pushed back by the chores of everyday life.

• • •

Now the dream had become a reality, but, like everything in my Whitbread endeavor, it was quite different from what I'd expected.

After Los Angeles, my way led me to Florida. The lady at the information booth in Miami airport, who handed me the list of local hotels, advised, "There's a sort of convention going on in Fort Lauderdale and all the hotels are packed. Don't even try. But I'm sure you'd find a place to stay here in Miami, and it's only a 40-minute ride. The hotels at the top of the list are more expensive, and going down, you'll find the cheaper ones. The motels are at the bottom."

I decided to start in the middle of the list.

"Yes, we have a vacancy, sir."

"How much?"

"One hundred eighty dollars a night for a single room."

Wow! I quickly moved a dozen steps down the social ladder. A few more calls revealed a problem at hand: as the prices became more reasonable, the vacancies evaporated. The situation deteriorated rapidly, as I progressed down the list, and soon I became completely desperate with only a couple of names left at the bottom.

"Yes, we have a room, thirty dollars and it's yours."

The woman had a strange accent. But what luck, I thought.

"Are you sure you want to go there?" the cab driver looked at me in disbelief when I handed him the address.

"What's wrong?"

"Oh, nothing. It's up to you, sir. I'll go anywhere as long as you're paying me."

After a 20-minute ride, he stopped at a deserted intersection, pulled my bags from the trunk and immediately took off. At first I didn't see a thing but as my eyes got used to a deep twilight, I noticed a low building at the end of a parking lot laying under the shade of gigantic palm trees. A weak light was coming from one of the windows, and I saw the sign "Office" as I approached the door. The lady at the counter requested the payment up front and handed me the key to my room. She might as well have not bothered because the lock was broken anyway. I started to get an idea of why there were vacancies here. The stories about crime in America, which were aplenty in Russian newspapers and which I had ignored, now started slowly surfacing in my mind. I looked around. The place looked like a classic desolate setting for a detective movie.

The furniture in my room looked like it was collected from various dumps of different historic epochs. Surprisingly, there was a refrigerator in the corner, which appeared almost new. When I opened it, a small bunch of frisky cockroaches darted away cheerfully in all directions, celebrating their newfound freedom. I wondered how those little guys survived in there. No, the refrigerator wasn't cold — it didn't work, it was absolutely empty.

I wasn't at all looking forward to the prospect of spending a night in this place, but there simply was no other choice. As a precaution, I pushed a heavy table up against the door — luckily it opened inside — and then, after some labor, added the refrigerator to the barricade. It looked impressive and probably would hold for a while if necessary. Then I checked out a possible escape route. It didn't look promising at all. A small window in the toilet gave out onto a wilderness, more like a real jungle, full of strange and frightening noises. After some wrestling with a rusted lock, the window opened with a screeching noise. A humid breath of tropical swamp filled the room. In the twilight I could make out a narrow creek, its waters reflecting the weakly lit starry sky — it looked like a perfect alligator habitat.

Not trusting the cleanliness of the sheets, I chose to sleep on top of the blanket fully dressed. This way I would also escape any embarrassment of facing potential intruders naked. Nervous but very tired, I fell asleep almost immediately.

I woke up to loud banging on my door, which shook the entire improvised barricade. Before I decided what course of action to choose — fight or flee through the back window, risking being eaten by crocodiles — the angry pounding stopped, and I heard two voices, a man and a woman, moving toward the next door. I glanced at my watch, 2 a.m. Through the blinds on the window, I could see the parking lot was alive now. Cars were coming and going, some strange dealing was going on, occasionally with a heated argument, and then I started hearing a methodical rhythm of intercourse coming from the adjoining room, separated only by a thin cardboard partition. Its pace was increasing and

increasing until it culminated in loud screams and cries. Oh, boy...
Where was I? Some sort of drag joint? An unofficial bordello?

Early the next morning, extremely happy to have survived the
night, I grabbed my bags and moved into a hotel in Miami Beach ranked
somewhere in the middle of the list from the airport. To hell with the
prices.

Back in Russia, the press had been quick to discover and expose
the problems of American society: crime, drugs, prostitution. I hadn't
believed them then, and was deeply shocked now to find that they were
not lying. Yes, they were telling the truth, but only a small part of it.
They simply failed to mention that besides this dark side of life, there
was another, real American life, free, wealthy, and beautiful. And probably nowhere was it more evident than in South Florida.

I unpacked quickly at my new location and stepped from my
room onto a wide balcony. And here it was, below, spread as far as I
could see, bustling and vibrant South Florida. The street beneath me
was a slow-moving parade of beautiful cars, most of them convertibles.
No one rushed. Instead, people were resting lazily behind the steering
wheels, oblivious to the thundering beat of monster sub-woofers, evaluating neighboring cars from behind dark sunshades. It was like a prom-
enade on the Champs Elisee, the only difference being that no one was
sitting at café tables facing the streets or strolling along the boulevard.
Everyone was in a car, which made the performance look even more
chic and expensive.

People weren't parading in fancy clothes from famous couturi-
ers; in fact, they were en masse almost naked, but rather clothed in the
shiny, sleek, and powerful steel armor they rode in. The car-king of the
moment was the torch-red Chrysler Le Baron convertible. It simply
dominated the crowd. But topless Camaros, Firebirds, and Corvettes
were almost as numerous, and their owners as proud — not to mention
the much more expensive Mercedes, Jaguars and Porsches, Porsches,
Porsches.

The boardwalk behind the stream of cars was paved in a pink-
ivory-teal stucco mosaic and lined with tall, perfectly straight palm trees,
their fan-shaped leaves whispering gently with the breeze. There were
no pedestrians on the boardwalk, and it was ruled unchallenged by a
beautiful mob of suntanned girls and men on roller blades. Who cares
about the men, but the girls — I couldn't take my eyes off of them, even
if I'd wanted to. Roller blades made them look even taller and more
slender. And those curvy shapes front and rear — girls were wearing
only mini bras and g-string bikinis, some of them were intentionally

tan-colored to create a complete and well-calculated appearance of na-kedness. Strangely, it didn't look vulgar or not even really sexy—maybe just a little bit. It was simply strikingly beautiful. I would probably get a pair of roller blades myself to chase bikini – clad skaters if only I were younger and wasn't sure that I'd break all my bones the minute I took a first step.

With an effort, I moved my eyes further toward the beach and the shining ocean, a mixture of turquoise water and white foam where it was breaking onto the shore, then gradually changing to a deep co-balt blue toward the horizon. The beach looked totally different from the narrow and cramped strips that I used to visit in the Crimea and Caucasus on the Black Sea. There people sunbathed lying like sardines in a can, so attempting to make your way toward the water, you'd in-evitably step on someone's foot or arm, provoking irritated and threat-ening remarks. Here the beach was not empty, but its sheer size was so enormous, stretching left and right as far as you could see and then disappearing in a light mist of moisture coming from the thundering breakers. It was simply so large, it appeared that each group of sun-bathers had its own private beach, paying no attention whatsoever to the others.

The ocean was crisscrossed by white wakes of Cigarette powerboats zigzagging in every direction. In the distance there were a few silhouettes of yachts heeled gracefully to the eastern breeze. Be-hind a line of breakers, another Cigarette was towing a paraglider, and above it hovered a couple of helicopters and a small bi-plane, towing a huge advertising banner.

I glanced at the whole panorama bursting with activity over again, and strangely it reminded me of something seen long ago but then lost among other memories. In the mid-1960s, as a teenager, I had subscribed to *Tekhnika Molodegie,* a Russian technical magazine for youth, sort of an equivalent of Popular Mechanics or Popular Science magazines. Like those magazines, it often featured a cover with a futur-istic picture jam-packed with all imaginable technical marvels: high-ways lined with beautiful cars, speedboats, helicopters, and white sky-scrapers disappearing into a blue sky—the pictures that were strikingly similar to the one before my eyes now. The dream world of Russia's communist utopia looked exactly like America's capitalist reality.

• • •

That morning Nicholas Pilugin, a journalist from Tampa, joined me. As a third-generation American with Russian heritage and fascinated by the changes in Russia, he had spent quite a bit of time as a correspondent in Moscow. Among the articles he wrote was one about FAZISI for an American sailing magazine, and that's how we had gotten to know each other. Now he volunteered to help me with initial contacts in America.

It was the same routine I had gone through many times already. First we drove to Fort Lauderdale to meet the local Whitbread organizers to get a first idea of what could be done to promote FAZISI and find out which local companies might be interested in sponsoring us. That night we had a dinner in Miami Beach with designer Bruce Kirby from Canada, the creator of the Laser (one of the most popular small sailboats) and with New Zealander Keith Taylor, sailing promoter. In preparation for the Whitbread arrival, the international yachting crowd was already invading South Florida.

The next morning I had breakfast at the Fort Lauderdale Chamber of Commerce. It started way too early and still jet-lagged and tired from the sleepless night in the Miami motel, I felt terrible. I don't even know how I managed to make a brief, fairly coherent speech and ended up with about a dozen business cards from people who were interested in talking further to me. A few meetings with reporters and an improvised press conference followed, which resulted in articles in the Miami Herald and the Fort Lauderdale Sun Sentinel. And of course, after the success of the merchandising program in New Zealand, I found guys who would start a similar program in Florida, and talked to a group of retail owners who were eager to sell The Russians Are Coming T-shirts. In all, after five days of hectic meetings and negotiations, I boarded my flight to La Guardia completely confident that the groundwork for Ray Glasgow's arrival had been laid, and if she were able to pick it up from there, we'd be all set. To make sure, I would fly back to join her immediately after the second Punta stopover.

• • •

Coming to America for the first time, I was not sure what kind of attitude I could expect from its people. Actually, I was ready for a cold reception, even for a dose of hostility, which would be totally understandable after so many years of the Cold War. I came absolutely unprepared for the openness and friendliness that I experienced everywhere. During those first days in America, my memory often returned to the pre-start period in England when Pepsi ended its sponsorship presumably because it had been afraid of "negative reaction in America." What negative reaction, I thought. It struck me now as rather very strange explanation. If those guys at the Pepsi headquarters really thought that supporting our team would result in any negative reaction, they must have totally lost their touch with the American public.

At about the same time that I was in Florida, Frank Lennon, editor and publisher of Palm Beach Illustrated magazine, who also published the official WRTWR program for the Fort Lauderdale stopover, got very interested and intrigued by the FAZISI story. He had performed his own investigation into the Pepsi sponsorship enigma. The result was his "FAZISI: It Ain't Easy" story, published in Palm Beach Illustrated and in the program.

Years later, while working on this book, I asked Frank Lennon to write a brief summary of his findings. Here it is.

Several blind people who knew nothing about elephants were brought up to the creature and asked to describe it. One held a tusk, another the tail, a third the trunk. A fourth rode on its neck. As you can imagine, each came up with a wildly different description of the el-ephant. That's the case with the ill-fated Pepsi-Cola sponsorship of FAZISI. Depending on which part of the story one was exposed to, wildly conflicting reports resulted.

Back in 1989 I had the advantage of objectivity (it was at the very beginning of my involvement with the project). As a writer preparing a feature story for a magazine, I also had access to various principals in the melodrama. Ten years ago I came to the conclusion that Pepsi really did go into the sponsorship in good faith, operating on the short-term belief that helping get FAZISI to the start line would make them look like good guys. They just never thought it through. The potential negative backlash that might result from leaving FAZISI sponsorless after she had gotten that far apparently never occurred to the Pepsi decision-makers.

Complicating the issue was the murky role of ASM, the German sports marketing firm involved as a middleman. Fazis was an unknown, Eastern bloc enterprise, competing for Western dollars in an unfamiliar, capitalist atmosphere. ASM simply took advantage of their naivete, and kept Murnikov and other Fazis principals away from direct dealing with Pepsi until it was too late.

Two facts are clear. Pepsi International did step in to bail out the venture when it appeared that the Soviet baby might never leave its womb. Then, after providing enough backing to get FAZISI's hull fitted out and ready to race, Pepsi chose not to exercise its option to sponsor the Soviets during the race itself. My own belief is that the well-publicized uproar about American companies sponsoring foreign syndicates while American challenges died on the vine was overblown.

Yes, race analyst and sailor Gary Jobson was on "Good Morning America" pointing out that no American boat could get sponsored, while American brand names such as Merit, Gatorade and MasterCard were emblazoned on European boats. (This interview was then picked up by the newspapers, one version of which was probably the paper crumpled up by Skip Novak when the news came out.) However, Pepsi's position has been misinterpreted by many observers.

"They fulfilled their commitment," Skip Novak told me. "Reports that Pepsi withdrew its sponsorship are technically incorrect. They just didn't exercise their option to continue."

David Ketchum of Hill and Knowlton, Pepsi's public relations firm in London, acknowledged concern about the negative publicity they received. He was frustrated as well, believing Pepsi had become the unwitting victim of the old adage, "every good deed gets punished." Pepsi's international division evidently felt this was an opportunity to be the white knight, dashing to the rescue and making a few points in the process. "Our understanding was that FAZISI would not make it to the start line without help. Their hull was lying unfitted in a Black Sea shipyard, and the start was only weeks away. We provided them with enough funding to get to the starting line, but it was never our intention to sponsor the entire race," concluded Ketchum.

According to Ketchum, Pepsi never really planned to go on and try to win the Whitbread. "Management's decision was firmly made early on that this was a short-term, goodwill gesture, and not a full-blown sponsorship," he said.

If that were the case, however, why did Pepsi have an option in their contract to continue as the major sponsor for the race? And, recognizing that getting the boat to the starting line did not ensure that it would finish even the first leg without additional funds, why even bother to get involved at all?

"Fazis SP and ASM felt confident they could get another sponsor for the race if we could just get them to the start line," said Ketchum. However, Pepsi's option tied the hands of Fazis; what other major sponsor would put time and effort into developing a program that was already locked up by Pepsi?

"I disagree," said Hill and Knowlton's sponsorship director Jock Wishart, who worked closely on Pepsi's sponsorship of FAZISI. "We

had been assured all along that other sponsors would be coming in. Had anyone come in, Pepsi would have been advised, and then they would have had to make their decision."

All that notwithstanding, with the fanfare and hoopla Pepsi put into their London promotion of FAZISI, the inference could be drawn that their intentions were longer-term.

"Perhaps that was an inference drawn by the crew," said Ketchum. "We got the impression that somehow they felt that our continuation would be based on how hard they worked and how well they performed... It's just one of those things. Face it, Pepsi is primarily marketed to young people. Michael Jackson is more in keeping with our marketing profile than a Soviet boat."

If there's an apparent inconsistency with Pepsi's major sponsorship of Dennis Conner's America's Cup campaign, Hill and Knowlton wasn't prepared to discuss it. "You'll have to ask Dennis Conner about that," said Wishart. In the Pepsi/FAZISI situation, "there was a lot of politics involved," acknowledges Wishart. Pepsi had been selling in the Soviet Union for 16 years; combined with the prompt from Dennis Conner, Pepsi felt that it should respond.

"It was really an unfortunate situation," Vladislav Murnikov told me from Uruguay. "Pepsi committed about $200,000 to us, and they spent another $150,000 on their own promotion and advertising primarily in England. We sailed to London in Pepsi colors, under the Tower Bridge. It was impressive."

But not impressive enough for Pepsi.

"They were just too trusting," said Novak, "I was the only westerner involved from the beginning. Fazis was like a kid in a candy store; they just thought everyone from the West was fantastic, and they simply believed what they were told, not realizing that a lot of the presentations made were full of hype."

Frank Lennon's findings had shed some light on the whole affair, though the exact motives of Pepsi's decision would remain known only to those who had made it. The thing that shocked me the most from Frank's findings was the fact, that according to the Pepsi executives, there never was even a plan to consider sponsoring FAZISI for the entire race. All our hopes were in vain.

As for Frank Lennon himself, he became so fascinated and hooked by the FAZISI story, he called me at Punta del Este during the second stopover there. Before long he had become part of the FAZISI team, working together with Ray Glasgow on a huge promotional program in Florida in anticipation of FAZISI's arrival.

•••

Returning home this time, I expected the "Syndrome of Coming Back," which most of lucky Russians who travel outside the Soviet Union experienced upon return. It was not just jet-lag. The initial shock of facing the surrounding gloom again made one feel physically ill and mentally depressed for days. Strangely, I was not getting used to the syndrome, its symptoms were always getting worse. I had probably spent too much time abroad. Or was it that Russia was falling apart at an accelerating pace during my absence?

The whole country was up for grabs now. Every official in every government ministry or state monopoly, who wasn't completely stupid or hopelessly lazy, was rushing to start his own private company, mostly joint ventures with an access to the West and bank accounts in Switzerland, Cyprus, the Caiman Islands or other "low control zone." Now they were methodically transferring assets and businesses into those private companies from the state enterprises that they ran. The time of quick money made by selling computers was long gone. Enough of that child's play. It was time for the big game now, an open hunting season, no limits applied. The name of the game was privatization, adding to that long list of historic Russian experiments: electrification, industrialization, collectivization, chemization, computerization and now — privatization.

It was a time of a battle for dominance, with newborn Russian capitalists fighting to become monopolists. After all, you don't need Bill Gates' IQ to recognize the benefits of being a monopolist. The means, though, were completely different in Russia. They ranged from bribing officials to blowing up the competitors' offices.

Those who had the nerve and were not imbued with morals, (who needs that old-fashioned ballast, anyway?) were on a roll. A few years later those guys who just happened to be in the right place at the right time would emerge as the richest men in the world. The real misfortune for Russia wasn't that they grabbed everything. After all, since capitalism had been chosen as the way of the future, it was necessary to transform the entire state-owned economy into a private one, and it was utterly naïve to expect that the change of hands might transpire in a civilized way. After all, at stake was one of the biggest fortunes in the world. The real tragedy was that the new owners of Russia had no clue as to how to manage all this wealth, other than for their own vain caprices. What a waste...

Truth be told, I was not surprised to watch this. It was, ultimately, just another way of pursuing individual happiness. How could it take a civilized form in a country that didn't know the law, morals, or religion? Actually, witnessing the chaos that swept over Russia, I was more amazed now at how different the Western countries were, and how the human race, despite an evident drive toward self-destruction, greed and aggression, was able to perfect a civilized society at all? Not an ideal one, not necessarily just, but at least fair as far as the human nature goes... Why some countries were able to accomplish this, while others didn't even try?

Well, it had taken mankind thousands of years of painstakingly slow development. From Jewish scriptures and the dawn of Christianity, which spread like a fire through the Roman Empire. From the sprouts of Greek democracy through the dark Medieval years to the Magna Carta and finally to the Bill of Rights... It took people thousands of years of tormenting advance, of making mistakes and painfully correcting them, slowly learning how to overcome their own weaknesses—by searching for God's Providence.

Tragically for Russia, all that time she had remained in obscurity, blindly dashing from one extreme to another. And she still keeps wandering without much of a clue—my poor Motherland...

19

SEA WOLVES' TALES

The Whitbread is often called the Everest of sailing. I like the comparison, as it clearly reflects the ultimate nature of the race. The mountains are my second passion next to the ocean. I am absolutely fascinated by them. I like to go to the mountains as often as I can, just to look at them, to admire their rugged beauty and to hike around. I'm not comfortable with heights and never did any serious climbing; nevertheless, the mountains have a lure that I, returning to them again and again, just can't resist. Even though I do not climb myself, I can understand why people climb mountains — after all, sailing is pretty much the same irrational activity.

Having read my share of books about Mount Everest, I found among the many similarities the two sports share, such as the primeval beauty of nature, challenge, hardship and ever-present danger, one striking difference between climbing and sailing deep into the ocean. Sailing definitely is more about exhilaration than torture.

Here's how the famous Tyrolian alpinist Reinhold Messner in his book "The Crystal Horizon" described the final stage of his ascent of Mt. Everest:

"When I rest, I feel utterly lifeless except that my throat burns when I draw breath ... I can scarcely go on. No despair, no happiness, no anxiety. I haven't lost the mastery of my feelings, there are actually no more feelings ... The longer I climb, the less important the goal seems to me, the more indifferent I become to myself ... My mental fatigue is now greater than my bodily."

Jon Krakauer's memories of the tragic 1996 Everest expedition described in his book "Into Thin Air" echo Messner's revelations:

"Above the comforts of Base Camp the expedition became an

almost Calvinistic undertaking. The ratio of misery to pleasure was greater by an order of magnitude than any mountain I'd been on; I quickly came to understand that climbing Everest was primarily about enduring pain."

There were many times during the race when Whitbread sailors could describe their emotional and physical state the very same way. Still, the attraction of the ocean is more evident, at least to me, because despite the exhaustion, anxiety, and danger, there was also present the real joy of riding the huge waves, which overwhelmed the inevitable pain.

When I started my Whitbread campaign, I wanted to sail the whole race myself. As it turned out, it was an unrealistic dream. Having gotten some glimpses of the sailing excitement, I know I missed a lot. Long after the race was over, I asked Edgar and Kuli, two of FAZISI's best helmsmen, to fill this void and recreate a record of their experiences. Relaxed comfortably in deep overstuffed armchairs, far from the chilling winds of the Southern Ocean, the seasoned sea wolves – the Russian equivalent of the English expression "salty sea-dogs" — shared the thrills and perils of extreme sailing, recalling the most memorable events of the race.

Edgar:
"The beauty of the ocean? Faraway places? That was all there, for sure. But for me the most exciting thing, naturally, was to steer the boat, the technique of it. I'd never been on the ocean before. I had sailed a lot on the Baltic, but that's different. I'd studied everything I could find on extreme sailing and felt theoretically well prepared. Funny, before the Whitbread, I'd seen big waves only on TV. Compared to surfing down the breakers off Hawaii, sailing FAZISI on the huge waves provided a pretty similar sensation, I think. When a massive, 83-foot yacht sits atop of a wave and planes like a light surfboard... This is the most incredible feeling! Especially at night, when you are flying at top speed in complete darkness. There is no horizon; instead, all you could see are just barely visible, constantly changing liquid mountains up front. It's hard even to know where's up and down.

"You need to steer within a sector of 10 to 15 degrees to keep the boat under control. The compass lags slightly, unable to catch up with the boat speed. Very challenging. You need to steer as if you're on a small dinghy, by instinct, following the feel of the boat's heel. The most important thing is not to capsize to windward. That would be a big mess and you'd break the spinnaker pole for sure. No matter how ex-

cited, I always tried to be careful. Or should I say calculating? Yes, you
need to act instantly, on impulse, but you also need to know what you're
doing. Always, a lot of brains are involved. Of course, I made some
mistakes at first, but then with experience, I became smarter. As long as
you feel how the boat is heeling, realize where the horizon is, hidden
behind the waves, and follow the apparent wind changes, you're okay."

• • •

Edgar:
"Big waves? The biggest? I think the maximum waves we met
were somewhere in the neighborhood of 100 feet from top to bottom."

Kuli:
"Oh, come on, don't exaggerate. It's all very subjective, as there's
nothing out there to compare with. Rather my estimate would be 50
feet, 70 tops."

Edgar:
"Believe me. I used to do a lot of downhill skiing and ski-jump-
ing and got a pretty good feeling of height. When I first saw the big
waves, my thought was they're just like animated mountains. You could
also compare them to tall buildings. Now, after returning from the race,
I often walk along streets, look at the buildings and see waves ... See
how they move and change.
"Some waves were really dangerous, tall and steep. They just
crashed above the boat, and she felt so tiny compared to their power. I
can close my eyes now and imagine a huge wave rising over my shoulder, its top so high, I almost can't see it. Initially, it was a bit scary to
steer the boat in such situations, just the thought of losing control ... I
always felt a burden of responsibility. After all, there were 14 guys on
board and at that moment their lives depended on me. But after I took a
few rogue waves correctly, I realized that I could manage them. It's an
incredible feeling of the unknown, just like downhill skiing. Falling
down the slope of the wave, you'd better be able to control the speed of
25 knots, make a correct landing, not letting the boat dive into the bottom of the wave, and get ready for a sharp change of apparent wind.
"It's easy on top. You have plenty of speed and the following
wave is approaching slowly. If there's enough time to put the stern right,
you're all set. But below at the bottom of the wave is the most difficult
moment. You either hit the previous wave and end up underneath it

with tons of water on deck, or sail too close to the wind risking broach. Or the guys on the spinnaker could mess things up at any time. There are so many ways to make a mistake. That's all it takes, just one small mistake that could turn out badly.

"FAZISI was the lightest boat in the fleet, and fortunately she didn't dive easily. We often had water covering everything past the helmsman cockpit, but that's it. Nothing like on the heavier boats, THE CARD or STEINLAGER. I've seen some scary video footage showing them completely submerged with just masts sticking out of the water."

Kuli:

"It's a cliché to say that steering in the Southern Ocean requires constant concentration. But, really, the margin of error is minimal, if it exists at all. After you start sliding down, you don't have many options. You're practically a hostage of the wave as you try to keep the boat on a very narrow groove. If you let her round up into the wind and broach, the wave will crash over, and she'll capsize the full 180 degrees. A broken mast would be the most likely outcome... But if you ease a bit more downwind, there is always a risk of an accidental gybe, and we all know what that means... So you pretty much need to make your decision, I mean the right decision, before you even start to slide down. And this requires not only experience, but also some gut feeling. I'm proud to say that I was the only one among all the guys who didn't broach FAZISI once.

"Was it scary? Sure, but also so exciting. Sometimes I wanted to cry out loud for sheer joy, and many times I did. Still, in the back of my mind was the constant thought that disaster was right there, looming over my shoulder. The risk was always much greater than you could reasonably comprehend, and just luck or God's will kept us from grim consequences. Remember MARTELA?"

MARTELA OF, the boat from Finland, lost her keel and capsized at the end of fourth leg, just 200 miles south of Punta Del Este. After hitting an underwater pipeline way back at the finish of the first leg, they had a persistent problem with her keel. Several repairs performed along the way had not taken care of it. In fact, MARTELA's crew knew that the keel was ready to go and sent a diver to check it just hours before. They were well prepared for the inevitable disaster, and there were a couple of other Whitbread boats on standby, which had rushed immediately to their rescue after MARTELA did capsize. No one was lost in the accident. Let's not even think of what the outcome might have been if it hadn't happened in broad daylight in warm water, and good weather, but on a stormy night deep in the Southern Ocean. Let's better get back to our sea wolves' stories.

Edgar:
"FAZISI had such excellent balance you could steer her with just fingertips, like a good car. It was a fantastic feeling... Riding along, spray everywhere, and looking around for another wave to catch. We had problems with boat speed in light wind close to the shore. But in the ocean, she was fantastic.

"I remember well the day when we set FAZISI's speed record. This was on the second leg when Skip didn't trust us in heavy weather, and allowed only a few, select crew — mostly foreigners — to steer. That day the wind was increasing steadily and, by the time my watch started, had reached gale force. When I asked to take the helm, Skip just simply said, no, and put on Bilou instead. I was upset but didn't give up hope. Skip never spent a long time on deck and when he was gone, Bilou wouldn't mind handing the wheel to me. He was a nice guy and we were already on friendly terms. Everything worked out as I expected and soon I was in charge of FAZISI.

"This was fantastic. The wind was great, the boat was flying, and I totally lost track of time. I noticed Skip back on deck again, but he just watched me and said nothing. It was getting dark and I grew tired, but no one came to relieve me. Skip was probably testing or just punishing me for ignoring his orders. Well, I didn't mind. I was having the ride of my life. I felt as one with the boat, as if I could predict her every move. It was completely dark by that time, but I could still occasionally see the silhouettes of waves, and some moments I had an illusion of being in the mountains again. One hill was in front of me, another farther forward, and I was on top of the highest summit. I could even see trees and bushes down below... Sound crazy? But I was in a really strange state of mind then...

"And then the boat started sliding downward, accelerating faster and faster. I knew we were doing great. A quick glance to the instruments confirmed my feeling: it was just a tick shy of 26 knots. Dave Tremain came and stood behind me, 'That's a record, man. Congratulations,' and he took the wheel.

"All in all, that day we covered 386 miles in a 24-hour period. As it turned out, that was the second longest day's run of the entire fleet during the race. Only FORTUNA did slightly better. We'd been on a roll. The boat was doing great and we'd been catching up with the leaders with every passing day. And than, just 2,000 miles from Australia, someone noticed small cracks in the boom where the vang fitting was attached. Our technical guys, Platon and Miron, started panicking. Especially Eugene, 'Oh, shit, it's disaster. In the middle of nowhere without a boom... How can we make it to the shore?"

" 'Come on, calm down. It is just a small crack, it's not over yet.'

" 'It can break any moment and there's nothing we can do about it.'

"Actually, we could do something, but not much, true. Two holes drilled at the end of the crack helped to reduce the concentration of stress and prolonged the boom's agony for a little bit. But once the cracks developed, it would be only a matter of time — it will break sooner or later. We just hoped for later and pushed really hard as every passing hour brought us closer and closer to Australia. Unfortunately, it didn't last long. In the early predawn hour of the next morning, I was off watch below when I heard Crocodile shouting: 'Boom broke!' Everyone ran up on deck. Two pieces of boom were violently swinging around at the height of our heads. It was a hellish job to get it down; the whole thing weighed more than 400 pounds.

"Anyway, we took the shorter piece below, but the longer one was too big, so we just tied it on deck. Our technical specialists concluded that the boom couldn't be repaired at sea, so we kissed goodbye any hope of a good position on this leg. We attached lines to the end of each reef line and led them to the stern in a sort of Chinese-junk rig fashion. At least, we got some control over the mainsail. And so we kept sailing slowly toward Australia..."

• • •

Edgar:
"The icebergs were just magnificent. It's impossible to describe — you need to see it. A huge glittering mountain rises ahead, shining under the sun in all imaginable shades of green and blue. The surrounding water is the brightest turquoise, better than in the Mediterranean. I've been there for windsurfing competitions and remember the color very well ... During the second leg, we saw just a few icebergs, but on the fourth leg, I counted at least two dozen and then stopped counting. Skip's interest in them seemed to be greater than in the race itself, and every time he sighted the next big one on the radar, he commanded a course change. We'd sail directly to the icy mountain, and Skip would

take pictures from all points. But there were so many of them, he finally got totally satisfied or maybe just ran out of film. Anyway, we stopped changing course and finally returned to racing in the right direction.

"Was there any risk of hitting an iceberg? Like the TITANIC? I don't know, never thought about that ... Thick fog was frequent, but it didn't cause much worry, as we knew there was no one around. During all the sailing in the Southern Ocean, we never saw a ship, never saw a plane flying above. Sometimes we could catch a glimpse of one or another Whitbread boat in the distance, but other than that, it was complete solitude. Icebergs could be easily spotted on the radar, unless, of course, there was a thunderstorm or a heavy downpour. Besides, immediately after one was spotted, all the boats would share information on the iceberg's locations. So we felt pretty secure. True, there were plenty of growlers, those small chunks of ice chipped off from the big bergs. Soaked with water, they'd float practically submerged, and though considered relatively small, they could still be sometimes the size of our boat. You could barely see them in the broad daylight, let alone at night or in fog. But, hey, this is the Whitbread and danger is supposed to be a part of the game, isn't it?"

• • •

Edgar:
"Sure it was cold and wet, but that was not a problem for me. I expected it anyway. We were well equipped and the dryer was a great help. I don't know if any other boat in the fleet had a dryer... As for me personally, I'd gotten used to the cold after sailing iceboats in my hometown of Riga. That is when you get cold. You could get serious frostbites, hands, face, feet ... Some guys got frostbite on FAZISI too, especially on the second leg, which at times was really miserable with sleet, freezing rain, wet snow, all that on top of the gale-force winds. Still, I enjoyed the Whitbread so much, who cares about cold. I knew it was for me; it was my race and small inconveniences didn't matter. Anyway, it's nature, and you should accept it as it is, or stay home. People, that's different. I got along well with most of the crew. But in the boat's tight quarters some brushes were inevitable. I think I will never forget our first cook, Doctor Drozdovski, who was with us for only two legs.

"I have a very vivid picture of him. In a faint red glow (we usually used only red lights below deck at night so as not to disturb those sleeping or blind you when you went back up on deck), covered in clouds of steam, he'd be furiously stirring something in a large pot, angrily murmuring, 'Just you wait, I'll feed you all right.' My bunk was next to the galley and I heard those words many times deep into the night, when everyone was asleep and he was casting his spell. It was exactly like a picture from my childhood fairytale book about witches and wizards. Sure, we were all afraid of him, sensing some deep power, or, as we call it in Russia, a 'bad eye.'

"I remember once after dinner he was distributing fresh apples to everyone, but passed me by. When I demanded my share, he just replied, 'tomorrow' and turned his back to me. The next day I was more persistent as fresh fruit was really precious at sea. Besides, I just didn't want to let it go, 'Hey, listen, doc, when will I finally get my apples, a double portion, one for yesterday and one for today?' He looked at me heavily for a while, then suddenly threw them at me with the words, 'Here, choke on them,' and kept staring. I took my first bite and sure enough, choked instantly. Yeah, the doctor, he had a really bad eye. Some guys in the crew had constant diarrhea, they were sure he'd poisoned them. There was a clear trend: people whom he disliked most would run into the toilet more often. Well, the guys paid him back in kind, connecting the ventilation hose, which led to the galley, to the sucking duct from the toilet…"

Edgar was silent for a moment, smiling. His memories of the doctor were more funny than scary, especially now, a few months later. Sure, Dr. Drozdovski was not an easy personality, but that's understandable after what he had been through in his life, having worked for a few years in a field hospital during the Afghan war. He came into our team late, when the boat was already built, and this didn't help the relationships either. Skip had requested that a doctor be aboard. On one of his previous Whitbreads there had been a medical emergency on his boat, and Skip had to face a tough choice: going back to port and abandoning the race, or continuing, risking the sick man's life. The worst thing was that he didn't know how serious the guy's condition was. He went on and continued racing, and the man was okay at the end. But since than Skip had always had a doctor on board.

We knew there wouldn't be enough work to justify a full-time doctor's position (we kept our fingers crossed), and we also needed a cook, as no one in the crew was looking forward to cooking. So we decided to kill two birds with one stone. Besides being a doctor, Drozdovski was a good sailor from Odessa; some crewmembers had known and recommended him. He was offered a combined position, doctor/cook. It seemed reasonable as both occupations had to do with crew health and well being. He accepted it.

The problem was he didn't like to cook. He also didn't know a word of English, so the labels on the packets of freeze-dried food meant nothing to him. He simply didn't know what he was cooking, and that didn't contribute to the quality of final product at all. The guys were able to find out what the menu was only after they'd sampled it, and in many cases even this wouldn't reveal what sort of dish he had mastered. Tensions grew higher. The worst part of this situation was that he didn't consider himself a cook, while no one treated him like a sailor. That could make anyone's life miserable. I felt really sorry for the man when he was replaced after the second leg.

• • •

Edgar:

"In general I expected more wind in the Southern Ocean. We had too many days with light breeze or even dead calm, but no matter what, storms were always coming, that's for sure. The wind would pick up and would be screaming soon, and the boat would fly eastbound again. The most furious storm raged for more than a week with winds of 55 knots and more. It was very wet, dark, and depressing. So when it finally started diminishing, and the sun broke through the clouds for the first time, everyone on board came alive again. During the storm we all were cautious never neglecting to fasten our harness, but when the skies cleared, all fears evaporated. The guys relaxed completely although the wind was still blowing 40 knots and waves had built up very high.

"Elephant was steering and I sat behind him in the windward cockpit. His harness was fastened, mine wasn't. A few minutes later Eugene showed up through the front hatch and climbed onto deck. Fully dressed in complete foul-weather suit armor, he looked rather like an astronaut. Moving slowly and heavily, he stepped into the central cockpit and sat down next to the mainsheet winch. He lifted up his broad face, closed his eyes, and let the weak sunrays caress his skin. Everything looked so peaceful despite the tall and steep waves dancing around. Elephant took one of the waves wrong and it hit the boat hard in a quarter. She heeled way too much, and I told him:

" 'Take it easy, Sergey, you are not doing it right.'

" 'Get lost,' he replied, 'when it comes to your turn, you will show us all how to do it right. Now let me do the job, as I know it. '

"The next wave hit and he made the same mistake. I told him

again, with the same result. You need to feel the wave. If not – it's practically impossible to explain. So I shut up, just grabbed the backstay tighter, knowing that the boat might capsize with any next wave. And sure, it happened. I saw a huge crest looming over our heads… Than it crashed and the boat capsized instantly. The next thing I saw was the mainsail sliding over the water, Elephant hanging on to his harness above the opposite cockpit, trying to get a hold of anything, and the boat still moving on its side, heeled a full 90 degrees. I held on to the backstay winch as tight as I could, trying to find support for my feet. And then I saw Eugene in the water down below, horrified when I realized that he wasn't wearing a harness.

"The boat began righting itself gradually and picking up speed again. Luckily for Eugene the mainsheet was in the water behind him, and he had gotten tangled up in it. Elephant was still wiggling in the lower cockpit, but Bilou had already grabbed the wheel as I ran to help Eugene. While I was trying to reach him, he struggled to pull himself closer to the boat using the mainsheet. Finally I got a hold of him, but he was so heavy, and the boat now was moving faster and faster. There was no way I'd be able to pull him on deck. He was submerging deeper and deeper, water now running over his head … Then I saw Elephant and two other guys running to help, and together we managed to pull him in. He was silent—in shock—for a couple of minutes and then started screaming: 'Elephant, what the fuck were you doing? How were you steering? Hadn't Edgar told you what to do?' Then he went below and requested some rubbing alcohol and didn't show up on deck for the next two days. After that he always wore two harnesses, snapping on both tethers."

The danger was not only that Eugene could have been lost in the ocean, although the risk was high. To stop a boat like FAZISI and then turn it back would require some time, and by then he would be at least a mile behind. To find him would present a challenge. In accordance with Whitbread safety rules, the boats were well equipped for such emergencies with Man Overboard Modules that would shoot out in the direction of the man overboard with a simple pull of the handle by the helmsman. Still, the risk was always there. An even bigger danger was hypothermia. The water temperature hovers just above the freezing level in the deep Southern Ocean, and a person would become unconscious only 15 to 20 minutes after falling overboard and dead soon after.

Seven people fell overboard during the second leg of this

Whitbread. All were recovered, and six survived. Tony Phillips from CREIGHTON'S NATURALLY was recovered as well but attempts to revive him failed, and he died from hypothermia. Here's how CREIGHTON's skipper, John Chittenden, reported the tragedy to the race headquarters:

"...We were hit by two huge seas at 0345 hours while running before a westerly gale. The yacht broached on the second sea ... and two men, Bart Van Dwey and Tony Phillips, were swept overboard. Both were equipped with life jackets, flares, and personal EPIRBs. Two life rings and the man-over-board poles were launched and the direction finder deployed. The headsails were dropped, and the yacht motored back on the direction-finding bearing of the two men. Van Dwey was located with the aid of white parachute flares at 0432. Tony Phillips was recovered and mouth–to-mouth resuscitation was started and continued until 0717 without success. Tony hit a stanchion as he went overboard and it is unlikely that he was conscious once in water."

• • •

Kuli:
"The fourth leg was supposed to be classic downwind sailing in the strong following westerlies. I've read a lot about the Roaring 40s and Furious 50s and looked forward to them. Besides, those would be the ideal conditions for FAZISI. Instead, we had moderate headwinds all the way to Cape Horn. The smart Whitbread tactic is not to tack upwind. We usually didn't go closer than 32 to 35 degrees of apparent wind in order to maintain good speed. Even if you go slightly off course this way, there is a good chance that you might end up in a better position when the wind finally shifts, than if you keep tacking, struggling to stay closer to the wind. So we went lower, pointing directly toward Antarctica. Finally, we ended up at latitude 61 degrees, further south than anyone else in the fleet, and surrounded by icebergs. The wind didn't show any sign of changing. Day in and day out it was from the east. Cape Horn by now was almost at our beam 200 miles to the north."

Edgar:
"Skip was worrying more and more: 'What if the wind doesn't change? If we tacked now, we'd be behind everyone...'

" 'Oh, don't you worry,' I said jokingly, 'If worse comes to worse, we can just make another loop around the world and hopefully the wind will be more favorable in three months from now.' But it was obvious the joke was pretty out of place. The situation was serious, if not desperate…

"And then, just like in a miracle, a couple of hours after our conversation, the wind started shifting to the north, and our course gradually led exactly to Cape Horn.

"We saw the famous rock, a dream of all sailors around the world, on a nice sunny day. The wind was very light and it felt warm after the Antarctic waters. Skip opened the champagne with a winch handle. His hand slipped and he broke the bottleneck. There were no glasses of course, so some guys cut their lips celebrating. It made rounding Cape Horn even more memorable with a slight pagan ritual flavor and blood sacrifice involved. Tierry, the French TV journalist, asked us not to use cameras. Some photo company sponsored him and they wanted pictures of the excited Russian crew rounding Cape Horn without any competitors' cameras in sight. He promised us that he'd send his professional quality pictures instead. I still haven't received mine."

Kuli:

"I don't know about the others, but I'd made some pretty good pictures. Why should I listen to that guy Tierry?… We came very close to Cape Horn. I could see it in every detail with some small structures and a lighthouse. In broad daylight, it was not as scary or gloomy or mystical as I'd read about it. Still for me, this was an absolutely magical moment that I had dreamed of all my life. This was not just Cape Horn for me; this was 'His Majesty Cape Horn,' nothing less. I even took a swim in its waters. Well, sort of. I just pulled a busket of water from overboard and showered myself. Man, I can tell you, it was icy cold…"

Edgar:

"We rounded Cape Horn slightly behind UBF, with three other boats, THE CARD, GATORADE, and NCB, following closely. It wasn't a great position, but not bad either. And then Skip started making some strange commands. Few hours after we had passed the Cape, when I was on the helm, he called for a tack. A few more hours of sailing, and what did I see again? Cape Horn of course. More strange tacks followed, but we were still there. Now I'd seen the damn rock from every vantage point and would remember it for the rest of my life. Maybe it was some weird current we caught or Skip just wanted to take a few more pictures, but finally we fell behind everyone…"

Kuli:

"By the next morning, as compensation for the serenity of our Cape Horn rounding, it blew 60 knots. After a few violent broaches, we ripped the main, and I was sent below to do repairs. I didn't mind now. We were on our way to warm waters off Punta again, away from the cold grasp of the Southern Ocean. The hardest part of the race was behind, it's all downhill from here."

20

TATIANA'S HOLIDAY

Our return to Punta was in sharp contrast to the tribulations and the tragedy that had marked the first stopover there. With sponsorship from Otegui, Amenco, and Comurex, we now had enough money to pull FAZISI through another leg, and it became evident that she'd be able to complete the whole race. In addition, Fazis SP finally fulfilled what Tikhov had promised the crew long ago: to bring their wives to one of the stopovers. The program was still very short on cash, but Aeroflot provided free tickets, and with help from local Russian immigrants, whom we had met during the first stopover, we received free housing in luxurious condominiums that line the Atlantic shore.

Now I yield to my wife Tatiana to tell her tale of the journey to Punta del Este.

"It was more like a fairytale …

"Until the very last minute, I was afraid to believe it could come true. We Russians were more used to the word *'nyet'* than *'dah.'* Just like our parents and grandparents, like countless generations of our compatriots, we were born and bred with the inner knowledge that relaxing after hearing 'yes' would only mean bitter disappointment in the end — who needed that?

"My trip became certain only three days before the departure. The preparations had been long and exhausting, going from one official to another to get the paperwork done, with hope changing to despair to hope again a few times a day. I wanted to believe that I would cross half of the globe and get to Uruguay, but only after the plane took off and gained altitude did I exhale happily and say to myself, 'Well, I guess I got very lucky this time …' And my adventure began.

"Vladislav, who had come back to Moscow a week earlier, the wives of FAZISI crewmembers, Alexander Kedishvili, and myself were aboard an IL-86 flying toward Buenos Aires. With a 24-hour flight and three stops — Algeria, Cape Verde and Brazil — ahead of us, it would truly be a time to relax and let my anticipation grow. As a child, I had somehow gotten the idea that I would die in a plane crash, so getting panicky even at the thought of being airborne, I hadn't taken a flight until I was 30 years old. But with all that in the past now, I found myself joyfully sipping cognac, looking out the window, and feeling totally comfortable in my economy-class seat.

"I concentrated on the things ahead. I would be discovering my own new world, not the world that I had lived in and had gotten so used to from my previous life. I would become acquainted with famous Whitbread sailors about whom I'd read in the magazines, world-renown yachtsmen like Peter Blake, Pierre Feldmann, and Lawrie Smith. I would see mysterious, faraway Uruguay. Well, most of the world has been unfamiliar and mysterious to ordinary Russian citizens like myself, even though I had traveled abroad several times. Those were visits to the Eastern Bloc countries with a group of tourists accompanied by a supervisor who mandated a long set of instructions on how to behave and what not to do. This trip was different. Now I would be able to act freely, go where I wanted, talk to whom I felt like talking to, try to get to know the customs and the traditions of this new land by my own means. Yes, it would be scary, very scary, but so exciting.

"For a long time I had dreamed about the ocean, about my first meeting with this immense wonder, about how I would finally come to the water's edge, touch it, go into it, and swim far out.

"And of course, the source of my greatest anxiety and anticipation, was FAZISI, my husband's brainchild. I would try to make peace with the boat that had nearly ruined our family but, in the end, had made it stronger, as I learned how to stand by my man. I would go sailing on FAZISI, would finally admire her grace, and would feel her speed and power. With my own eyes, I would see, straight to the heart, my husband's dream came true.

"Should I recall the sleepless nights and bitter doubts associated with this boat? Or Vlad's laborious work that resulted in the most beautiful yacht in the world? At least, I think she is the most beautiful. My feelings at the moment were truly discrepant. There was a mixture of pride for Vladislav, joy in anticipation of new meetings, new emotions, new impressions, but also doubts, even fear. Lacking self-confidence was not my normal state. But I was not surprised with all these confused feelings, considering the uniqueness of the situation. It was almost too much for me to comprehend entirely.

"Moscow was getting farther and farther behind. Time had stopped for us as we traveled through the darkness of the night. But soon the dawn will come, we will arrive at our destination, and it will be wonderful. Go away worries and fuss of my everyday life, my daily problems and troubles. I wanted to forget about everything for the next two weeks, to close my eyes and shut the old world out, completely giving myself to the power of new sensations and emotions—oh, God, let me be free!

"Twenty-four hours of travel flashed by. I was gladdened by the sunrise over the ocean, darkness fading away slowly, giving way to the first timid sunrays that painted the plane's wing pink. I was cheered by the friendly smiles of the flight attendants serving champagne as we crossed the equator. After a short dive into the humidity of the Brazilian summer for a brief landing in Recife, a few more hours of flight, and there it was, Argentina on the far horizon. It is the home of my favorite writer, Julio Cortasar, the country that I came to know so well through his numerous books, all of them fondly displayed on the bookshelves in our Moscow apartment. Buenos Aires was fast approaching as the plane descended, with ribbons of roads, houses, fields, and forests visible, and finally the airport. We applauded the pilot—a perfect landing—and the flight was over.

"Moscow was so far away; I wasn't even sure anymore if it even existed. I was in South America, walking the Argentinean land, and all forthcoming was finally just as real to me as the smile of the immigration officer. Hurrah, I'd made it!

"Having to change airports for the local flight to Montevideo just across the La Plata estuary, I took only a brief look around through the car window, comparing the Buenos Aires of my imagination, where I'd lived the lives of Cortasar's characters, with the real city. Wouldn't it be great to take a walk, visit places I knew of, stay a while—but not a chance. The destination of our trip was different. The small jet delivered us to Montevideo in 20 minutes. Dusk had already enveloped the airport, and I could see a brightly-lit landing strip far below, as the plane made a sharp descending turn. I was feeling nervous and excited, just like the rest of my travel companions. It was such a long way; there were such great expectations. What would be next?

"What followed were smiles, greetings, and introductions. I savored a state of complete happiness. Just yesterday I had been in snowy Moscow, and now the warmest evening covered me all over, with new inexplicable smells filling the air, with luxuriant tropical plants sway-ing in melancholy. My skin felt tender touches of this mysterious night, and all I wanted was to hurry no more, to stand still and listen, to be left alone. But the sensation was brief, it was passing by ... then gone. We were already in the car speeding toward Punta del Este. I didn't see much but the road in front, dark houses, and trees flashing by, emerg-ing for a moment, illuminated by the headlights, only to disappear in the darkness behind. It was only my first glance at Uruguay and every-thing was still ahead. It was so important not to hasten. There would be enough time for everything, one just had to use it wisely.

• • •

"Although it was already after midnight, the day was not over yet. Leaving our luggage in a small cozy flat in the center of Punta, where Vladislav and I were going to stay, we were on our way again. Vlad led me about to show me the town and to show me FAZISI. Deep in the night, silence surrounding us, we walked the streets toward the pier, and slowly before my eyes appeared the small town-resort, its numerous hotels, dark and sleeping, with half-illuminated lobbies. Closer to the shore, the solitude of beautiful villas, stylish and sophisti-cated, took over. Every villa was different, custom designed and built to the owner's caprice, yet they all were in wonderful harmony with one another, with trees and flowers surrounding them, with the dark ocean heaving heavily behind. It appeared to me as if I was taking part in a fairytale, as if I was just imagining all this. There were no words to communicate my sensations. Should I say that I was excited, charmed and stunned — maybe tomorrow I'd find the proper words, but all I wanted then was to give in to this endless gentle night.

"Then we were on the dark pier. The Whitbread boats were rock-ing silently, lighted by the moon. I saw STEINLAGER, NCB IRELAND, THE CARD, other boats, looking exactly as in the photographs and on TV. And finally, there she was, our FAZISI. What a great boat! What I had seen in Poti during the first launch was just a gray hull, barely resembling the beauty in front of me. She had come to life now, a sleep-ing creature — night-dreaming, resting.

"And in my thoughts I went back to the very beginning, to CHAMPION, the first boat that Vlad had designed and built in our Moscow apartment. I recalled our life then: strange, uneasy, filled with arguments, and misunderstanding. I recalled our nighttime discussions, when Vlad tried to convince me that building that boat was the only way for him to keep going, to get somewhere. And I remembered when I had stood stubbornly against his venture in an attempt to maintain the order of things as I knew then. Just like my parents, my friends, like all Russians, I wanted nothing out of the ordinary. And I wanted my husband to be the same: to build his professional career like the rest did and take care of our son Pavel and me.

"One of my reasons then was that our son's happy childhood was being taken away. I insisted that he couldn't grow up in an atmosphere of constant noise, a mixture of hammering or sawing sounds and rock music that at times was so loud we couldn't even talk. I was annoyed by the construction tools all over the place, the air filled with dust, and much more. Those arguments didn't lead us anywhere, and the relationship became worse as the construction progressed. Vlad was very dedicated to his project.

"Now, looking at FAZISI, I realized that those years long ago were the first steps on the ladder that had led us onto the deck of this boat. That experience of growing up in such an unusual environment had not only taught our son the first lessons of craftsmanship, but also, perhaps, had given him a chance to see life from a different perspective—to think independently, to make his own decisions, to take on challenges. Does this sound like a total re-evaluation of my own attitude? Well, yes, it was. I guess all that our small family had been through to get to this particular place in time was meant to be.

"Vlad took my hand and helped me climb aboard. Finally I could touch FAZISI's smooth shiny hull and, raising my eyes upward, find the top of the mast among the stars, far up in the black sky. Tomorrow we would go sailing and I was sure I would be accepted by FAZISI. She would eagerly show me what a good boat she is, and we would become friends. With these thoughts, my first day on Uruguayan soil ended.

• • •

"And then time went flashing by in a kaleidoscopic blur of events, faces, and conversations. With only short breaks for night rest, my schedule was filled to the limit. There were meetings with new people, long walks exploring Punta, many official events, parties, and squeezed in between long hours in the office with Vlad, blissful short getaways to the beach to swim in the ocean. The weather couldn't have been better—bright sun, cloudless skies, a rainbow of colors — all the spectacle of South American nature celebrating summer.

"I had to get to know the guys in the crew a little better, as I'd met them only briefly during the launching ceremony in Poti. They surely looked different now — stronger, more confident, suntanned, more muscular, smiling more openly without shy reservations as before. Of course, they had sailed a major portion of the globe by this time. They had gone through tragedy and remorse, through personal problems and mistakes, and had definitely learned a lot about life outside the Soviet Union.

"Still, I couldn't call FAZISI's team united. In my opinion, Russians are not capable of being 'one for all, all for one.' We each have too much self-importance. That's why every FAZISI crewmember considered himself the smartest, the only master of his trade. I was beginning to realize what a huge job it was to manage a team like this, and how challenging it was for Vlad to unite so many masters on one boat.

"It seemed as if most of the crewmembers expected Vlad, Chumakov, and Kedishvili to take care of everything. They simply didn't want to know about problems, particularly the financial situation. Not that financial problems should be the headache of the crew; no, I don't mean that. But they could have shown a little understanding. They might have, at least, reduced the number of requests and been a bit friendlier toward management. It would have made the job easier for everyone, both crew and shore people—maybe.

"Of course, for me there was no news in the fact that people bred by the Soviet system, with all its lies and corruption, did not feel respect toward their leaders. For too long the system had oppressed its citizens, not letting their initiative and free spirit grow and develop, and as a result, people learned to automatically resist any governing. It might take not just years but generations to pass before we, Russians, would be able to overcome this antagonism.

"On a brighter note, according to Vlad, the FAZISI crew had made huge progress compared to where they had been at the start of Whitbread. Certainly each to a different degree, but they all had grown more mature, more agreeable, and more willing to accept the leadership; and definitely more responsible. The guys had changed for the better and were still changing, which meant that there was hope for a more united FAZISI team — and hope for a better future for all of Russia.

"It was difficult to find the time to take a break. Vlad was busy practically all day long, and I tried to help. Even knowing that the ocean was there, with its alluring coolness, I spent most of the time in the office with Vlad, dealing with the endless everyday routine—taking care of correspondence, faxing, making arrangements. Translating from

and into English took too much time, and I realized how poor my vocabulary still was. Only then did I begin to understand the scale of the
FAZISI project, to see the aspects unknown to me before. With this new
knowledge, my appreciation for people like Valery Chumakov, who
worked side by side with Vlad, grew immensely. Although I saw him
every day in Punta, he was still a puzzle to me. I sensed that he had his
own hidden goals in all this, in addition to honestly wanting FAZISI to
succeed. Dark waters of the human soul—who could see through it?
Or, perhaps, it was just my imagination, nothing more. I loved detective stories and sometimes could see intrigue in simple and ordinary
happenings. And of course, I'd heard the rumors that Chumakov was a
sort of KGB man. Who knows, but just in case, I would be careful with
him.

"To Chumakov's credit, I must note that he handled his financial responsibilities excellently, and FAZISI's books were in perfect order. I also noticed that he was a skillful communicator. Having worked
for a long time as a coach for the Soviet Sport Committee, he had learned
to understand people's psychology, their strengths and weaknesses.
Combining this experience with intuition, he was able to get results.
Despite the stark contrast between him and Vlad, they seemed to work
well together and in a peculiar way complemented each other.

"Sometimes Vlad took me to FAZISI. It was just a nice ten-minute
walk from our office in the Palas Hotel. There was plenty of work to be
done on the boat as well—all the usual stuff in preparation for another
leg. Vlad showed me how they checked every piece of equipment and
rigging—things that looked really complicated and even slightly intimidating to me—to make sure that everything would work properly
and not break in the middle of the ocean. In the sail loft next to the
Palace Hotel, Kuli and Valery Safiullin were repairing the mainsail torn
into pieces during the fourth leg. Often Vlad, with me in tow, would go
there to check on the progress of the work, or just simply to help.

"In addition to all this, there was the media, the journalists. Often we received calls from the United States—they already knew about
the Russian contender, and, it seemed, were anxiously awaiting our arrival. For the first time Vlad started sharing with me the idea of a future
joint Russian-American participation in the next Whitbread. It would
be a true joint venture from the beginning. For us Russians it would be
a great learning experience, and for Americans it would be a chance to
get to know personally their one-time enemies. Everyone would benefit. I very much liked the idea of a joint team. Certainly much would
depend on the results of the next stopover, the first one in the history of

the race on American soil. Well, we'll see. Since FAZISI had managed to compete in the Whitbread despite all odds, I was beginning to think that nothing is impossible.

"But first she needed to complete this race.

• • •

"In the evenings before sunset, Vlad and I would take a walk with the camera, looking for new unseen corners, admiring the ocean and the red sun slowly disappearing behind the horizon. We would talk a lot during those evening walks, discussing current problems and potential ones, or just talking about ourselves and our future. Time was going very quickly. The quiet of the evening, the dusk with its half shades between the day and night, and the relaxed conversation gave us both a feeling of peace, even if short lived, but so soothing.

"Later, when darkness grew thicker and night fell, we would go out to Gorlero, the main street of Punta. Filled with advertisement lights and colorful displays, noisy and alluring with a frivolous sensation of celebration, it was a different world that would instantly draw us in. Blending with the promenading crowd, we walked along, exchanging greetings with acquaintances, maybe stop at a small craft market where local proprietors sold their hand-made items—bags and purses, shoes, jewelry, knitted sweaters and gloves, practically everything that a person might fancy. Surrounded by the same gay, throbbing hubbub we would stroll along and finally end up at a small restaurant on the beach, with the sound of surf and the cries of seagulls in the distance. We would finish the evening with quiet small talk, an exotic meal of unknown name, and a glass of beer or wine, all within the cozy atmosphere of friendly faces and a strange language.

"Oh, those charming nights, my short southern summer in the middle of the cold Russian winter, now eons ago—I still remember the smell of the ocean and my feeling of happiness.

"Walking the streets of Punta one evening, I caught a glimpse of Skip with his girlfriend Julia in tow. He was almost running, his pace wide and swift, several times passing through the same intersection, following the same route. He seemed uneasy, nervous, preoccupied with his thoughts. Probably again trying to solve his dilemma: whether to continue or not sailing on FAZISI?

"There was neither solution nor peace for Skip. It seemed he had no desire to continue on. It was also obvious that the crew could do as well without him. Who would want to sail just as extra ballast? Besides, he was already writing a book about the Whitbread, and that in itself was enough excuse to stay ashore. But it was also so tempting to complete the route; then the book would have a proper ending as well.

"Alexander Kedishvili added to the confusion. Trying to convince Skip to sail at least one more leg, he was worried that FAZISI would meet a cold reception if she sailed to the US without her American co-skipper. Vlad didn't think so:

" 'Of course, you can keep insisting that he goes,' I heard him tell Kedishvili, 'but I'm sure it won't change a thing… only cost us another 10 grand for Skip's salary.'

" 'Could you guarantee then that without him we wouldn't reduce our chances of getting sponsorship at Fort Lauderdale?' replied Alexander.

" 'I don't know … The further we progress, the less I understand all of these sponsorship games. Isn't this funny? But there's one thing I do know. The Americans will welcome us. With Skip or without him. I've been there and experienced it. Anyway, sailing-wise Skip has already effectively removed himself from the captain's position. There is no doubt in my mind that our guys are able to sail FAZISI themselves without any problem.'

" 'Okay, I'll talk to him,' Alexander agreed.

Later that afternoon, I saw Skip leaving the office, bent down by the weight of all his belongings, including a computer he was carrying. Despite being overloaded, he moved swiftly, in his usual way, almost running. Noticing me, he changed his course and slowed down.

" 'I am finally leaving. I think it's about time. I have pretty much done my job. The Russian guys can sail without me just as well… Anyway, it was very nice to meet you. Who knows, maybe we'll meet again some day. Good Luck.'

" 'Good luck to you, Skip, as well.' I really felt sad at that farewell moment. He hadn't become our personal friend, but he was a nice guy, and did so much for FAZISI. That had been a long, long time ago, when Vlad had brought him for the first time to our Moscow apartment. It seemed like ages ago. Isn't it a pity how life crosses our paths with so many interesting people only to split us apart again after a brief acquaintance?

"Good luck to you Skip—and good-bye.

"The next morning I woke up early. The dawn was marvelous with a deep blue sky visible from my window, and I decided to walk to the ocean to take an early swim. At the hotel entrance I almost ran into Skip who was hurrying inside, carrying his computer and the rest of his stuff.

" 'Oh, hi, morning,' he said as he ran through toward the office. As it turned out, he had changed his mind and agreed with Kedishvili that he would stay on FAZISI for one more leg after all. But after that, he changed his mind again. For a while it became almost a Shakespearean drama, rising to the height of the everlasting question: to sail, or not to sail. All the while Skip was getting good exercise moving that heavy computer from the office to his apartment, then back to the office, changing his mind almost every other day. Finally, he went sailing on FAZISI, I suspect simply because the start had fallen on the day of his 'to sail' mood.

• • •

"During one of our traditional evening walks, Vlad led me to the ocean shore and we sat at the edge of a cliff. No one was around. Waves relentlessly washed the rocks down below. A full moon spilled a shimmering silver patina over the ocean. The air, a rich mixture of tropical aromas, was filled with romance.

"I don't think Vlad noticed the beauty surrounding us. He was unusually reserved and serious.

" 'We need to talk,' he said slowly, as if not sure whether he wanted to start the conversation.

"I knew this was coming.

" 'I'm not going back to Russia after the Whitbread. I don't know exactly what's going to happen, but I certainly don't want to go back... I mean, of course, all of us, you, me and Pavel... I don't want us to live in the Soviet Union anymore. Well, you've known all along that I've never surrendered to the fact that I was stuck there...' He kept his voice very low and unemotional, as if he were speaking to himself, but there was a determination about it that scared me.

"Then he continued, faltering, 'I always had this idealistic vision of the West, where harmony rules, where laws are natural, and the very fact of individual freedom made everyone eternally happy. Wrong. It's a very tough world, it's a jungle there, and everyone has to stand for himself. But that's okay. Freedom should come with responsibility. I think that's a fair price.'

"For the first time during his monologue, Vlad looked at me and a hesitant smile lit his face.

" 'I have no idea where we'll end up and how we'll survive, but

I have no doubt that we will. Millions of people have done it before us and we will. With God's help. He has already brought us this far, He will lead us to a Promised Land... '

"Again he smiled lightly and continued, 'You knew, of course, I've been dreaming of America ... That is why I have this idea for the next Whitbread, a joint team with Americans. But at this point ... who knows what's going to happen?... Maybe we'll start in England. I haven't had a chance to tell you, I actually got an offer from a publisher in London to write a book about FAZISI ... Can't imagine how I'd do it with my English. We could probably stay with Jim and Liz in the beginning until we're able to afford our own place. They are wonderful people. You'll love them. They just moved into a new bigger house... Eventually I will find a job as a designer or even open my own studio... Wouldn't it be great?'

"He was talking and talking not leaving any space for me to say a word. But then he stopped and silence hung between us. There was only the sound of the waves brushing the shore. I wanted to respond but all the right words eluded me. 'I understand how it would be better to live in America or in England,' I finally started slowly, 'and surely there are many other countries, much better than ours. But there is only one Motherland...'

" 'And so it is. And always will be, and nothing can change that,' he said, impatiently interrupting. 'And in a sense I'll always love Russia. But it's the same, as when you grow up, you don't need to necessarily live with your parents anymore. I want to make my own choice. I want to be free at last... Anyway, I don't feel connected to my old country any longer. Remember, at the beginning of the Whitbread project I was stupid enough to believe that I was doing it for the pride of Russia, among all the other reasons. As if she cares!'

"He went silent for a while and from the expression on his face, I could see how tough this conversation was for him. He was literally spilling his guts out.

"He continued, 'Now, that I've seen what's outside, no way am I going back. Don't you understand, it's not really a motherland, it more like the bad stepmother of an old fairytale... I often felt as if I was in prison there. I had no space to do anything, to fulfill myself. No room to breathe freely... And now, that I've escaped, I am not going back to the cell again.'

" 'But it's all changing now. In just a few years Russia will be like any other civilized country in the world, and we all will be free...'

" 'Do you believe that?'

"Well, I wanted to. With all my heart I wished my country to emerge finally from darkness and obscurity. But I knew Vlad was right. Deep inside, I didn't really believe that Russia would ever use its opportunity.

"There were people there, people who were brave and romantic, who sincerely wanted changes for the good, but I doubted that they had a plan or even a clear vision of what should be done. Others, dependent, without initiative, a silent majority, didn't want any changes. Could my country ever change, could its people ever change? Oh, my dear, poor Russia ... I hadn't noticed that I had started to cry.

"I knew Vlad was right. I would follow him wherever he went, but I was scared, absolutely terrified facing the unknown, having no idea what the future might hold. After all, I had never been a fighter, living my routine, uneventful life ... not happy, but reasonably comfortable. I wanted changes for so long ... but now the reality of these changes was terrifying.

• • •

"Surprisingly, my fear didn't last long. It soon gave way to anticipation. I felt deeply relieved having this conversation behind us. Nothing was decided for good, yet now I knew what Vlad wanted and was glad to realize that, deep inside, I wanted it too. I felt strangely relaxed and enlightened, like a heavy weight had been lifted from my shoulders. Now, with only a few days until the start of the next leg, the Punta stopover and my holiday were about to end. I wanted to enjoy what was left to the fullest.

"During those few short days we joined the others at parties practically every night. The crews of the Whitbread boats each took turns hosting, with everyone invited. Rivers of beer and wine, sea tales and anecdotes accompanied by loud laughter, dancing, and singing—all the parties were alike. Only MAIDEN's party was properly organized—we women like order. Each member of their team had prepared a performance; some were humorous bits, some were musical numbers, and we, the audience, united in our gay mood, happily applauded every performer.

"The next day we went to the prize-giving ceremony. In the reception area of the Punta Del Este Yacht Club the best pictures taken by the sailors during the last leg were exhibited in a traditional photo contest – an amazing multicolored display of ocean beauty and human courage. At the podium Admiral Williams and a few other race committee officials awarded prizes to the last leg's winners and made appropriate speeches. Best of all, I liked Sam Whitbread's speech, probably because he talked really slowly and clearly so I understood at least something of what he was saying.

"The atmosphere was really festive with many women dressed up in beautiful evening gowns. But others, like myself, preferred the sporty-casual look. Oh, I would love to dress up as well, but at that time my wardrobe consisted of creations of my own hands, and the clothes that I made were all of a practical, work-leisure style, no evening gowns at all. There had been no need for them in my previous life. Finally, I got a chance to see all the crews together, each of them wearing their team colors — handsome, assertive, suntanned men, looking already somewhat distant, ready for the ocean.

"After the prize-giving the crowd drifted into a nearby building, a fishermen's club, where people finally relaxed, shaking away the solemnity of the official part. We drank something very strong with the guys from UBF and BELMONT (nobody could drink vodka better than the Russians except for the Finns), exchanged T-shirts and crew polos, then, unexpectedly, some of the sailors appeared wearing fur hats (they were sold around the corner). More toasts followed, elevating the festive atmosphere to a new level. At some point, the whole scene reminded me of the carefree spirit of early Hemingway novels, as if everyone was living only for today, as if there was no tomorrow, no ocean with its dangers — and I didn't need to return to Moscow's winter.

"Multilingual conversations filled the small, smoky room with no one having difficulty, understanding each other. And of course, there was dancing later, and then the walk home along the dark boardwalk. And, all of a sudden, a sharp feeling of closing farewell and realization that the time had come to part with everything new that had come into my life during these two short weeks. What a pity, I didn't feel at all like leaving.

• • •

"From what I knew through Vlad, their first stopover in Punta had been totally different. It had been a tragic time. The death of Alexey Grischenko had planted grave doubts in Vlad's mind and almost put an end to it all. Should this death be taken as a sign that they had gone too far, that the whole affair was too risky and its continuation would bring only more trouble?

"On the rocky shore, there is a tiny shrine built of sea stones where after Alexey's death Vlad had gone to think, to regain his strength, to search for answers and support. He had told me about this place and we went there together several times. The simple shrine that protected the statue of the Virgin Mary from the ocean spray, wind, and rains, was indeed a sacred place. It could move you to deep reasoning—to a conversation with yourself, with God. Like Vlad before me, I stood there, in the roar of the ocean, listening for the answers, feeling peace and comfort enter my mind and soul.

"Vlad had decided then that FAZISI would not stop, allowing a painful memory of her first captain to pass into his heart. And now, after several months, FAZISI was here in Punta again, the living proof that his decision had been the right one. There were two more legs to go in the race, but perhaps the most difficult part was already behind. It had been a continuous struggle, not only with the obstacles and the elements. So many people had tried to find their position within the project. And how many of them were left unsatisfied, disappointed, holding a grudge?

"Anatoly Verba, for instance. Initially he was invited to enter the competition to become FAZISI's captain, along with a few other candidates. The competition, which was supposed to be fair, like the sport of sailing itself, turned out instead to be a bitter struggle. Not an ordinary man, a person of great ambition, persistence, and vanity, an excellent photographer, with his exceptional pictures winning prizes during the race, he was unable to find his place in the team. Anatoly would fly back to Moscow with us, angry, with black circles under his eyes, silent, reserved. I knew that both he and Eugene Platon had each plans to run his own project in the next Whitbread, four years ahead, and I hoped each of them would find a better purpose for their ambitions as leaders of their own team. I wished them luck.

● ● ●

"But, hey, enough about these strong personalities. There I was, still in sunny Punta, surrounded by the ocean on three sides. I was standing at the embankment, watching the raging water down below. Sometimes, when a big wave splashed over the parapet, I'd have to take a step or two back. The foam would settle down on the pavement, sticking to my feet, leaving tiny drops on them. I had to leave tomorrow, and soon I'd recall my life here as something unreal, as a beautiful episode seen in my dreams, or maybe read in a book—or maybe as just someone else's story, told by a friend during one of those long dark Moscow evenings, when there was time for everything: talking, listening, reflection, recollection.

"I didn't know what would happen next in my life, had no idea of where it would go from then on, after this beautiful side-tour, but I did believe that a continuation would follow. And I had high hopes for it. But I was leaving it all to the future. And then, when there was still a little time left, we would go for our last walk around town to say good-bye to this now-so-familiar corner of the world, where the summer was so hot, the ocean was so blue, and the people were so joyful.

"Yesterday we saw FAZISI off, but because of confusion caused by Tierry Raneu, the French TV-journalist, I didn't get a chance to say good-bye to her crew. Tierry, who was supposed to sail on FAZISI for this leg and produce a TV documentary, should have arrived well in advance to discuss with Vlad and Alexander the conditions of his sailing as well as the future film for French TV. But, instead, he didn't show up until just before the start. And then they discussed the copyright and all other legal stuff. Tierry was arguing up to the very last minute, while I was so anxious to see the start. We ended up too late to catch the spectators' boat, which had already left the dock. The Frenchman, after a long kiss good-bye with a suntanned beauty, who probably was the reason for his late arrival and exhausted look, threw all his stuff into a rubber dinghy and went to catch FAZISI. At this point the boat was already close to the starting line. All we could do was to drive around the bay to watch the start from the shore.

"A great number of people gathered on the beach and the surrounding hills to wave their farewells to the Whitbread sailors. The beautiful boats were moving slowly near the starting line, and our eyes immediately spotted FAZISI. 'Come on, baby, you've done so much already, there's not much left now. Go for it! Fair wind!' The starting gun fired and the boats rushed forward, so swift, so graceful and lovely. It was impossible to take my eyes off of them. But we wanted to catch one last glimpse of the fleet from the faraway cape so we jumped back into the car to drive back around the bay and through the town.

"I waved a little more, yelled and cheered for the last time, feeling so close to this great race — almost like a participant.

"My holiday ended when the boats sailed into the ocean. That day, yesterday, was truly exceptional. And today my parting with Punta could, in a way, be called formal. Tomorrow would be the flight to Moscow, and as always before departure, there would be a lot of fuss about small things, packing, checking that I didn't forget anything, and then – driving to the airport.... But I was still there though, in Punta, trying to concentrate on my beautiful holiday already fading away into the distance, thinking happy thoughts of gratitude for those days filled with sun, discoveries, and overwhelming emotions.

"No matter what the future held, for me these days in Punta would always stay unique and unprecedented. I would treasure them in my memory like a keepsake so that later, after years had passed, I would look through my old photo album and smile at the familiar faces looking back at me from the Uruguayan pictures and find myself back here, in Punta again, feeling so free and happy as never before in my life."

21

THE RUSSIANS ARE COMING!

While we all, FAZISI, the crew and myself included, were still in Punta del Este, Ray Glasgow had already arrived in Florida, picked up all the preliminary sponsorship contacts that I'd developed, and moved ahead. First she took care of our future accommodations either for free or at a good discount. The deal she made with Bahia Mar, a luxury resort right on the Fort Lauderdale's beach, included free office space, assistance of the resort's PR staff, and a few rooms. That's where the bosses would stay, yours truly included. Crew quarters would be located not far away, in the more modest but still decent Best Western hotel next to the 17th Street Causeway Bridge. It was a convenient place at the very hub of Fort Lauderdale, with the Pier 66 Resort, location of the Whitbread headquarters and all future activities, right across the street.

Initially I was slightly taken aback by Ray's aggressive and straightforward manner. She used to raise horses in Australia, and now was doing business in the same forceful way that she would use to train a wild mustang. Nevertheless, she had endless energy, was able to motivate people, and in the end did a great job for us in Fort Lauderdale, even if never delivering on everything that she had promised. But then, who had?

I never understood how in the first place Ray was able to convince Tikhov that she could do a better job finding sponsorship for FAZISI than anyone else involved earlier. By the end of the Auckland stopover, when she came into the picture, I was in temporary disfavor with the Fazis SP administration, and they shared very little with me. I'd heard some bits and pieces, and it appears that Ray promised to raise $500,000 during the Fort Lauderdale stopover alone. This was a figure unrealistic enough to take seriously for all of us who already had some idea of the sponsorship games. But that's not all. There was another, totally astronomical number circulating, which Ray promised to raise using her International Rotary Club contacts. It was even higher than the wildest dreams that Alexander Manenko made other Fazis SP executives believe at the beginning. No wonder Ray immediately received unlimited credentials to represent our project. Impressed with the outrageous numbers, Tikhov gave her full carte blanche and sent to America. I was amazed at how easily he shook off the previous sponsorship fiasco and eagerly embraced a total stranger who promised him fields of gold. But then, I probably was simply biased and bitter after he had challenged my leadership position once again.

Ray's carte blanche was a relatively short letter signed by Fazis SP authorities and stamped with an impressive seal. With the pride of a young lawyer displaying her fresh diploma, she laminated it and hung it over her desk in the Bahia Mar office. According to this letter, she was authorized to perform sponsorship-search activities not only in Florida but nationally and internationally. Some authority! So it could be understood why my knees were shaking slightly when I first made eye contact with Ray in such an imposing place. The only thing that helped me bear the moment was the memory of the similar letter that granted total authority to Klaus Wawer — and then later a slightly smaller honor to Radio 89FM.

Surprisingly, Ray turned out to be a friendlier person than her first appearance had led me to believe, and we got along just fine. She understood perfectly well that by this time I already knew much more about managing and financing the project than she did, so she played it smart, never challenging my efforts. Chumakov was a different matter. From day one, Ray let him know that by Fazis SP's decree, she was in charge of all finances, and his involvement was no longer welcomed. The sad irony for poor Valery was that he had eagerly promoted Ray in Auckland, after he had been pushed aside by Radio 89FM. Now she was doing exactly the same thing. One more *deja-vu* for Chumakov.

Another key person who contributed probably even more than Ray to the success of FAZISI's Florida stopover was Frank Lennon, editor of Palm Beach Illustrated magazine. After he had learned about our project, he reached me on the phone while I still was in Punta del Este to offer his services and support.

"Mr. Murnikov, I'm calling you from Palm Beach, Florida. It's a very small community, but I'm sure you've heard of it." Indeed I had. Even back in Russia, we knew about the place where the mansions of

Yoko Ono, Donald Trump and Senator Edward Kennedy were located.

Frank continued, "It's one of the wealthiest places in the United States, on par with or even higher than Beverly Hills and Palm Springs in California. What better place to look for sponsorship money than one bursting with wealthy people? As publisher of a local magazine, I am well integrated into the very fabric of Palm Beach life and know personally many of its most prominent residents. I think a man of my position would have a lot to offer to your project. I am well aware of your difficult financial situation and would like to help."

Great, but what about Ray Glasgow? I explained Frank that Fazis SP already had an agent in Florida, and told him a little bit about the history of Ray's involvement with us.

"It's too bad that you've already given her the exclusive rights. But then… it really doesn't matter. I am not looking for any rights here. I simply know that I am in a position to help you and I want to help."

I gave Frank the phone number of our office in Bahia Mar, got him in touch with Ray, and together we started developing an ambitious plan of promotional events. When I finally arrived in Florida, I noticed a bit of rivalry going on between Frank and Ray, but all in all, we made a great team. Surprisingly enough, Valery Chumakov got along with Frank very well, which had never happened before in his relationships with foreigners. He simply either didn't like them or didn't trust their good intentions. However, with Frank he quickly found a common language, and both of them liked to joke that their mutual respect came from the idea that Chumakov was a former KGB officer while Lennon had connections to the CIA. I never found out if there was a grain of truth in their jokes, but Frank did seem to know suspiciously a lot about Russia, and while he spoke very little Russian, I was always under the impression that he understood it much better than he ever led us to realize.

While FAZISI was still sailing somewhere east of the coast of Brazil in the middle of the fifth leg, we had already lined up an impressive USA program. That included numerous fundraising parties in Palm Beach, an auction of Russian art donated to the FAZISI fund by young artists eager to help us while getting some recognition in the West, and even a boxing match between our own Juki Tsomaya and the strongest guy from THE CARD. Mohammed Ali was invited as a guest of honor. Our boxers were not professionals, so we laid down strict safety rules that helped the participants save their faces for future celebrity activities, but probably made the match less exciting. Nevertheless, we raised a lot of money from it, which was equally split between FAZISI and THE CARD.

Oh, yes, by the end of the race, we were getting so proficient in the art of raising money that we even helped our wealthy competitors raise some.

• • •

Sailing-wise, the fifth leg of the race was a bummer for FAZISI. Designed for heavy winds, she performed poorly in the baking heat of the doldrums. In all it turned into a slow and uneventful leg with the entire Whitbread fleet crawling, mile by mile, toward Florida. The only surprise to spice it up was ROTHMANS' big lead developed for the first time in the race. The British yacht, with its all-star crew and supported by a budget rumored to be $10 million, had never lived up to the high expectations placed on her. At times her performance was sparkling, yet never consistent. But it seemed now that Lawrie Smith, ROTHMANS' skipper, had finally gotten a grip on the race and led the fleet for more than two weeks, gradually putting more than a hundred miles between his boat and the rest of competitors. For a while it appeared as if Peter Blake's monopoly on leg victories would come to an end. But the New Zealander was just incredible, and his team — simply the best. After crossing the equator, STEINLAGER started gaining on ROTHMANS, day after day shortening the distance. And in the end, it was the New Zealand yacht that crossed the finish line first again.

Sailing in the doldrums is in a way even more strenuous than sailing in the bitter cold waters surrounding Antarctica's frozen ice fields. In the Southern Ocean there are always ways to deal with the cold, like putting on an extra sweater and a pair of socks, or better yet, replacing your exhausted pal at the coffee-grinder for a nice 20-minute workout. Soon you'd find yourself breaking a sweat and wanting to take off those extra clothes. And then, after watch, there are the simple pleasures like going down to the galley for a hot meal or just a cup of tea, exchanging a few words with Rami, sitting next to the warm stove. Wind is plentiful in the southern latitudes most of time, and any discomfort becomes an afterthought when you're sliding down those awesome waves, shouting for sheer joy as the boat hits 25 knots.

The heat is a totally different matter. There is simply no escape from it. Anywhere. Your choices are limited either to the scorching sunlight on deck, which reflects so brightly it hurts the eyes even through sunglasses, or to the humid, suffocating environment below deck. Day and night the temperature inside FAZISI never dropped below 100 degrees, and her aluminum shell was too hot to touch.

The high-pressure zone...

FAZISI suffered probably more than any other boat in the fleet. In addition to the extra displacement she was carrying due to the keel change, her sails entered the last phase of their life span, after serving endlessly for almost 30,000 miles. They still yielded enough thrust in a fresh breeze, but in lighter air their sorry shape would just hang hopelessly, discouraging the crew from any attempts at trimming. FAZISI just glided lazily over the glassy water. Discussing our plans for the fifth leg before the start in Punta, it was clear that with FAZISI's poor sail inventory, she stood no chance of holding her position in the race. The only hope was successful fundraising in Fort Lauderdale, which would enable us to build a few new sails. But it's one thing to understand and make peace with your shortcomings before the start, and a totally different thing to feel powerless, stranded on a sitting duck of a yacht.

The high-pressure zone.

I could only imagine how sorry Skip felt now about his decision to sail this leg after all. Totally frustrated, he revealed his agitation in a series of boring and rude interviews broadcast over the radio. His dissatisfaction was not limited to FAZISI and overflowed into the whole Whitbread race, its organizers, and the choice of the Fort Lauderdale stopover. Eventually he pissed off everyone he possibly could, and it became obvious that he had finally made his decision to leave and was just burning the remaining bridges.

• • •

FAZISI arrived in Fort Lauderdale in 13th position, late but in style. The first-ever Soviet yacht to sail to America, she was destined to become a celebrity, no matter how poorly she performed on the last leg. From that point on everything transpired in a blur of endless parties, fundraising events, and honest-to-goodness fun. Finally the organization was great and all this non-stop action was not distracting us from taking care of all the necessary boat maintainance and repairs. We even built a new mainsail and a spinnaker, which our yacht needed badly.

Upon FAZISI's arrival in Fort Lauderdale we parted with Skip coldly, and I thought I would probably never see him again. That was it. Or was it?

Well, Skip wouldn't have been Skip if he were to just disappear without a trace. After Punta I should've known better how easily he could change his mind. Only a few days later, he reemerged and before we could even come to our senses, he was back in full swing again, deeply involved in FAZISI's promotional activities, now simply as a volunteer.

One of FAZISI's main fundraising events was held in Palm Beach on May 1st. In Russia this day is one of the most celebrated holidays, known as the Day of Workers Solidarity, the day when the proletariat in all countries supposedly unites together against the world's capitalism. Now, as FAZISI crew, who could be considered representatives of the Soviet working class, were mingling with the richest people of Palm Beach, Frank Lennon suggested renaming the holiday the Day of Solidarity of Proletariat and Bourgeoisie. Well, the new name, perhaps had its merits, but sounded too cumbersome and the suggestion didn't fly.

Back in the Soviet Union, May 1st was the day of a mighty military parade, with heavy tanks, artillery, and mobile missile launchers parading across Red Square for a good couple of hours. An even longer demonstration of the masses followed. Very festive and cheerful, with singing and dancing and shouting slogans, it was, in fact, a carefully staged celebration, rehearsed for weeks in advance. All those who participated received two *otguls,* extra days added to their vacations. No wonder the celebration was so popular and cheerful.

Now, in Palm Beach, there was also a demonstration of a sort. When we arrived at one of the local restaurants for lunch and a press conference, there were a dozen people in Baltic national costumes pacing around carrying harsh signs: "Russians Go Home," "Free Baltic Republics from Russian Tyranny," "Gorbachev — Bloody Butcher." But in sharp contrast, the demonstrators smiled openly and even became engaged in friendly conversation with Rami Leibovich in his native Latvian language. They definitely had nothing against us, or against Russia for that matter. I couldn't help wondering whether this demonstration had been staged and rehearsed in advance as in the good old Soviet Union, and if the participants would receive a couple of *otguls* added to their vacations as well. But there was no time to ask.

Late at night, after the grand fundraising gala was over, Skip and I were returning back to Fort Lauderdale along beautiful Route 1-A. Skip was driving a Porsche, borrowed from the Bahia Mar Hotel's PR manager.

"Look at this car. Can you imagine a Porsche with an automatic transmission? What an oxymoron! For me this car epitomizes America in a way. Isn't it silly to take a perfect European sports car and equip it with automatic? All the flavor's gone. Do you know you can't buy a

Mercedes with a stick shift here? Not offered even as an option."

"I'm afraid I cannot share your disappointment. I'm not in the market for a Mercedes yet," I said.

Approaching a sharp 90-degree turn, Skip tried to reach for the stick to downshift, then glanced at me: "You see what I mean..." Braking slightly, he took the turn at 50.

"So you moved to Europe where you could drive real cars, with a manual... "

We both laughed. In a strange way, despite all the rivalry between us, we were somewhat alike, and in moments like this could understand each other easily. Especially now, that he was no longer a part of the team, just a friendly volunteer.

Skip continued, "Not only that. But in a way it's probably true that after all my wandering around the world I can see America in a more realistic light."

Beautiful villas, dimly lit with the night illumination flashed by, looking absolutely gorgeous to me. But apparently not so to Skip.

He continued, "Look around... It's all fake. Just a few decades ago there was nothing here but a swamp. This place has no more meaning than it has history, trying to cover up what it lacks in character with all this hoopla... Have you noticed all the thousands and thousands of boats hidden on canals behind the houses? It's all vanity. How many of them ever sailed out? Hardly a dozen on any given weekend. What a joke."

I didn't want to answer. I was on my honeymoon with America and my feelings couldn't be further from Skip's bitterness.

He continued, "But it's not all America. If you drive west toward the Everglades, where the real locals live, or south to the Miami ghettos ... People there have no hope, no chance."

A trivial conversation was getting more meaningful, approaching issues too important for me to keep silent. The more time I spent in America, the more I liked this great country. If it wasn't exactly as I had imagined in my idealistic dreams, it was pretty damn close. So I felt now as if I needed to retort.

"Granted, there are problems in America, life even in the best country in the world could be tough. But it doesn't come even close to the miserable existence the Soviet people are doomed to bear. No matter how different the Americans are, they all have equal rights. They all have opportunities to pursue if they want to. And to a large extent, it's their own choice to live the life they do."

"It's not all that simple."

"Who's saying it's simple? Human beings are complex creatures, not perfect... I don't bear any illusions that an ideal society could ever exist. But one thing I know for sure: people should have the right to make their own choices, and unfortunately this right comes with penalty of responsibility and potential for failure. But there's no other way; the alternative is too scary. I lived in Russia under Big Brother's watchful care and I know how bad it can be. They can call it communism, or socialism, or whatever – but it's all pretty scary stuff."

We drove in silence for a while.

"You know, Skip, sometimes I understand you very well. After all, we both are rebels in a way. But the irony is that I was lucky to have been born in the Soviet Union to have a real enemy to rebel against ... I've seen life there and I see it here ... It's a great advantage to be able to compare."

Deep in his thoughts, Skip didn't answer, probably contemplating the fact of how unlucky he was to not have been born in the Soviet Union. We had already arrived in Fort Lauderdale, merging into the slow parade of cars toward Bahia Mar. Our Porsche blended perfectly into the stream of Corvettes, Mercedes, and Jaguars.

• • •

Never during my entire round-the-world journey had I felt so comfortable as in America. It was like coming home.

FAZISI was docked at the most honored place, Pier 66, and attracted the utmost attention and interest. Of course, all the Whitbread teams enjoyed celebrity status, with Floridians paying respect to the magnificent fleet of the best sailing machines from all over the world and their brave crews. Endless crowds swamped the docks, happy to mingle with the sailors from Great Britain, New Zealand, Germany, France, and other countries, who had already sailed some 30,000 treacherous miles before arriving in Fort Lauderdale. And yet, foreign sailors were not big news in Florida, an extremely cosmopolitan place, flooded in winter with hoards of tourists from Europe and Japan, and with thousands and thousands of boats from faraway places that made their home in the beautiful canals of this American Venice.

But never before had Floridians seen a yacht from the Soviet Union. FAZISI was the first dove that gave Americans an opportunity to see, to talk to, and to shake hands with Russians, to find out for themselves that we have much more in common than anyone before had ever thought. We were like the messengers who brought to America the firsthand knowledge that Russia is not the Evil Empire anymore, that our people are yearning to live in a free society, like everyone else. And it's not their fault if they have not yet learned how to achieve it. They will eventually, I hope.

The arrival of the Soviet yacht would've been impossible just a short time before. Who could have imagined that there were sailing yachts in the Soviet Union after all? Actually, in accordance with American customs regulations, there was no such category as a pleasure vessel under the Soviet flag. There were only categories for military or commercial ships, that's all. We were considered a military vessel, otherwise we would've been slapped with a hefty customs duty. Military's fine. We didn't care. No matter what category we were in, everyone around understood very clearly that we came to America with the mission of peace, bringing the news that Russia was changing, that the Cold War was over.

Everyone around was eager to help, to see us successfully finish the Whitbread. Our promotional merchandise became such a hit that, walking along the Fort Lauderdale beaches, it seemed that every third person was wearing a T-shirt or a hat with "The Russians Are Coming!" on it. In addition to the events we scheduled, spontaneous fundraising parties erupted almost daily. One of them, organized by Bob and Bernie Thompson, managers of the local condominium complex, was just a fun night at the swimming pool. The next morning, when the smoke had cleared, the hangover subsided, and the contributions counted, the party yielded more then $10,000! Just one fun night!

It certainly seemed that the results of our fundraising campaign in Florida were even more astonishing than in Auckland. Finally, it became clear that FAZISI will complete the entire route around the world. Only a short, four thousand mile sprint across the Atlantic separated us now from the finish of the Whitbread. The job was almost done. Now, again, I could treat myself to sailing on FAZISI for this final leg.

The American stopover became so successful that I was not at all surprised when during one of the parties while sharing drinks with Frank Lennon, he casually asked, "What do you think, Vlad, about doing the Whitbread again? We've already laid out the basics for the fundraising campaign here in America and it would be a shame if it all ended with your departure. With all the interest you're attracting here and the changes in Russia dominating the news, I think we could put together a strong and well-financed project, a real joint venture. I will handle all the promotion, PR, and the sponsorship search."

Long ago, somewhere down in Australia, after so many big problems of the current project had been overcome, thus giving me at least a glimpse of hope that FAZISI just might finish the race after all, I had started thinking about the future. This campaign had become a real torture, nothing but a mere fight for survival. I had made my share of mistakes but I also had learned a lot, became more mature and experienced. Of course, I wanted to put this newfound experience to good use in the future. I was confident that many mistakes could be avoided the second time around and a new project could become a much better, brighter one.

I was perfectly aware that I was dreaming about a "proper" campaign, the one where everything would go right, the ideal venture that Skip, Ludde Ingvall, and many others tried to build before me. And almost everyone failed. Certainly not a good sign. But then, right in front of me, during the whole Whitbread was an encouraging example. Peter Blake, who in a span of over 20 years, had gone through a chain of bitter disappointments, yet persistently kept moving forward to his goal, had finally put together an excellent campaign, where everything fell perfectly into place and worked like the precise mechanism of a Swiss watch.

He had a great boat, his crew was simply the best in the race, and even if there were problems, no one knew about them. STEINLAGER, nicknamed "Red Devil" more for her tenacity than for the color of her hull, just kept charging forward, unstoppable, winning leg, after leg, after leg. With an overall lead of one day and 11 hours over her next rival, another New Zealand ketch FISHER & PAYKEL, and with only one more leg to go, it was perfectly clear that she was untouchable. Seemed like proof that the perfect campaign was possible after all, didn't it?

In conversations with Frank, we often came back, in more detail, to the subject of a future American-Soviet team. Soon I knew for sure that I would return to America to work with Frank on another Whitbread project. Isn't that exactly what Tatiana and I had dreamed about during our long, late-night talks in Punta?

In the meantime, the Fort Lauderdale stopover was quickly coming to a close. The grand finale featured a long-anticipated art auction and the visit of the Soviet Ambassador Yury Dubinin, who came from Washington, D.C. especially for the occasion. Both these events required a tremendous amount of preparation. As we found out, shipping art from country to country was subject to strict customs regulations, of which we were totally unaware. As a result, the whole collection was almost seized upon arrival at the Miami airport. Transporting the Soviet Ambassador across the United States wasn't an easy task either, and was surrounded by similar mountains of red tape and regulations. Only Frank's delicate handling of the State Department helped to ease the situation. Finally, just a few days before the start, all was taken care of. The art was released and Dubinin arrived.

The day before the start, May 4, 1990, the NBC crew led by Curt Gowdy descended on FAZISI to film an interview with our crew and the Soviet Ambassador. For the occasion, Yury Dubinin was wearing all FAZISI paraphernalia including a signature hat "The Russians Are Coming."

He said into the microphone, "This boat and her crew are the real ambassadors of peace and goodwill. During their incredible voyage, they have helped people of different countries to understand each other a little better, to work together, trying to reach a noble goal. I hope it will become a great lesson for world diplomacy."

Then we all, including the NBC crew and Dubinin, went to the farewell dinner organized in FAZISI's honor by the local Chamber of Commerce and the mayor of Fort Lauderdale. It was arranged at Port Everglades at a waterfront restaurant famous for its seafood. I'd been there once before, enjoyed it greatly, and was looking forward to the last real dinner before I would be restrained to the nutritious but tasteless rations aboard FAZISI.

The main course this time was a fantastic swordfish steak, tender and juicy, more than an inch and a half thick. I cut a small piece, picked it up with my fork and took a bite. Absolutely delicious. Grilled to perfection with herbs and spices, slightly sprinkled with lemon, it simply melted in my mouth—I even half closed my eyes, so that nothing would distract me from the simple pleasure of enjoying such great food. The best swordfish I'd ever had.

"Vlad... Hey, Vlad," Frank Lennon tightly tapped my shoulder, bringing me back from the trance.

"The ambassador is going to make a short speech after dinner and I would like to reply in Russian. Here, I wrote a few sentences. Please translate this, but write it with Latin letters, so that I can read it."

"Oh, come on, Frank, not now. Don't you see, I am trying to eat here?"

"But the ambassador will be starting his speech in just a few minutes. We don't have much time, Vlad. Please... I think it would really be terrific if I made my speech in Russian, don't you agree?"

I pushed my plate slightly aside to make space for a notepad and started writing: "*Uvazaemiy Gospodin Posol ...*" I finished in five minutes, during which time the dish with my swordfish disappeared, I hadn't even noticed when. The waitress must have decided that I didn't like it.

Oh, boy, what a miserable life—if it's not one thing, it's another. Being so busy all the time, I missed so many things that I knew I would have enjoyed. Like all those fun parties for the crew that I didn't have time to attend, the beautiful Florida beaches, the trip to the Disney World sponsored by Continental Airlines, the wet T-shirts contest at Shooters, where Juki was a chief juror—he told me later that the babes and the boobs were top class. I trusted him.

Yeah, I surely needed to do the whole thing over again. And the next time it should be a much better organized project and definitely well financed, so that I could take it easier and have a chance to relax and enjoy. Then I would see it all.

22

BACK TO THE SOLENT

May 7, 1990. Evening.

The third day of the last Whitbread leg was slowly fading away. My watch was over and I went to my favorite place on the afterdeck, settled down comfortably on top of the spare genoa and started dictating into a tape recorder my first impressions of this leg.

The gigantic orange disc of the sun had already touched the horizon to port, disappearing behind the invisible Carolina coastline. The wind was light and variable during the first three days after the start, as we sailed north, turning eastward gradually following the North American coastline. With wind of 10 to 12 knots tops, most of time even lighter, we averaged only 100 to 120 miles in the 12-hour periods between mandatory radio call-ins with the race headquarters. As usual, the leading boats were doing better in light winds. Not much better, really, yet covering an additional 7 to 10 miles every 12 hours, they had already put almost 50 miles between us.

The major strategic question of this leg was to decide how to play the Gulf Stream. An extremely powerful current that at some points reaches a speed of three or four knots, it's a mighty river of warm water traveling across the Atlantic Ocean from the Gulf of Mexico to the Polar Seas north of Russia. It's not a steady, predictable stream. It winds out and meanders like a real river, making sharp turns, leaving huge whirlpools, tens of miles in diameter, where current can flow in an opposite direction. It narrows, widens and branches out. It can speed you up and it can slow you down, and any mistake could cost you dearly in the Gulf Stream.

There are many theories on how to sail the Stream and get the most from it, but practice doesn't make it any easier even if you know the theories, which we really didn't. Our navigator Sergey Akatyev had gathered some information about the current prior to the start but it wasn't much, and I had a definite feeling that his strategical decisions were based more on guesswork than on solid knowledge.

The Gulf Stream couldn't be recognized visually. Its waters share the same blue color as the rest of the ocean surrounding it. The only difference — it's warmer. You have to constantly monitor the water temperature in order to know where the current is. FAZISI's instruments included a very precise temperature indicator, which could be mounted on the boat's bottom, and it was one of Elephant's duties during the stopover to install it.

As we sailed away from the start and Sergey Akatyev occupied his position at the nav-station, the first thing he attempted to do was to locate the Gulf Stream. But there were no temperature readings on the display.

"Probably a bad connection," suggested Valery Alexeev, who had just come below to take a look at FAZISI's course. "Elephant, could you check it out, please?"

Elephant didn't move and Valery glanced at him inquiringly. The silence lengthened as the atmosphere inside the boat grew heavier.

"...Oh, well... I didn't install the indicator..." Elephant finally uttered.

"What? How are we supposed to locate the damn Gulf Stream now?" said Alexeev, his voice calm but annoyed. "At least, try to figure out how to install it while we're under way..."

Elephant hesitated, then responded, "I'm afraid I left it in our container on shore."

"Damn it!" Alexeev swore and darted up the companionway ladder, then turned and said:

"I can understand now why Skip got so frustrated at times."

Despite some minor bickering, I noticed significant changes in the crew attitude from what I'd seen five months before on the leg from Fremantle to Auckland. Sailing FAZISI for the second time, I was now getting a totally different impression. We had reduced the crew to 12 people and they more efficiently did the job that earlier required a complement of 16 guys and lots of screaming, shouting, and butt kicking. True, there still were problems, like a missing temperature indicator or lack of enthusiasm for light-air racing; but, at least, there were no serious arguments or conflicts. The guys seasoned, learned a lot, gotten used to each other, and the atmosphere on FAZISI had improved dramatically. In part I attributed this to the fact that Anatoly and Eugene were gone. It was also the first time we sailed without Skip on board, and it was so far so good.

The next day, looking for some tools, Elephant found the missing indicator in his storage box. He hung it off the transom and let it drag from its wire. Though hardly installed as it was intended, the device worked nevertheless, and our ability to make strategic decisions was immediately elevated to a new level. That afternoon Dave Matthews, the new crewmember who had joined FAZISI in Fort Lauderdale, walked back to the leeward transom corner to answer nature's call and noticed the small gizmo jumping and bouncing in the wake.

"What the hell is this dragging behind us?" he said while pulling up the wire, ready to snap it.

"Hey, hey, careful!" shouted Elephant. "That's our new secret weapon. Nobody in the entire fleet has anything like this."

"Oh, I see... Another example of Russian ingenuity..."

Dave Matthews was an American from Fort Lauderdale, and this time the inclusion of a foreigner in our crew didn't cause any problems. Actually, he was more of a businessman than a sailor. Dave paid for his ride with a combination of cash and free maintenance for FAZISI before the start, provided by the marina he owned. A nice outspoken guy, he was a pleasure to talk to while sitting on the quarterdeck after watch. We discussed everything from politics and economics to books and music. Just the previous evening we'd had an almost two-hour-long conversation. A few other guys had joined us, recalling memories of the American stopover, comparing the ways of life in both our countries, and arguing about Russia's future.

Everything the crew had seen for the almost year-long around the world voyage had changed them a lot. They had seen it all and were prepared for almost anything. Yet for some it was still difficult to digest the amazing life they'd witnessed so briefly in Fort Lauderdale, to comprehend the level of freedom, prosperity, and opportunity. They were confused, even suspicious that some of the things they had seen were really just like a fake façade put on only to impress and mislead them. Sort of an American *Potemkin's Village.* Yes, the last year had definitely changed them, but they still remained Russians, a very tough bunch to make believe in anyone or anything. But for how long? How soon would it be until they accepted the facts and surrendered beliefs implanted long ago in their heads by Soviet propaganda?

Eventually the discussions with Dave would become regular and we all ended up learning something and having lots of fun explaining and arguing our points of view. We called those meetings on the quarterdeck "The Fazisi School of Business."

• • •

While I was dictating into the tiny microphone, darkness completely enveloped the boat and the ocean around us. The night was clear and bright, with a myriad of stars above. A full moon rose over the horizon and started climbing slowly, changing its color from dark gold into silver. To my eyes, already adapted to the darkness, it was almost too bright. The wind swung around a little, and the moon hid behind the mainsail, shining through, transforming its functional structure with all the seams, reef lines, patches, and reinforcements into a magnificent transparent spider's web. A few puffy clouds to starboard were completely black with a shimmering silver border outlining them. It was a dream-like night.

The next day the light wind persisted. The ocean remained empty and apparently uninhabited, except for flying fish periodically jumping out of the water. Something scared them out of the deep dark waters, hinting that there definitely was some life down below, only we couldn't see what it was. Occasionally a bunch of flying fish would hit our sails and fall onto the deck. If we saw them, we would throw them back into the water. Victor Pogrebnov, in particular, tried to take good care of those poor fish, periodically looking around and saving unlucky representatives that were hopelessly flopping around on the deck. But if it was too late to revive the fish, or Victor, paying attention to other things, hadn't noticed them, someone would pick them up and send right down to the Rami's kitchen. After our boring rations, fresh fish, artfully grilled and served with a touch of onion and dill, was absolutely delicious.

The wind increased a bit but swung more to the south, changing our course to dead downwind. The apparent wind felt even lighter and FAZISI slowed down. She rolled from side to side in the long swells that began to come from the east, signaling that there was wind somewhere. If only it would reach us.

Nothing is more boring than sailing downwind in a light air. On our watch, we continued to constantly trim the spinnaker, trying to squeeze out any extra tenth of a knot of boatspeed. But now, off watch and sitting on the quarterdeck with Dave Matthews, I viewed the scene, which belonged more to a beach resort than to a racing yacht.

"This is not how I had imagined the toughest race on the planet to look," Dave said.

Valery Safiullin was at the helm, while the rest of the crew was sitting or lying on deck in totally relaxed poses, reading or sunbathing. The spinnaker sheets were cleated. If the wind changed direction slightly, Valery would jump forward, trim the sail, cleat it again, and run back to the steering wheel.

"Hey, guys, if one person can sail the boat alone, why do we need a crew?" I said trying to appeal with irony to the guys' sense of responsibility, knowing perfectly well that it wouldn't change a thing. "We should've had just two helmsmen on board to stand watch and relieve one another, that's all. Imagine how fast FAZISI would go without all the extra food, supplies and water... and without the crew for that matter?"

"Very funny," said Elephant without raising his eyes from the book he was reading.

Juki slowly looked up at the main. "Come on, Vlad, it's not the wind for this boat. I'm sure, stronger wind will follow these swells, then it will make sense to fuss around. "

Not discouraged, I continued, "Don't think I am trying to tell you that I am more interested in the race than anybody else... It's just that I'm sure we could sail a little bit better. And that's all that matters."

Our navigator Sergey Akatyev, who left the chart table to catch a breath of fresh air on deck, reinforced my point. "I mingled with the guys from STEINLAGER and FISHER & PAYKEL during the last stopover. They told me that the entire race's result is determined by the crew's performance in light air. Those guys keep one sheet in the right hand, another one in the left, and sometimes even one between their teeth. And they constantly trim like crazy, picking up on even the slightest movement of air."

Encouraged by his support, I went further. "You've seen videos or pictures of their boats in the race. And what a contrast to ours. If only someone could see us from the outside... This boat in light winds represents a pretty weird picture."

Suddenly I got an idea.

The boom, stopped from swinging by the preventer, was now all the way outboard. It was the perfect point from which to gain an outboard view of the boat. I ran below, grabbed my camera and safety harness — what a smart idea, I would soon discover — and climbed on top of the boom. Walking its length of 37 feet on the narrow top ledge required some acrobatics, but I made it safely. I took a few pictures — now it would be easier to make the point the next time, in the future, if we argued about light-wind sailing techniques.

At that moment a gust hit, FAZISI accelerated, and the mainsheet tightened like a string between the boat and the end of the boom where I stood. Suddenly it looked like an interesting way of returning back to the boat by climbing along the rope. With luck I'd make it back safely if the puff lasted only a few more minutes. The preventer held the boom in place, not letting it get closer to the boat, and keeping the mainsheet from sagging. I clipped my harness and hung on to the mainsheet, grabbing it with my arms and legs. Everyone on the boat now watched my manipulations with great interest.

The puff didn't last. I was half way home with about 15 feet to go when I felt the line began to sag, and the next thing I knew I was submerged under water. How far-sighted I was to place my camera in a waterproof bag! At seven knots of boatspeed, the water hit me really hard and my feet lost their grip. Now I was hanging on only by my arms with my lower body dragging in the water. I tried as hard as I could to make my way back to the boat. I was safely clipped, lightly dressed, and the water was warm. It was just a fun exercise. Still it was tough. I couldn't even imagine what it would be like to fall overboard in full foul-weather gear somewhere in the Southern Ocean...

Juki started trimming the main, pulling the line closer to the boat to help me, and soon I felt hands grabbing me and bringing me back on deck.

Valery Alexeev looked pretty angry, "That was a really stupid thing to do."

"I am sorry... Guess I wasn't thinking. But there was no danger anyway," I replied. At least I had chased away the boredom on the boat, I thought to myself.

Valery looked around.

"Don't any one of you even think of repeating this trick."

• • •

The wind gradually increased overnight, changing its direction a few times, and forcing us to trim and change the sails endlessly. We replaced our largest spinnaker with the Aeroflot logo to the No. 1 genoa, then changed to the No. 3 genoa, as the wind swung north and increased to 17 knots. Soon the reaching spinnaker was hoisted, then we went back to the large Aeroflot spinnaker as the wind died slightly. The cycle was repeated again and again all through the night.

What a change from the tranquil atmosphere of the previous day! By the end of our watch, we were all totally exhausted, but it was worth it. In a 12-hour period we had sailed 171 miles, better than anyone else in the fleet. STEINLAGER covered two miles less, and FISHER&PAYKEL sailed 163 miles. By morning the wind stabilized at 23 to 25 knots and about 90 degrees apparent. Conditions were tricky for carrying the spinnaker and required constant trimming and non-stop attention. Still occasionally the boat would run out of wind, the spinnaker would collapse and start flapping like a giant flag. Then, with a deafening bang, it would fill again. We could have probably sailed almost as fast — and without all this hassle — with the large genoa, but the brisk pace of sailing energized everyone, and we simply didn't want to risk losing even the smallest bit of this speed. For the last two hours, FAZISI averaged 16 knots — it couldn't have been any better.

The waves grew 12 to 15 feet but were too short for comfortable surfing. Frequently the bigger ones would hit the hull hard on the starboard side, blasting up vertically before falling onto the deck and breaking into a spray that glimmered like a diamond dust in the soft glow of the withered sun.

The wind brought a change in the weather, filling the air with a light transparent mist. Thin streaks of clouds seemed themselves to emit defused light. FAZISI's deck, usually too bright to look at in direct sunlight without sunglasses, now was glowing like sugar candy as if gently lit from within. Bright and soft simultaneously, the ocean around us shimmered like liquid silver. Juki brought the waterproof speakers out on deck, put "Gypsy King" on the tape deck, and we flew through all this beauty in a state of total enchantment.

Kuli was at the helm. He glanced over his shoulder at another big wave coming from the rear quarter and turned the wheel slightly to let the boat slide down and accelerate. It was a really steep one and FAZISI tilted her bow down graciously, going faster, faster, faster!

"Yes! Yes! *Davay!*" cheered the chorus from the afterdeck, shaking outstretched arms and clenched fists as the speedo reached 22 knots. At this moment the bow hit the previous wave, dove down, and tons of white water rushed on deck.

The effect was like hitting the brakes. The speed fell down to 7 knots in an instant, knocking down anyone who'd been standing on the deck. Most of the boat was covered with at least two feet of water, but the afterdeck remained dry. FAZISI hadn't broached, hadn't even attempted to. A few seconds later the bow re-emerged, shaking the water away, and, as Kuli turned the wheel to starboard, bringing the boat closer to the wind and Victor Pogrebnov trimmed the spinnaker, the numbers on the repeater jumped up again: 12 knots… 18… 20!

"Yes! Yes! *Davay! Davay!*" cheered the crowd on the afterdeck.

• • •

May 14, 1990, morning.

After a few days of beating, we were having a good southeasterly again and were doing great. During the last few hours, FAZISI's
speed had never dropped below 13 knots with prolonged periods of
surfing at 20 to 21 knots. And the result showed. We had moved into
seventh position in the fleet, and what was even better, the leaders were
not that far away. STEINLAGER and FISHER & PAYKEL were only 80
miles in front; THE CARD, a mere 40. MERIT, UBF, and BELMONT
were just slightly ahead of us, but much farther to the north.

Everyone was in a great mood, working enthusiastically to hold
on to this position. Edgar was steering, Kuli was trimming the mainsail,
and I was working with Victor at the spinnaker sheets. One of us sat
next to the huge drum of the primary winch and eased the sheet when
the boat slowed down to make the spinnaker shape fuller and more
powerful. When FAZISI started surfing and the apparent wind swung
forward, the person on the coffee grinder trimmed the sheet, trying to
keep the spinnaker working as long as possible, not letting it collapse.
It was a strenuous job, requiring non-stop attention, and also an uncomfortable one to perform, bent over the pedestal in an awkward position with your head facing upward, constantly watching the spinnaker. Twenty minutes of trimming and I was toast. We changed positions
with Victor. Twenty minutes later we changed back. Then, after two
hours, we were relieved and got to trim the main or, best of all, steer the
boat.

I liked working with Victor. He'd been on FAZISI since Auckland
and had developed a perfect sense for the boat. A massive bear of a
man, he had surprisingly lightning-fast reactions. It was a pleasure to
watch him moving on the wildly bouncing deck with cat-like grace.

Now, as I pondered the decision on the next Whitbread project,
I was looking at the guys with different, more critical eyes, evaluating
everyone, choosing whom I'd like to have on the crew the next time
around. Victor? For sure. Then Edgar, of course. He was simply amazing, no doubt the best helmsman on FAZISI. He was also a natural-born
leader, always calm, always confident, always knowing what to do.
Sometimes he reminded me of Skip, only without Skip's occasional
hysteria or overreaction. No matter how tense the situation gets on the
boat, I'd never seen Edgar scared or even nervous.

Juki — another very brave man. Last night when the genoa sheet had snapped under tremendous load and the monstrous sail was violently flapping around, slapping the deck with its giant whip-like, inch-thick line, it was Juki who ran forward and in complete darkness managed to attach a new sheet. Like many Georgians, Juki, a heroic man, could easily become unmotivated when the going got easy. Well, nobody's perfect. He is also a genius of communication, and I couldn't think of anyone who could represent better the crew on shore during all those press conferences and non-stop sponsorship activities. I certainly wouldn't start a new project without Juki on the team.

Among the others, I'd been watching Kuli closely and constantly. He was really good, a natural helmsman on par with Edgar, but at times he could be too temperamental and occasionally exploded for no particular reason. But then he was the youngest in the crew and would probably calm down eventually. All these guys together would make a very strong core for the future crew. If I were able to find American sailors to match their talent, we could have one of the best teams for the next Whitbread.

Well, I guess I had again allowed dreams about a future "proper" campaign to carry me far away.

• • •

Three hours later in a powerful gust, our largest Aeroflot spinnaker blew apart into two equal pieces right along the center seam. The wind came so strong that the lower ripped half blew forward horizontally and kept flapping like a giant blanket without even touching the water. It was a relatively easy job to pull it back on deck, but in order to lower the top piece, Edgar had to go up the mast to wrestle with the wildly flailing, 1,000-square-foot sheet of nylon. We held our breaths for 15 minutes watching him as he swung with the movements of the boat 80 feet above deck.

Then it was all over, and we were speeding again under a much smaller reaching spinnaker. But our largest and best one was gone for good. No way could it be repaired. Now we didn't have a sail for light downwind sailing. And, sure enough, after that violent gust, the wind began to diminish.

Our sail inventory was getting smaller and smaller. The biggest genoa started showing its age long ago but was still holding on thanks to Kuli and Valery Safiullin's constant repairs. Of the seven spinnakers we started the race with, only three were left. During the Fort Lauderdale stopover, we added a new mainsail and spinnaker; still, FAZISI's inventory was as meager as Cinderella's wardrobe. The sails are the source of power for a boat, the same way as a car's engine. There isn't much you can do when you lack power. We started at a disadvantage with total inventory fewer than 20 sails including all the genoas, staysails, spinnakers and even the storm jib and trysail. This was roughly the same number of new sails that the leading syndicates were adding for each leg of the race. It was a losing game to compete with such a disparity. And yet we kept holding our own just fine.

A big change in the weather occurred within an hour after we blew our spinnaker. The wind became light again but freezing cold. The temperature dropped from 75 degrees to 40 in a matter of minutes. The difference was stunning. Fog came from the northeast, light at first but getting more and more dense. After the bright sunshine we had been enjoying just a short while ago, the wet damp air was chilling to the bone. We all quickly changed, putting on thermal underwear and a full set of foul-weather gear.

We had arrived at the Grand Banks of Newfoundland.

The waters around us teemed with marine life now. First came the dolphins, gaily jumping mere feet off FAZISI's bow. The large number of noisy seagulls indicated plenty of fish. A couple of seals stuck out their sympathetic faces, curiously watching us passing by. I was amazed to see so much change in such a short span of time. Why do all these species prefer to live here in the icy-cold waters and not in the warmth of the Gulf Stream? I couldn't understand this at all. Wet, miserable and shivering cold, I was already missing the warm weather we had left only so recently.

The Grand Banks is the world's major fishing ground. We'd already spotted a few fishing vessels before the fog had grown too thick. Now we could only hear their radio communications. There was Russian talk as well and Valery Alexeev conversed with them for a while. We observed them on the radar screen. Each produced a pretty sizable bright dot and was clearly recognizable. We weren't worried about a collision with the fishing vessels. A much bigger threat were the icebergs.

We were now right in Iceberg Alley, the most dangerous place in the entire North Atlantic, where the cold Labrador Current carries huge chunks of ancient ice chipped from the eternal Greenland glaciers. THE CARD, which was three hours ahead of us, reported seeing before nightfall a few gigantic bergs. Now the freezing rain, heavy at times, arrived with the darkness. Each small drop of water falling from the skies reflected a radar emission, creating a chaotic, sparkling glow on the screen. Was it just the rain or was there something more ominous lurking behind all those green splashes?

We were sailing in about the same area where the TITANIC had sunk, and the mood on board was gloomy. The watertight bulkhead separating the front compartment was sealed tight. For some strange reason no one wanted to stay below deck, and even the off-watch guys gathered tightly on the afterdeck. The wind freshened as the air chilled. Now we were making a good 12 knots, speeding blindly forward. Illuminated by the navigation lights, the fog glowed red and green around the bow and soft milky white behind the stern light. The rest of the world disappeared. FAZISI seemed suspended in a strange eerie space — water underneath, water above — and mountains of dangerous frozen water somewhere up ahead. It was the moment, when disturbing thoughts were entering my mind and I asked myself, "What are we doing out here? Why?"

There was no one around to answer... Only the silent ghost of the boat that kept piercing through the cold, wet darkness.

• • •

Supposedly a downwind leg, this crossing of the Atlantic had plenty of upwind sailing. All in all, the weather conditions of the Whitbread were quite different from what we had anticipated. There was much more light wind and more upwind sailing than our weather studies revealed during the preparation for the race.

It was again mostly upwind beating along the final leg across the Atlantic. Some boats chose to make frequent tacks, which eventually led them to a more northern route and allowed them to stay longer in the Gulf Stream. We, instead, had made the general decision to stay on the same port tack, which pushed us out of the current and led farther and further south. The wind blew from the east-northeast day in and day out, reminiscent of the situation on leg four before rounding Cape Horn. Again we just stubbornly held onto the same course, hoping that eventually the wind direction would change and we'd end up in a favorable position. But now, as Europe grew closer and closer, we were still pointing somewhere to the corner of the Bay of Biscay where France meets Spain. The sad joke of the moment was "Which do you prefer: Spanish wine, or French women?" What we preferred was a good cup of English tea!

It wasn't until we came only 200 miles within the Spanish coast that the situation, similar to our Cape Horn rounding, miraculously repeated itself. The wind slowly started shifting to the north leading us directly to the Ile D'Quessant and the entrance to English Channel. Now, with a mere 200 miles to go, for the first time we shared fourth-fifth position with MERIT, which had sailed much farther north, passing near the Isles of Scilly, but was the same distance from the finish line as we were. This had been our best strategic decision of the entire race! And, for a moment, it looked like it might lead to a fantastic Whitbread ending.

Not so fast. It was not finished yet, and those last miles proved to be very tricky. Just as with many good things in life, our luck didn't last long enough. Sergey Akatyev, who had been a navigator on a Russian nuclear submarine before coming to FAZISI's crew, was a very independent guy. I've always wondered how he managed to survive all those years within the restriction of the Soviet military forces and in the tight quarters of a submarine.

Navigation on a Whitbread yacht involves a lot of weather forecasting, which is a tough thing to do even for weather specialists with all the computer power behind them. Considering the scarcity of information we had available at sea, it was always a creative process with lots of guesswork. On most of the boats it was a joint effort of the navigator, captain, and watch-captains. This way the risk of mistakes was greatly reduced. But Akatyev vigorously protected his turf and wanted to be the sole boss of the nav-station. Being the only guy on board with navy background, he felt he was a cut above the rest of us, land rats.

Sergey was capable of smart decisions, which he demonstrated many times, but he also proved to be a stubborn guy, who wouldn't change his mind easily even when the mistake he made was so obvious. And what foolish mistakes he made at the end of the race!

The first blunder came as we entered the English Channel. My watch started at 8 a.m. and coming up on deck, the first thing I noticed was an endless chain of merchant ships moving along the Channel in both directions. Separated by intervals of less than a mile, at least a dozen of them were visible at any given time. After the vast expanse of unpopulated Atlantic, it seemed almost like a traffic jam.

One thing alarmed me right away: the direction in which the ships were moving was wrong. Or was it FAZISI that was sailing in the wrong direction?

"Aren't we sailing backwards?" I asked Valery Alexeev.

"Well, I was thinking that the other tack might be better too, and checked it with the navigator. He assured me that our course was okay," he replied.

It certainly didn't look okay to me. I went below to look at the chart. I knew that Akatyev was a very sensitive guy, so I started carefully, trying not to step on his toes.

"Sergey, could you please double-check the direction? It seems to me if we tack now, we would be sailing almost our general course into The Solent."

"The wind is going to change. I've analyzed recent weather faxes. If we hold on to this direction, we'll be in a much better position later," he responded.

"I am only asking you, please check it again," I said, pleading as persistently as I could and returned to deck.

A few minutes later, Sergey popped out through the hatch and told Valery, "We need to tack." The tone of his voice indicated clearly that he wasn't happy admitting his mistake.

After we tacked, I asked Valery, "How long had we been sailing this course?"

"Almost three hours," he replied.

Oh, no, that's about 25 miles in the wrong direction. But that wasn't the last of our troubles. By the end of the same day FAZISI caught a strong counter current near Start Point— a very strong one, indeed. Start Point, a long cape which protrudes far into the Channel, is notorious for having a lot of tidal current around it. An ebb and flow of four to five knots is not unusual in these waters. Changing direction every six hours, it could add four knots to your boatspeed if you are in synch with it, or, if not in synch, it might slow you down by the same amount. Simple wisdom tells you never approach the cape when the current is against you, as the farther out you sail into the open waters, the weaker the current becomes.

It remains a mystery to me why Sergey had not checked the tide schedule, but we did come to the Start Point right at the wrong time. The wind was dying and FAZISI was barely holding her position against the strong flow. At one point we'd even started drifting slowly backwards.

"It's time to drop the anchor," said our captain looking at Juki.

FAZISI's main anchor weighed 100 pounds and was stored deep in the bilge. On those rare occasions when we had to use it, it was normally Juki's job to bring it up on deck.

"I think this time the navigator should do it." Juki said, expressively glancing at Akatyev. Without a word, Sergey turned around and disappeared below. We heard noises of clanging and banging metal deep in FAZISI's belly, and then saw Sergey struggling to push the anchor up through the hatch.

"Hold it…" Alexeev's attention was glued to the jumbo repeater, where the boat speed numbers started slowly climbing. "Seems like the wind is increasing and the current is getting weaker. I think we'll make it through."

All in all, we lost almost three hours there. That's in addition to the time spent on the wrong tack earlier at the Channel!

Well, that's racing. Everyone makes mistakes. Those who make the fewest, win. We were not in a winning situation in this race; we were newcomers to the Big League. Coming from the Soviet Union for the first time, without any experience, but with too much of self-confidence, we were doomed to make more mistakes than our Western, more-seasoned fellow competitors. And sure enough, we made our fair share of them, all of us, myself included.

Well, in a sense, we were on a voyage of dilettantes, like each of us is at time, when trying to achieve something never done before. And, all things considered, our performance wasn't so bad at all.

23

MISSION ACCOMPLISHED?

Land was somewhere there in front of us, hidden beyond the pale mist that covered everything from horizon to horizon. Our anticipation grew ever more tense, as this would be our last landfall before the finish of the race. Finally, in the distance, the first contours of the Isle of Wight appeared through a slowly lifting smoky curtain. A majestic panorama of chalky rocks ending with the chain of the piercing Needles that guarded the entrance into The Solent slowly took form in front of us. An expanding fleet of various vessels that had motored out to greet us soon surrounded FAZISI. It was great to be back after sailing around the world, yet it was a strange and sad feeling to realize that it was all over, and there was nowhere to sail tomorrow.

It seemed as if even nature was in a melancholy mood. Huge cumulus clouds towered over the horizon, and the sun, slowly disappearing behind them, was sending us farewell rays, painting the sea and the sky in all shades of pink and purple. The wind had almost died as the day faded away and FAZISI was gliding slowly over the glassy water. We've almost done it, haven't we?

Only 15 miles to sail were remaining — out of 33,000. The boat was moving slowly; still it seemed to us that those last precious miles of the Whitbread were vanishing too quickly. We felt strange. We wanted to make this finish as good as we could, and the crew work and the boat performance during these last moments was nearly perfect. And yet everyone wished it could last longer. Only 10 miles left. Five...

Leaving Cowes to starboard, we bore left into Southampton Sound, a very special place for us, where 10 months before FAZISI had set her sails for the first time. No one believed then that the untried boat with her inexperienced crew would be able to complete the most grueling sailing marathon, to climb the sailing equivalent of Mt. Everest. In a symbolic sense our odyssey started even earlier, on the shores of the ancient river Fazisi, where according to the legend the hero Jason led the Argonauts in search of the Golden Fleece, the epitome of glory and prosperity. No wonder we called our boat FAZISI and, high in the belief that we were new Argonauts, expected that reward would follow the challenge and struggle. Little did we remember that, according to a legend, the Golden Fleece did not bring Jason the happiness he seemed to deserve, and the whole story was a tragedy with its full share of horror, betrayal and death. Everybody forgets this part...

Our route, like the Argonaut's, turned out to be extremely rough and beset by many trials. It often felt as if we had reached a dead end. Yet there was always hope, which led us through oceans and tribulations. We never gave up, never ceased fighting. Even if things had not worked out the way we'd wished, at the end we came out winners — not of the race, finishing eighth on this leg and 11th overall — but of the struggle against time, obstacles, and our own weaknesses.

A child of perestroika, our entry FAZISI was like a dove sent out into an uncertain future. Like perestroika itself, FAZISI was an experiment of survival. In retrospect our safe return to the British shores was a victory against all odds.

A white cruise ship leaving Southampton harbor passed on the opposite side of the channel only a few hundred yards from us. As it towered 10 stories high abeam of us, it sounded its powerful horn in salute. In the thickening dusk, we could see a brightly-lit wide red stripe on its stack with a golden hammer and sickle. The next moment, as we glided under its stern, we saw the name in large letters: FEDOR DOSTOYEVSKY. Its red flag was waving above, the same flag that waved over our transom too. It was an appropriate moment to feel sentimental. All of us on FAZISI had different feelings toward that red flag with the hammer and sickle that represented the Soviet Union. But at that particular moment we all felt as one: extremely proud to sail aboard the first-ever Soviet entry to successfully complete the Whitbread race, extremely proud to be the crew that took her around the world.

A few minutes later the gun fired.

After crossing the finish line we dropped the sails and motored slowly toward the entrance of Ocean Village Marina, trying to make our way among the chaos of hundreds and hundreds of spectator boats, deafened by a cacophony of cheering, and blinded by powerful searchlights focused on us. I hadn't sailed FAZISI enough during the Whitbread, but I certainly was the lucky one to steal the two best finishes, in New Zealand and now this final one. Thousands and thousands of people were everywhere, covering the docks, standing on the balconies, even on the rooftops of surrounding condos, packing decks and even climbing masts and rigs and straddling spreaders of boats docked in the marina. The Russian words they'd learned last summer were thrown back at us: "*Zdrastvuytie! Privet! Nah Zdorovie*," they shouted. Overwhelmed by the squall of cheers, we listened to the Soviet anthem floating from the loudspeakers above.

As usual, the first person meeting us at the dock was Admiral Williams with the traditional huge bottle of champagne, only this time it looked even bigger than at the other finishes. Juki shook it violently, let the cork shoot high into the dark sky, and the entire contents of the bottle exploded in a firework of white foam spraying everyone around. A noisy mob of journalists had already climbed on board and in a flash was all over FAZISI's deck, with outstretched microphones and TV cameras pointing at us.

"What are your first impressions now that the race is over?"

"Are you satisfied with the results?"

"Are you glad to be back?"

We were mumbling confused answers, overwhelmed, happy, and slightly lost. The only thought clear in everyone's mind was, "Yes, we did it. We had completed the Whitbread!"

• • •

The race was over, all the fleet was in the harbor, and the sailors were gradually leaving to return home. We had other plans.

A few days after the finish I called a crew meeting with two things on the agenda: first, we shared our experiences, both good and bad, talked about what we had learned and what could be done better the next time, if we entered the race again. I then told them about plans for the next Whitbread. Obviously they already knew that and were ready for a new adventure. During the last leg, I had spent a lot of time on the phone coordinating things between Frank Lennon in Palm Beach and Tikhov in Moscow until the whole future program finally had taken shape. Since some of the guys would go home for vacation and rejoin us later, FAZISI would sail back to the U. S. with a smaller crew. She would immediately jump into a six-month long, event-packed promotional tour along the East Coast.

After we finished the business part of the meeting, I took out my miniature tape recorder, which had served me so well along the entire Whitbread route, and asked the guys in the crew to share some of their impressions and memories, to preserve them for the years to come. Maybe one day, much later, we would recall them together.

Rami Leibovich:
"...I am still feeling kind of sad after the finish. It's the beginning of summer here, but in my mood it's like fall. We started the race last September, and then everywhere in the Southern Hemisphere at each stopover, in Uruguay, Australia, and New Zealand, it was always summer, the sunshine was bright and flowers were blooming. It's over now... With the finish of the Whitbread, I almost physically feel the cold winds of the upcoming Russian winter.

"Ending something is often sad ... And the end of such a great adventure as the Whitbread is almost heartbreaking. True, it was an incredibly tough ordeal, but now, looking back, if only a few days back, it appears in a totally different light... It looks like a great achievement. And the more time passes, the better we'll realize what we have accomplished, the more we'll miss this controversial and beautiful time when we sailed on FAZISI...

"...I want to call what had happened 'the Russian miracle.' It is true that we all came from different nations and even from different countries. But I still want to use the word Russian, admitting clearly all the good and all the negative meanings that people associate with this word. Yes, we all acted like Russians, we overcame obstacles, we made a lot of mistakes, we fought against the obstacles and against each other, we had a great time, and we went through a tragedy. But in the end, everything that has happened to us is nothing short of a miracle."

Sergey Stanetsky (Elephant):
"Sadness was exactly my feeling as well immediately following the finish. It was the great race, the one I had dreamed about since I don't remember when... Certainly the most interesting period in my entire life ... And now it's all over... Well, anyway, one thing I know for sure: my thirst for sailing has not been satisfied yet. And I don't know if it could ever be satisfied. If I were back home now, I'd be restless and start looking for a new sailing opportunity immediately. To go racing or to do deliveries, or whatever, but to be on boats. Sailing is my life, period. So when I heard about a new program and about a chance to sail back to America and cross the Atlantic again, I didn't think twice...

" ... It's too short a time since the finish and I haven't had a chance to think about the results at any length. But one thing I know for sure after sailing the Whitbread: there are no losers in an ocean marathon like this. Everyone who has crossed the finish line is a little bit of a winner. And the fact that we demonstrated outstanding performance at times and surprised many with our results makes me really happy. Remember those silly bets against us at the beginning? Hah, hah, hah … Now we can laugh at them. We deserve that."

Valery Alexeev:
"I believe that our greatest achievement at the end was the fact that we were able to overcome our differences and finish the race as a team. There were a lot of small and not so small things that contributed to that: like improved organization at the end, more clarity to the entire project, better defined responsibilities. Everyone finally knew who was who and who was doing what. Unfortunately it got sorted out only at the end, but hey, there will be new races, for sure… Well, life is life and even in very good families, conflicts do happen. When the 'family' is so large and consists of unruly, free-spirited sailors, each member is under the constant pressure of extreme situations, so you inevitably face clashes of egos and personalities. We had our fair share, but all in all it wasn't all that bad…"

• • •

While still on the ocean aboard FAZISI, I had called Tony Castro in Hamble and asked him to send official invitations necessary for Tatiana and our son Pavel to obtain visas to get to England. I was really tired of being alone for so long. I wanted to start a new project together with them. And it looked like our reunion would become a first step toward the realization of the plan Tatiana and I had made in Punta.

The rules had already started easing in Russia but still, even with Tony's invitation, my family's leaving was more like an escape. Trying to reduce the risks and afraid of suspicion, Tatiana didn't tell anyone in Russia that they were leaving for good. To fool everyone she flew to the West with only one duffel bag, which for a while contained all of our belongings. She didn't even tell her mother about our plans. We had already made our decision and knew that we wouldn't return to Russia, but we had no idea where we would end up, and what kind of life lay ahead. I only prayed to God that I was not making a mistake by changing my family's future so dramatically.

For a while I considered sailing with Tatiana and Pavel back across the Atlantic on FAZISI, but then settled on a more traditional route, by plane. This would give us a couple of weeks in England to relax, visit the friends I had made during the Whitbread, and then fly to New York to meet FAZISI and start it all over again. I would prefer not to rush, to take a good break, to leave all the pressure of the previous campaign behind. I wanted to put to rest all the bad things that had happened, all the troubles, disappointments, and failures. And probably all the excitement, happiness, and achievements as well—it was all too much. All I wanted was just a few months of peace.

But Frank Lennon was pressing harder and harder, eager to start the promotional tour as soon as possible.

He was calling from Florida every day, "We cannot afford to lose momentum. FAZISI is a hot thing here, but for how long? The American public has a very short memory. We need to capitalize on your status now, immediately. Every day counts!"

So be it. As soon as all the formalities with FAZISI's return to America were completed, she would be on her way.

In the meantime, my family and I had a wonderful time, staying with Jim and Lisa Saunders in Hamble. We also visited Ted and Sheila Lonsdale, whom I met briefly the previous summer during FAZISI construction, and who became our good friends now. We stayed at their home on Hayling Island and spent a weekend together driving through the English countryside. I finally got a chance to see this beautiful country without haste. We visited Salisbury cathedral and Stonehenge and even once had a dinner in the ancient castle where every guest at the table was attended by an individual waiter.

We spent quiet evenings in Jim's beautiful house, recalling over dinner and a bottle of good port our work together on FAZISI. Along with sailors from different corners of the world — Australia, France and Switzerland — we shared his hospitality. And while talking about ocean racing and the Whitbread in particular, more and more often we would try to answer the question, "Why are we doing this? Why do people do such irrational things like sailing the Whitbread or climbing Mount Everest?" Probably the simplest and the most famous answer came from the British alpinist George Mallory, who snapped back at the irritating nagging journalists: "Because it is there."

Well, as good as it is, this answer never satisfied me. Neither had I agreed with Reinhold Messner, the Everest soloist, who on the question, "And what do you do for the community (by climbing)?" responded, "Nothing. On the contrary I love experiments, adventure, I am therefore a danger to this industrious, timid and unimaginative society". Well, with all respect to Messner, an incredible man who individually achieved things thought impossible, I could not agree with this answer.

I knew there was much more to it than just a selfish desire to satisfy one's own dreams, something that would rightly justify all that we had gone through during our voyage, but I just didn't know how to put it in the right words yet.

• • •

Finally FAZISI was ready to sail back to America. Her crew was rested, their visas taken care of, provisions packed and stowed, her water tanks filled. We called customs, FAZISI got cleared and received permission to leave. Together with Valery Chumakov, I stood on the pier ready to wave the guys good-bye as they left Ocean Village Marina.

Then, all of a sudden, we saw Nodari, who was replacing Sergey Akatyev as FAZISI's new navigator, running in a panic across her deck and then jumping down to the dock. A customs officer stood in his way.

"Sir, you cannot leave the boat now."

Nodari dove past him.

"Sir, sir," the officer said as he tried to chase him, but he was no match for Nodari, who kept running toward the shore, shouting at us. "We do not have any charts on board."

"Where are they?"

"I don't know, probably Akatyev took them when he left for home. "

Chumakov looked at me in disbelief. "Oh, no, not again! This boat is a total madhouse. There is still not the slightest hint of order, even after they have sailed more than 30,000 miles. Amazing!"

Then he turned to Nodari. "It's all your fault, you should've checked everything before Akatyev left. How did it happen that you have discovered this only now?"

After a short emotional debate, interrupted several times by the customs officer, Nodari finally disappeared in search of the charts. He returned more than an hour later, during which time the officer, who was completely pissed off initially and wanted to arrest everyone left and right, finally got into the situation, relaxed, and ended up on almost friendly terms with us. Nodari had found only one chart, the general large-scale map of the whole North Atlantic region with little detail.

"No problem, we'll make it," said captain Valery Alexeev as he stood at the wheel. He started the engine and to the official's great relief, they finally cast off. We watched as FAZISI maneuvered out of the crowded marina and departed for a new adventure.

EPILOGUE

August 19, 1991 saw FAZISI docked at Port Jefferson on Long Island's north shore, as hurricane Bob approached. It was a relatively small, compact, but mean storm, packing winds of more than 90 miles per hour. At first, it seemed as if it would swing out into the ocean, but after changing its mind, the hurricane picked up more speed and hit directly on the tip of Long Island. By that time there was no crew left on the boat, only my small family desperately trying to save her. But it was an uphill battle. Extra mooring lines snapped like strings and the more than a dozen fenders that I had hung on FAZISI's sides proved to be inadequate protection.

Earlier in the morning, just before the hurricane hit in earnest, while the wind rapidly increased from 25 knots to 50 in a matter of minutes and kept strengthening, blowing rain in sheets, I received a phone call from Fazis SP in Moscow.

"We have bad news. There has been an anti-government coup, the streets are occupied with tanks ... Gorbachev was arrested ... No one knows what will happen next."

"I have bad news too. A hurricane's coming. I have to run back to the boat. Sorry, no time to talk." I hung up, struck by the ominous coincidence of these events.

By late afternoon, the hurricane had already passed and an unusually bright sun came out to shed light on the wreckage of more than 30 yachts sunk or tossed onto the rocky shore. FAZISI had survived but was left with a 20-foot long scar of tortured aluminum on her port side.

The coup was short lived as well. In two days it was over. A few months later Boris Yeltsin came to power, and Gorbachev was thrown out of the Kremlin. A bully of a politician, a populist, who would promise people heaven and hell just to stay on the top, Yeltsin had an endless zest for power but very little in a way of an agenda. Gorbachev's thinktank, all the economists, new politicians, and civil leaders like Andrey Sakharov, were replaced by Boris' hunting and sauna buddies;

personal fitness coaches and bodyguards became his political advisers. First only as a joke, and then more and more seriously and solemnly, the Russian media started calling Yeltsin the new Tzar. The ghost of the past had descended on the Kremlin again.

Perestroika as I understood it was over.

• • •

Both Anatoly Verba and Eugene Platon did put together their own campaigns for the 1993-94 Whitbread. True, both came as a far cry from being the "proper" ones, especially Anatoly's, but, hey, they pulled it off nevertheless. Anatoly's project, unfortunately, turned into a complete disaster, as he desperately struggled to build the boat in the crumbling Soviet Union, then tried to bring her to the start line, falling deeper and deeper behind schedule. It was like FAZISI, only much, much worse. He finished the race last, 19 days and 12 hours behind the next boat.

Eugene did better, beating not only Anatoly, but also two other yachts, finishing seventh out of the 10-boat fleet.

Despite their poor results, I do respect them more now, after they proved that our rivalry, as bad as it was, at least was based on their honest and substantiated drive to be leaders in their own right. I can appreciate that.

• • •

On the other hand, I was unable to pull off my own "proper campaign" for the following Whitbread. There were plenty of solid objective reasons but the main reason was I myself. I was simply too exhausted and didn't have enough stamina to begin it again. Maybe I would have if I'd taken at least a short break to gather myself, to regain strength mentally and bodily. But I had instantly plunged into a new project, and it turned into the same nonstop rush, struggle, and defeat.

Later on I read in "The Perfect Storm" by Sebastian Junger:

"Anyone who has been through a severe storm at sea has, to one degree or another, almost died, and that fact will continue to alert them long after the winds have stopped blowing and the waves have died down."

Not the legs that I had actually sailed, but the whole FAZISI project had been one endless storm. It took me some time to realize that all my energy had been drained and, utterly exhausted, all I wanted now was a little peace to try to make sense of everything that had happened.

Still, I put up a good fight. I found a sponsor in Russia to build a new boat. I had designed this boat to be much faster than FAZISI and far more optimized for light air and upwind sailing. I even came close to landing a major American sponsor. But it was all too different from the first time. Then I was charging ahead unstoppable, now I was running on half cylinders and my tank was on empty.

And then Ted Hood, arguably one of the most prominent American designers and boat builders, invited me to act as a consultant for his company. I felt honored, and I learned a lot. Soon thereafter I started my own design office. Now I could see clearly that there was much more to this life than racing on high seas. The endless opportunities that I discovered in America in a way helped me to make the decision. Reluctantly, I withdrew my entry into the next Whitbread. Maybe one was enough, maybe this was not just the right time... Surprisingly, I was not disappointed. Okay, maybe just a bit. But at the same time I had that incredible feeling of being absolutely free to make my own choice, of being able to overcome the desire, the temptation -- and the pressure -- to continue on out of the last drop of energy. It was not "now or never" anymore, as it had been during my FAZISI venture. Like a wise climber on Mount Everest, who has enough will to turn back when further advance is impossible, I knew that there would be another opportunity.

I went on happily with my life, designing and building new boats, some of them even more radical than FAZISI. As time passed, the storms abated and the memories healed. I have found a new life in America, a land full of opportunities. I cherish every new day in my newfound home and look boldly into the future. I have made it to my Promised Land.

Yet occasionally, for no particular reason at all, I become restless, and the idea of another great adventure fills my imagination. I start toying with it, trying, testing, only to find out — no, it's not my time yet, maybe one day... But as the saying goes, once a junkie, always a junkie. Who knows, maybe there is still a Big Project for me somewhere in the future.

• • •

Most of the FAZISI crew ended up living all over the world. Edgar Terekhin, Victor Kamkin, and Igor Mironenko settled in Australia. Victor Pogrebnov lives in Fort Lauderdale where he has recently discovered his own talent for designing and building high-performance racing multihulls. The succession of his catamarans, each called ORCA and painted with black and white spots like a killer whale, proved to be very fast as Victor keeps winning one competition after another all over Florida. Valery Safiullin lives not far from him, building his own sailmaking business.

Kuli has gradually risen into professional sailing superstardom. Always in high demand, he stretches his racing grounds from Florida to New York City, to Bermuda, to Philippines. He did sail another Whitbread on both Anatoly's boat ODESSA 200 (only the first leg) and Eugene's HETMAN SAHAIDACHNY (the rest of the race), but he didn't like it very much. Later he told me, "You know, it was nothing like the first time... True, the Southern Ocean legs turned out to be faster in 1993-94, with more wind, and I had some pretty wild rides then... Still, the time on FAZISI remains simply the best."

As with everyone who tried it and got hooked, Kuli is dreaming of another Whitbread, this time his own. Well, good luck, my friend. As we all proved, there are no impossible dreams.

• • •

In the summer of 1995, I was invited to a dinner at the New York Yacht Club's mansion in Newport, Rhode Island, where finally, I guess, I got the answer to the question that has haunted me, "Why do we do such irrational things like racing the Whitbread?" The guest speaker at the dinner was Dodge Morgan, the first American to circumnavigate the globe alone non-stop. In his short presentation were these words as I remember them:

"By sailing around the world, I certainly did fulfill my dream and satisfied my individual desires. But I reflected a lot later on whether or not it was just a selfish satisfaction or that I did, in fact, achieve something for humanity. And I think I did. All those crazy things like crossing the oceans or climbing the highest mountains or driving racecars as fast as you can... they all do show that there still is a place for adventure and dream in our routine and ordinary lives. Just imagine for a second that nobody does these extreme things anymore, and you'll instantly see the average attitude of human society shifting tremendously into boredom."

AUTHOR'S NOTE

It took me almost nine years in all to complete this book. Language became the first and obvious challenge. I had arrived in America in 1990 with a very basic English. It was okay to communicate, but certainly not sufficient to write a good book. Over the years, as my English progressed, the manuscript went through countless revisions. I didn't rush. All those years of digesting slowly the wealth of information gathered in numerous diaries, notebooks and audio tapes that I had made during the Whitbread, of going through the necessary introspection, and replaying the story against events still unfolding in Russia, had enabled me to put everything into the right prospective. The leavening factor of time helped me to filter the events that comprise this tale, separate the important from the insignificant that only seemed vital at the time it happened.

The story is so personal that initially I had been afraid that my feelings, too raw and painful, would lead me to an overly emotional and perhaps biased account, if I put it on paper too soon. Even after nine years, elements of this odyssey are still painful, but at least I can now recall the whole story with a cool head.

Of course, the passage of time faded the memories somewhat, and I do not claim that mine is the most precise and objective account of what happened. No doubt, it is greatly affected by my own perceptions. It is therefore my personal tale of FAZISI's journey as I remembered and understood it and tried to tell as accurately and honestly as possible. Nothing more and nothing less.

• • •

There were times, when I reflected with regret on the missed opportunities and misfortunes that plagued our venture.

If only the boat wasn't overbuilt and had shown her full potential... If only we hadn't had ambitious fights in our design cooperative, wasting so much invaluable time... If only there had been no conflict in the crew and they had worked as one motivated team... What the result of the race might have been, had we had on FAZISI a truly professional crew on par with STEINLAGER's? Could we have won if we had had the best skipper like Peter Blake? What would have happened if PEPSI had not ended its sponsorship, and we had had sufficient funding throughout the race? What if Alexey Grischenko hadn't died?

So many things had gone wrong...

But then, I always remember that each of these misfortunes had the potential to stop the entire project dead in its track. Yet it had not. We all were dilettantes in the beginning, starting everything from scratch. We had no experience -- had no clue -- and we had learned the hard way from our mistakes. Considering all circumstances, it is truly incredible, what we were able to accomplish after all, finishing the race successfully.

By good luck, good fortune -- by God's grace -- my impossible Whitbread dream, and in a wider sense a desire to achieve something significant, to fulfill my life, had come to fruition.

Deep in my soul, there was another, even more ambitious, totally unrealistic dream. Only a few people knew about it back in Russia, and they thought it was crazy and dangerous. It was a dream about coming to America.

It too, has become a reality.

Probably, I am one of the luckiest men on the planet. Or, maybe, God has heard and answered my unrelenting prayers.

I know He did.

• • •

In writing this book I benefited greatly from the friendship, help and professional advice of many people. My special thanks go to Ellen and Dick Gower, Fred and Anne Hallett, Micca Hutchins, John Carlson, Frank Lennon, William Schanen, Brian Hancock, Jene Hircshel, Dallas Murphy, Jon and Irene Belinsky, Henry Shapiro, Diane Dimond, Mark Langlois, Patricia Lehto.

I am grateful to all my FAZISI companions and to all sincere and generous people who supported the project and made it a reality. It is impossible to mention all their names here, but I will always remember them all, especially Nadia Ovsjannikova, Igor Pronin, Vladimir Gladishev, Valery Zakhovaev, Skip Novak, Alexey Grischenko, Alexander Struzilin, Michael Tzarev, Oleg Gulinsky, Oleg Larionov,

Alexander Manenko, Victor Tikhov, Alexander Kedishvili, Dennis Conner, Valery Chumakov, Wilfred Post, Gerd Budzek, Tony Castro, Ted and Sheila Lonsdale, Vladimir "Kuli" Kulinichenko, Clive Tremain, Jim and Liz Saunders, Dick Saint, Monica Tingay, Paul Smitt, Barry Everard, Leonid Farvarschuk, Rae Glasgow, Valery Alexeev, Victor Pogrebnov, Sergey Akatyev, Sergey Borodinov, Jumberi "Juki" Tsomaya, Nodari Teneishvili, Yuri Doroshenko, Victor Kamkin, Gennadi "Crocodile" Korolkov, Rami Leibovich, Edgar Terekhin, Sergey "Elephant" Stanetsky, Eugene Platon, Dale Tremain, Thierry Rannou, Anatoly Verba, Victor Yazykov, Alexey Drozdovski, Valery Safiullin, David Matthews, Vladimir Musatov, Oleg Belomiltsev, Mark "Herbe" Hauser, Roland "Bilou" Jourdain, Roger Vaughan.

My wife Tatiana not only helped to re-type and re-edit the countless versions of this manuscript, but provided me with the inspiration and courage to see this project through to its completion. The final stage of my writing of this book coincided with her brave fight and victory over breast cancer, the fight that made all my tribulations and achievements look insignificant.

And finally, my gratitude goes to my son Pavel. Representative of a young *e*-generation, he is of course a computer wizard, not necessarily a big book reader and a person not easily impressed. Yet he told me many times how great this book is going to be. It inspired me a lot. Pavel also helped me to cope with the computer's hardware and software shortcomings. He set up and maintains this book's web site.

The process of writing this book has been at times exhausting and frustrating, and yet I enjoyed it immensely. I hope, at least part of this joy has been passed on to you, my reader.

APPENDIX I

MAIN CHARACTERS.
Literally hundreds of people on four continents have been involved in the
FAZISI project. It would be impossible to name them all. Listed below are
only those who played key roles in the FAZISI story and on the pages of this
book.

	Pages:
FAZISI CREW.	
Skip Novak, USA	2, 4, 17, 102-106, 108, 112-116, 118-128, 130-132, 134-135, 137-138, 140-141, 143-144, 151-158, 160, more...
Valeri Alexeev, USSR/Russia	42, 93, 193, 214-215, 276, 280, 284, 286-288, 293-295, 302.
Alexei Grischenko, USSR/Ukraine	40-43, 66-70, 99-101, 105-108, 128, 136, 139, 158-159, 161-164, 168, 173-174, 259, 302.
Sergei Akatiev, USSR/Ukraine	4, 275-276, 279, 286,286-287,303.
Sergei Borodinov, USSR/Russia	193, 214, 303.
Yuri Doroshenko, USSR/Ukraine	3, 6, 118, 303.
Alexey Drozdovsky, USSR/Ukraine	157-158, 240-242, 303.
Brian Hankock, USA/South Africa	143-144, 151-158, 302.
Marc "Herbe" Hauser, NZ	303.
Rolland "Bilou" Jourdain, France	157, 238-243, 303.
Victor Kamkin, USSR/Ukraine	299, 303.
Gennadi "Crocodile" Korolkov, USSR/Ukraine	66, 152, 239, 303.
Vladimir "Kuli" Kulinichenko, USSR/Ukraine	66, 118, 129, 189, 206, 235-246, 253, 281, 283, 300, 303.
Rami Leibovich, USSR/Latvia	67, 201, 204, 278, 283, 292, 303.
Dave Matthews, USA	277-278, 303.
Igor Mironenko, USSR/Ukraine	66, 118, 132, 152, 162-163, 203-204, 206, 239, 299, 303.
Vladimir Musatov, USSR/Russia	66, 132, 303.
Eugene Platon, USSR/Ukraine	4-5, 100, 118, 162, 164, 177, 203-204, 208, 214, 216, 239, 242-243, 260, 276, 298, 303.
Victor Pogrebnov, USSR/Russia	193, 214, 278, 282, 299, 303.
Thierry Rannou, France	245, 261, 303.
Valery Safiullin, USSR/Kazakhstan	118, 129, 189, 253, 278-279, 283, 303.

OTHER WHITBREAD SAILORS:

INITIAL SUPPORTERS AND FRIENDS:

FAZIS SP:

APPENDIX II
FAZISI'S Design

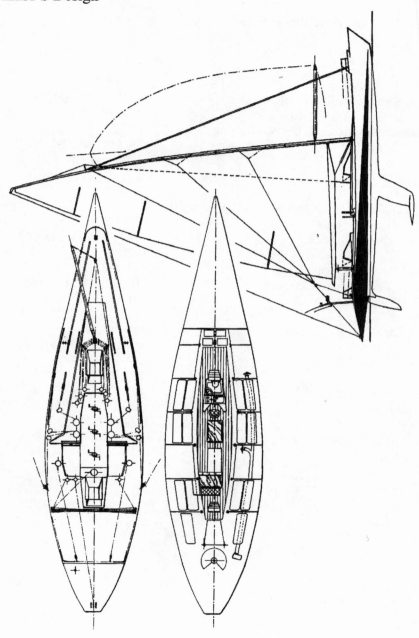

APPENDIX III

RACE RESULTS
Whitbread Round the World Race 1989-'90

Boat Name	Elapsed Time			
	D	H	M	S
1. STEINLAGER 2	128	09	40	30
2. FISHER&PAYKEL	129	21	18	22
3. MERRIT	130	10	10	14
4. ROTHMANS	131	04	54	23
5. THE CARD	135	07	15	43
6. CHARLES JOURDAN	136	15	14	51
7. FORTUNA EXTRA LIGHTS	137	08	14	11
8. GATTORADE	138	14	30	12
9. UNION BANK OF FINLAND	138	16	38	12
10. BELMONT FINLAND II	139	04	31	13
11. FAZISI	139	09	01	04
12. NCB IRLAND	139	19	22	38
13. SATQUOTE BRITISH DEFENDER	143	12	42	23
14. EQUITY&LAW II	148	23	50	33
15. LIVERPOOL ENTERPRISE	151	04	52	22
16. CREIGHTONS NATURALLY	162	06	34	58
17. L'ESPRIT DE LIBERTE	164	21	36	16
18. MAIDEN GREAT BRITAIN	167	03	06	53
19. SCHLUSSEL VON BREMEN	167	19	07	34
20. WITH INTEGRITY	170	16	19	07
21. LA POSTE	181	22	56	17
22. RUCANOR SPORT	Did not complete legs 4 and 5			
23. MARTELA O.F.	Capsized on leg 4			

APPENDIX IV

GLOSSARY OF NAUTICAL TERMS.

Apparent Wind. The direction and strength of the wind as it appears
    to blow aboard a boat. It is a combination of a true wind and a
    wind caused by a boat's motion.
Beam. The width of the boat at its widest point.
Bear away. To alter course away from the wind.
Bearing. The angle between the centerline of the boat and direction to
    another object.
Beat. To sail to windward in a series of tacks.
Backstay. A stay running from the upper part of the mast to the stern
    to keep the mast from moving forward. There are two types of
    backstays: standing and running. The latter can be adjusted
    during a sailing to alter the mast bend, and therefore the shape
    of the sails.
Ballast. Weight (usually led) put into the bottom of the boat or keel for
    stability.
Bilge. The lowest part of a boat's hull.
Boltrope. A line running along the mainsail's **luff** used to attach it to
    the mast.
Boom. The horizontal spar that hold the foot or bottom of the mainsail.
Boom vang. A system using tackle or hydraulics to keep the boom
    from rising up.
Bosun's Chair. The canvas or wooden seat used to hoist man on the
    mast.
Broach. A boat broaches when, while running downwind it inadverten-
    tly swings and broadsides to the wind. Very dangerous, and
    could result in broken equipment or sails.
Broad Reach. Sailing with the wind coming from a stern from one
    quarter or the other.
Close reach. To sail with the wind somewhat forward of abeam.
Cockpit. The recessed area in which the crew including helmsman and
    sail trimmers work during a sailing race.
Coffee-grinder. Winch pedestal, which is connected through series of
    gear shafts and switches to main winch drums. On FAZISI
    there were three pedestals connected together so that six people
    could work simultaneously trimming a single sheet or halyard.

Come About. To change direction from one tack to another while sailing to windward (upwind). To tack is to come about. See also **Port Tack** and **Starboard Tack**.

Displacement. The weight of water displayed by a floating vessel; hence, the weight of the vessel itself.

Fender. A portable anti-chafe device, usually tubular, placed between a boat and a dock or another boat.

Foot. A lower edge of a triangle sail.

Foredeck. The part of the deck between mast and bow.

Forestay. The stay running from bow to mast on which the jib or genoa is set.

Freeboard. The distance from the water to the deck.

Genoa. A large jib whose clew (aft corner) extends aft of the mast.

Head. An upper edge of a triangular sail.
Also a marine toilet.

Headsail. Sails set forward of the mast. For upwind sailing triangular-shaped jibs or genoas are used, for downwind sailing – balloon-shaped spinnakers.

Headstay. See **Forestay**.

Halyard. A line used to hoist a sail.

Inclining Test. Part of the measurement procedure in order to establish a boat's rating. The purpose of inclining test is to check the boat's stability and compare it to the requirements of the racing rules.

Jib. Alternate term for headsail. Jibs are usually smaller than **genoa**s and do not overlap the mast.

Jybe (jibe). To jibe is to change course while sailing downwind. Requires to move the mainsail and spinnaker from one side of the boat to the other. In an accidental jibe the boom swings uncontrollably and quickly from one side to another, placing great stress on equipment and sails. Accidental jibe is extremely dangerous and often results in serious damage to the boat.

Keel. A protruding section under the boat that provide stability and prevents sideways drift.

Ketch. A two-masted sailing vessel with smaller aftermast.

Leeward. Downwind.

Luff. A triangular sail's leading edge. To smoothen the air flow, luff is often set on a special plastic or aluminum headfoil mounted on a **forestay**.

Mainsail. The sail hoisted aft of the **mast**. Its foot is attached to the **boom**.

Mainsheet. The line used to trim the **mainsail**.

Mast. The vertical spar that holds up the sail and itself is held up by stays and shrouds.

Offwind. On reach or run you are sailing offwind.

Preventer. A line running from the foredeck to the end of the boom that keeps the boom from jybing accidentally as the boat sails downwind.

Port. The left-hand side of the boat as you look forward.

Port tack. Sailing with the wind coming over the port side of the boat. The sails would, therefore, be on the starboard side.

Rail. The deck's outer edge.

Reach. To sail with the wind abeam. On a **close reach** the wind is somewhat forward of abeam. On a **beam reach** the wind is directly abeam. On a **broad reach** the wind is aft of abeam.

Rig. Arrangement of boat's sails, mast and rigging. Depending on the rig configurations, a boat could be classified as a **sloop, ketch**, shooner, etc.

Rigging. A general term applied to all lines, shrouds and stays necessary to support spars and trim sails. Shrouds and stays constitute standing rigging. Sheets and halyards are a part of boat's running rigging.

Rudder. An underwater flap (foil) operated by steering wheels in the cockpit that changes the boat's course.

Run. To sail directly downwind.

Runner. Running **backstay**.

Sheerline. The edge of the deck as seen from aside.

Shrouds. Supporting wires on both sides of the mast. They give the mast lateral stability.

Sloop. A single-masted sailboat. Usually sails upwind with mainsail and jib or genoa. Spinnakers are added for downwind sailing.

Spinnaker. A light balloon-shaped sail used when sailing downwind. It is set with the aid of a spinnaker pole.

Spreaders. Struts on both sides of mast that spread the shrouds out to enhance their stabilizing effect.

Starboard. The right-hand side of the boat as you face forward.

Starboard tack. Sailing with the wind coming over the starboard side of the boat; the sails are therefore on the left or port side.

Stay. A wire that provides fore and aft support for the mast; part of the standing rigging.

Strongback. A ragged and precisely built frame used to assemble the boat's hull.

Tack. To tack is to change direction while sailing to windward (upwind)

Topsides. The upper parts of the hull sides located above the waterline.

Transom. The back of the stern.

Trim. The way a boat floats on the water – on an even keel or down by the bow or by the stern.

Also **trim** means to set a sail in correct relation to the wind using a sheet.

Trysail. Small ragged mainsail for stormy weather.

Upwind. Sailing toward the direction from which the wind is blowing.

SELECTED BIBLIOGRAPHY

William Bradford, *History of Plymouth Plantation*, 1898.
John Jourdane, *Icebergs Port and Starboard*, 1992
Sebastian Junger, *The Perfect Storm*, 1997.
Jon Krakauer, *Into Thin Air*, 1997.
Reinhold Messner, *The Crystal Horizon*, 1989 (1982).
Skip Novak, *FAZISI, The Joint Venture*, 1990.
Captain Joshua Slocum, *Sailing Alone Around the World*, 1956 (1900).
Andrey Voznesensky, *Juno and Avos* (musical), 1980.

ORDER FORM

RACE TO FREEDOM *by Vladislav Murnikov*

Please send me _____ copies of RACE TO FREEDOM
at $19.95 per copy $ _____

Massachusetts residents include 5% sales tax $ _____

Shipping and Handling for the first book $ 4.50

Add $1.00 for each additional book $ _____

Total payment included $ _____

Ship the order to:

Name:_____

Address: _____

City: _____ State _____ Zip Code _____

Country _____

Mail your check or money order to:

7 Seas Publishing
P.O. Box 394
Sudbury, MA 01776
www.fazisibook.com

Thank You for your order